COMPENSATION FOR DAMAGE

Compensation for Damage

An International Perspective

Edited by
Sheila A.M. McLean

Dartmouth

Aldershot • Brookfield USA • Hong Kong • Singapore • Sydney

Published by
Dartmouth Publishing Company Limited
Gower House
Croft Road
Aldershot
Hants GU11 3HR
England

Dartmouth Publishing Company
Old Post Road
Brookfield
Vermont 05036
USA

A CIP catalogue record for this book is available from the British Library.

Library of Congress Cataloging-in-Publication Data
Compensation for damage : an international perspective / edited by
Sheila McLean.
p. cm.
Includes bibliographical references and index.
ISBN 1-85521-169-6
1. Damages. 2. Torts. 3. Compensation (Law) I. McLean, Sheila.
K923.C66 1993
346.03—dc20
[342.63] 92-27240
CIP

ISBN 1 85521 169 6

Printed and bound in Great Britain by
Hartnolls Limited, Bodmin, Cornwall

Contents

Contributors

Margaret Brazier is a LL.B Barrister, Professor of Law and Legal Studies and Director of the Centre for Social Ethics and Policy at the University of Manchester

Benjamin Browne is a Solicitor and Partner with Clyde & Co. Solicitors, Guildford.

Françoise J. Hampson is Senior Lecturer in the Department of Law and Human Rights Centre at the University of Essex.

Peter Kaye is Reader in Law and Director of the Centre of European Law and Practice at the University of East Anglia.

Sheila A.M. McLean is the International Bar Association Professor of Law and Ethics in Medicine and Director of the Institute of Law and Ethics in Medicine at the University of Glasgow.

Christopher Newdick is a Barrister and a Lecturer in Law in the Department of Law, University of Reading.

Ruth Redmond-Cooper is Lecturer in Law, University of Leicester, Director of Education, Rubinstein Callingham Polden and Gale.

Introduction

To the observer, it must seem as if interest in the legal processes and methods underlying compensation for harm has seldom been greater. Recent disasters, such as oil spillages, increasing awareness of the dangers run by all of us as we go about our everyday business, and increased coverage of harms allegedly caused by pharmaceutical products and medical care have all served to bring what might in the past have seemed to be a somewhat esoteric part of the law into sharp public focus. Any of us, at any time, might be directly or indirectly affected by the actions of others, so the question of how damages are awarded now has an immediacy which, some might say, is long overdue.

Perhaps not surprisingly, heightened awareness brings with it heightened controversy. Increasingly, people are challenging the efficacy, and sometimes the justice, of the systems currently in place, questioning whether better models could not be made available and demanding that attention is paid to the rights of alleged victims. In tandem with this is the interest of individuals, companies, states and other authorities in monitoring spiralling costs and seeking to balance the consequences of this against the legitimacy of grievances. Attention, then, has come to be focussed not just on the problems which are sometimes found in current systems, but also on other nations and other systems for innovative ideas and models which might assist in ultimately providing a better, fairer and more equitable system. This book seeks to address some of the areas in which change has been contemplated or has been effected over recent years, and to assess critically the systems in place and the benefits (if any) of the changes which have occurred.

Many of the chapters emanate from a series of conferences organised by the University of Essex. As will be seen, they cover a wide variety of issues relating to compensation for harm, both personal and commercial. The book, therefore, has no overt theme, representing as it does a wide and diverse range of topics. However, it also has a number of chapters with certain similarities in terms of the topics discussed and for this reason it has been split into two sections.

The first part deals with issues arising from accident or harm as a result of the involvement of the individual in medical care. The inclusion of such topics is perhaps inevitable in a book of this sort, since it is from these cases that a large amount of the demand for law reform has emerged. In the United Kingdom, the United States and many other jurisdictions throughout the world there is, for many, a real need to modify the basis on which liability for harm is calculated. Most often, these demands for change concentrate on the development of a no fault system of liability to replace the more traditional fault based system. For this reason, two of the chapters consider the model of no fault liability established in a radical move in New Zealand. Not surprisingly, perhaps, it is not only in the countries which still substantially rely on the traditional model that the systems of compensation are closely monitored. Since these chapters were written, New Zealand has itself reassessed its system and has promulgated new legislation. Whilst the comments and criticisms contained in these two chapters remain valid, it is worth at this point making brief reference to the changes which have been effected from 1st July 1992 by the Accident Rehabilitation and Compensation Insurance Act 1992, and in particular to those which refer specifically to medical cases. Indeed, the reader may well notice that the chapters in some ways predicted the fact that change would probably occur and even, on occasion, the shape that these changes would take.

From 1st July, following on a somewhat gloomy budget in the summer of 1991, financial constraints play an even bigger role in the operation of the New Zealand Scheme and on the availability of compensation. Sometimes criticised for excluding some victims rather than living up to its all-inclusive image, the new legislation enhances that criticism. Medical mishap will now be compensated only where the injury is both rare and serious – it must be a risk no greater than 1 in 100. The person who suffers an adverse reaction which occurs more frequently than this will be considered to be a victim of sickness and not 'personal injury by accident' and therefore will not be entitled to compensation under the Accident Compensation Scheme. There are further changes, again unashamedly based on financial exigencies. Doctors will be required to pay a premium in addition to their subscription to Defence Organisations to help fund the scheme and lump sum payments will no longer be available.[1] Although the changes are greater than this, for the purposes of this book they represent the most interesting and significant ones.

There have also been some changes in compensation awards in the United Kingdom which are relevant to the chapter dealing with Consent to Medical Treatment. At the time of writing no award had been made in excess of £1 million – this is no longer the case. Given that the Crown

Indemnity Scheme has also come into effect, meaning that hospital boards and authorities are now responsible for allegations of negligence in the hospital setting, the implications of spiralling costs on their ability to set budgets and maintain health care provision seem clear.

This section also considers strict liability compensation with specific reference to pharmaceutical products and to the changes made in UK law – changes designed to facilitate the award of damages.

The second part of the book considers some other issues of compensation, including the commercial need for damages, from an international perspective. In introducing the areas covered in this part of the book, it can be seen that the scope of this book on compensation is widened beyond the traditional and the reader will, in some cases, be introduced to aspects of compensation schemes which are often relatively inaccessible. Chapters cover oil pollution (surely of particular contemporary relevance following the Gulf War), the French no fault road traffic scheme, vitally important matters concerning jurisdiction to litigate and the place of the European Convention on Human Rights in the compensation debate.

It only remains to thank the contributors to this book for their hard work. As will be obvious, in the time between writing their chapters and the process of preparing the manuscript for publication, things have changed rapidly and I am extremely grateful to them for their patient and generous agreement to update and amend where this was possible. Anyone reading this book who has ever attempted to write on these aspects of the law will doubtless sympathise with the almost impossible struggle in being absolutely up-to-date, but the intellectual and analytical input of the chapters, even given these constraints, remains relevant and vital. I must also thank the staff at Dartmouth Publishing, particularly Sonia Bridgman, for their unfailing kindness and help throughout. They too have suffered as a result of the changes and amendments which have been made and have, as always, been unflappable and encouraging. Thanks are also due to Professor Norman Palmer, formerly of Essex University and now of University College London, whose brainchild this book was. Quite how I found myself in the position of editing it is another of Professor Palmer's contributions which I will gloss over, but it has been an interesting experience! Finally, my personal thanks for unfailing encouragement and many practical and other contributions must go to my parents and friends, especially to Maggie Carle who has made my life much easier with both her efficiency and her friendship, to Cara for being there and to Allan for immense personal support.

Note

1 For a brief discussion of some of the changes made by the new legislation, see Paterson, R. (9 May 1992), 'New Zealand Doctors Must Pay for Medical Misadventure', *British Medical Journal*, Volume **304**, 1203.

Sheila A.M. McLean,
Giasgow University
May 1992.

PART I

1 Special Problems of Compensating Those Damaged by Medicinal Products

Christopher Newdick

The Committee on the Safety of Medicines (CSM) estimates that drugs caused 616 deaths in Britain during 1986 and 1987. It described a further 9 718 adverse reactions to drugs as serious.[1] These drug-induced (iatrogenic) reactions arose from a total of over 390 million prescriptions in each year. Some of these reactions were expected by the pharmaceutical manufacturers, the Department of Health (DoH) which licensed them and the doctors who prescribed them. Others were novel and unforeseen. The category of product most commonly associated with side-effects was the non-steroidal anti-inflammatory drug (NSAID),[2] often used in treatment of the elderly who suffer arthritis. The most common form of damage from NSAIDs was to the gastro-intestinal tract, to the liver, kidneys and skin.[3]

For two reasons, these statistics probably represent a significant underestimate of the numbers of those killed or injured by drugs.[4] First, the CSM depends largely on general practitioners to report incidents of suspected adverse reactions. The Committee makes available yellow cards on which doctors are encouraged to notify the authorities of these incidents, but less than 20 per cent are in the habit of using the system.[5] Secondly, the reports are of 'suspected' reactions. But the problem of whether a particular drug caused the damage in question is extremely difficult to resolve, particularly in patients who are already seriously ill.

Given this background, how should compensation for drug damage be awarded? The question is relevant now in the light of the European Directive on Product Liability (1985) which has been effected in the UK by the

Consumer Protection Act (1987). This Act seeks to introduce a form of strict liability compensation for those injured by defective products. In doing so it will tend to encourage those injured by drugs to seek compensation for their loss. This chapter, therefore, will consider (i) the criteria by which a drug should be considered 'defective', (ii) the 'development risk' defence whereby a manufacturer will be absolved from liability for damage caused by undiscoverable defects, (iii) the problem of causation, that is of associating a product with a particular reaction and (iv) the difficulties raised by mass litigation, in which large numbers of plaintiffs sue a single manufacturer.

When is a Drug Defective?

Strict liability under the Consumer Protection Act turns on the notion of a 'defect'. The word is defined in Section 3(1): '... there is a defect in a product... if the safety of the product is not such as persons generally are entitled to expect...'. How much safety is a person entitled to expect from a drug? We are probably *entitled* to rather less than we actually *expect*. Many appear to be largely unaware of the inevitable risks connected with pharmaceuticals.[6] Perhaps it is fair to say that we are entitled to expect as much safety as is reasonable, taking all the circumstances into account. How much is that?

The question of defectiveness depends on at least three issues: the need to balance the benefits with the risks of taking drugs; the relevance of the warnings and instructions that can make drugs more safe; and the significance of the fact that no drug can be made generally available until it has the approval of the DoH.

Balancing the Benefits of Drugs with the Risks:

No drug is entirely safe and the risks it may present are infinitely variable. Some drugs, particularly those supplied on request and without prescription, may be dangerous only if taken in excess, and present the same form of risk to all those using them. In this sense their risks can be foreseen and assessed quite easily by those taking them. Other drugs, however, are capable of causing catastrophic damage, or death, to a small and unidentifiable group of people, even though they may have been used in accordance with the manufacturer's instructions. Risks of this sort are more difficult for patients to quantify. How can the risks presented by a drug be measured against its benefits?

Weighing up the various risks and benefits presented by a drug is an imprecise art:

> How does one weigh a slightly increased risk of mortality against an easing of crippling arthritic pain? How is it possible to ensure that there is adequate evidence on the adverse reactions and efficacy of the product to reach an informed judgement or enable the patient to give informed consent? Is it possible or even desirable to establish a specific formula, for example, for a non-steroidal anti-inflammatory drug that postulates that a mortality rate is 'acceptable' at, say, below 1 in 20 000 patients?[7]

There is no objective yardstick against which the relative safety of a drug can be measured. Drug companies, the licensing authority, doctors and patients all have to make judgements, on the basis of different considerations, as to whether the risks presented by a product are justified by its overall benefits.[8] In the crudest terms, these foreseen risks of drugs can be considered under two broad headings.

Side effects common to most patients Medicines designed to treat serious conditions of illness are often expected to cause generalised side-effects, for example, nausea, fever, lethargy, or hypertension. Some are known to be addictive. The extent of the reaction which should reasonably be tolerated depends on the nature of the patient's condition, the urgency of the treatment and the availability of suitable alternative treatment. A more serious complaint may require a more powerful drug and result in a correspondingly severe incidence of side-effects. Tablets for car-sickness and insomnia ought to present less danger than those designed to treat heart failure. These are matters initially for the drug producer and the licensing authority, and subsequently for the patient and the prescribing doctor. With adequate advice, however, the patient ought to understand the need to balance the costs and the benefits of treatment, and be in a position to make a choice whether or not to accept them.[9] If the overall benefit to be gained from the drug outweighs its drawbacks, it is 'reasonably' safe. It is not defective. This is entirely a matter of fact.

Adverse reactions in particular individuals A more difficult issue concerns the drug that causes idiosyncratic damage. The chemical composition of each of us is different and we are all subject to a small, 'one-off', risk of catastrophic harm from a drug out of all proportion to its intended benefits. It might cause blindness, dermatitis, a blood disorder or death. Should loss of this type, to a small number of people, be said to have been caused by a defective product? There are a number of reasons for thinking that it should not.

First, in the case of life-threatening conditions, patients may well be prepared to accept a significant risk of adverse reaction to a product. Similarly, those who suffer debilitating diseases with the prospect of a long and painful future may prefer to run the risk of harm from a product which holds out the prospect of alleviating their suffering. Provided they have understood the risks of treatment, and decided to undergo them, it should not be possible to say that the product did not provide the safety they were entitled to expect.[10]

Secondly, if, on the balance of risks and benefits, a product is considered to be in the overall interests of the public, there may be an overall detriment to that public interest if the product is considered to be defective. The strong inclination of a company responsible for a 'defective' product must be to withdraw it from circulation. Indeed, it would probably be required by the licensing authority to do so. However, withdrawal of a product from the market carries its own costs. If, for example, a form of treatment reduces the risk of post-operative infection in the large majority of users, but causes liver damage to a small minority, there is a loss both in public and private terms if that product is withdrawn.[11]

These considerations do no more than state the obvious – that drugs, in common with many other products on the market, present both risks and benefits. A decision as to whether they should be made available depends on the balance of those risks and benefits. In the case of drugs, the question of whether the balance is in favour of release or not is a delicate matter. Reasonable people may disagree about the answer. How serious is the illness in question? With what likelihood will there be an adverse reaction? How serious will it be if it happens? How long will it take to materialise?[12] It is on the basis of these types of question that a judgement has to be made. But they do not suggest that all those who suffer injury from drugs should necessarily receive compensation under Section 3 of the 1987 Act.[13]

Warnings and Instructions for Use

The question of the safety of a drug cannot be isolated from the condition it is designed to treat. The nature of the instructions and warnings attached to the product are, therefore, crucial to the question of defectiveness. Products that would otherwise be unreasonably dangerous may be made safe by the inclusion of adequate warnings or instructions for use. Under the 1987 Act, the 'safety persons generally are entitled to expect' turns, amongst other considerations, on '...any instructions for, or warnings with respect to, doing or refraining from doing anything with or in relation to the product;...'[14] When should warnings and instructions be given? How much should be said? To whom should it be said?

The general principles of the law of negligence require warnings and instructions to be given whenever they are necessary to make the product reasonably safe. The same general criteria appear to govern the information required under the Consumer Protection Act 1987.[15] The dangers present in some products are sufficiently obvious not to require notification. Drugs, of course, will generally be considered defective in the absence of such notice because information about the correct dosage, the frequency of use, the categories of patient for whom the drug is unsuitable and the potential for adverse reactions is essential to their safety and not otherwise available. Only with this information can the product be made reasonably safe.

The nature of the manufacturer's obligations under the 1987 Act will be coloured by the existing regulations under the Medicines Act 1968. The general obligation may be considered in three stages: the manufacturer's obligation to the patient; the manufacturer's obligation to the doctor: and the doctor's obligation to his patient.

The manufacturer's obligation to inform the patient The extent of the manufacturer's duty to supply the patient with information depends on whether the medicine in question is a non-prescription (over-the-counter), or prescription only medicine.

Non-prescription medicines are controlled by the Medicines (Labelling) Regulations 1976[16] and the Medicines (Leaflets) Regulations 1977.[17] In general terms they require manufacturers to supply the following information direct to patients via labels and (if they choose to include them) leaflets: the name of the product, the quantity of the product, its quantitative particulars, directions for use, contra-indications, warnings and precautions, the expiry date and the name and address of the supplier. Judging from a random selection of non-prescription medicines the information supplied is generally brief and does not discuss improbable reactions. On the other hand there is a premium on brevity if information is to be communicated effectively to patients.

Prescription medicines are subject to a different code. No obligation is imposed on the manufacturer to supply the patient with information directly (though if he chooses to supply a leaflet with the prescription then the 1977 Regulations [above] apply). In this situation, therefore, the patient is largely dependent on his or her doctor for the supply of information about the product.

It is arguable that these statutory obligations mirror the standards of disclosure imposed by common law. In *Sidaway* v *Royal Bethlem Hospital*[18] the House of Lords considered the extent of the doctor's obligation to disclose the risks associated with a surgical operation. The court said that doctors are not obliged to tell the patient everything about an operation, or even as much as they believe the patient would like to be told. They must disclose as much as they believe, in their professional judgement, the patient needs to know to enable them to make a reasonable and balanced decision whether to undergo the operation.

This reasoning may also be applied to the relationship between drug companies and patients. If the patient is under the supervision of a doctor it is preferable for the supply of complicated and detailed information to come from that source, where it can be disclosed in the most appropriate manner. As a US court decided:

> In such cases the choice involved is essentially a medical one involving an assessment of the medical risks in the light of the physician's knowledge of his patient's needs and susceptibilities. A warning to the medical profession in such cases is the only effective means by which a warning could help the patient.[19]

If this is right, the question now arises how much ought the manufacturer disclose to the doctor?

Manufacturer's obligation to inform the doctor The manufacturer's obligation to the doctor is governed by the Medicines (Data Sheet) Regulations 1972.[20] Before a representation or advertisement is sent to a doctor by a company about its products, a data sheet must have been sent within the preceding 15 months. The data sheet should give comprehensive details about the name of the product, its ingredients, both by approved name and quantity, its uses, dosage and administration (distinguishing children from adults), contra-indications warnings, including the main side-effects and adverse reactions, requirements as to storage and product licence and manufacturer details.

In principle, therefore, the manufacturer must disclose as much as the doctor requires to allow him to prescribe the product with reasonable safety. But the ease of stating the rule may hide the difficulty of applying it to particular facts, because even this degree of disclosure must have its limitations. The manufacturer will inevitably possess large quantities of information from which a selection must be made. This is a more fertile source of litigation. Did the producer incorporate sufficient information in the data sheet? When reports of adverse reactions were received, was the data sheet updated with proper speed? Why was a warning included in the data sheet for America, but not in the UK? Did a statement to doctors in a medical advertisement over-promote the drug, so that a warning in the data sheet was undermined? Inevitably these questions involve matters of judgement and may provide grounds on which to bring an action generally for negligence or specifically for breach of Section 3 of the 1987 Act.

Once the doctor is furnished with information about the product he intends to use, how much should the patient be told?

Doctor's obligation to the patient The case of *Sidaway* governs the obligations of doctors to their patients. As a general proposition it is for the doctor to decide how much and in what way information should be disclosed to the patient. For reasons that are not entirely clear, patients and doctors seem prepared to accept much higher risks from surgical operations than from drugs.[21] Similar caution is also expressed by the CSM and by manufacturers. Both tend to withdraw products with levels of risk which, in surgical operations, would be regarded as acceptable.

How can this difference be justified? Why should a risk from one sort of treatment be acceptable when the same risk from another sort is not? Has the memory of Thalidomide made both manufacturers and the licensing authority overly cautious about drug-risks?[22] There is a strong case for saying that patients, with the guidance of their doctors, should be allowed more discretion to decide for themselves whether the benefits of treatment justify the risks. Perhaps the licensing authority should be prepared to grant licences which, at present, would be refused. A concomitant obligation would fall on the producers of such 'high risk' products, to inform both doctor and patient of its characteristics. Some work has been done on ranking risks in order of magnitude and this may be helpful to some patients.[23] With this in mind, there may be scope for extending the obligation of the doctor to disclose risks by making available products that are currently considered too dangerous, on the understanding that there will be greater discussion with the patient of their relative risks and benefits. Inevitably the numbers to benefit will be matched by an increase in those who suffer. But provided the risk to which the patient has been exposed is considered to be reasonable by both patient and doctor, the product cannot be presumed to be defective, and compensation under the 1987 Act could not be available.

Significance of Department of Health Approval

It is an offence for a person in the course of a business to sell, supply, export or manufacture any medicinal product without a licence from the DoH to do so.[24] The DoH, with the advice of the CSM, conducts lengthy investigations into the safety, efficacy and quality of products submitted to it for approval. In addition it approves the purpose of use and the literature supplied with a product, and may vary or suspend a product licence in the light of new information.

Do these facts have any bearing on the issue of the liability of the manufacturer for releasing a defective product? They are relevant only to the extent of contributing to the evidence in a case – that the product ought to be regarded as reasonably safe. They do not provide conclusive evidence of that fact. How persuasive is the approval of the DoH?

In the circumstances, it must be substantially persuasive.[24a] Provided all the relevant facts have been disclosed to the authority, its decision, taken on the advice of the CSM, is bound to carry considerable weight. As the decision in *Sidaway* shows, the courts are extremely reluctant to interfere with the decisions of doctors *vis-à-vis* their patients; similar deference would be likely in this context. On what principles could the DoH be held liable?

There are two stages at which the decision of the licensing authority may be attacked: the decision taken on grounds of public health to promote a particular drug; and the decision relating to the manner in which a product should be made available.

Decision to promote a particular drug Only rarely does the DoH become involved in the promotion of a drug. When it does, it does not do so for the benefit of a pharamaceutical company, but rather on grounds of protecting public health. The most obvious example of such a decision concerns the routine vaccination of children against whooping cough, pertussis and diphtheria. There is virtually no chance of successfully challenging a decision of this nature. An attempt to do so was made in *DHSS* v *Kinnear and Others*.[25] The DoH had a power under the National Health Service Act 1946 to introduce a policy of immunisation. The plaintiffs were vaccinated under the policy and alleged that they had suffered brain damage as a result. They said that the policy of immunisation ought never to have been introduced, because no proper study had shown the risks from vaccination to be substantially less than those from the illnesses they were supposed to prevent. Consequently, they argued, the introduction of the immunisation policy was negligent.

The claim failed. The Minister was exercising a discretion conferred on him by statute. So long as he did so in good faith and with reasonable care, it was impossible to say he had strayed outside his powers. There is always a margin of latitude in the exercise of discretion. Provided the Minister has taken the advice of those qualified to guide him, and has responded to it reasonably, it is effectively impossible to overturn the decision.

Decision concerning the manner in which the drug is released Lawyers distinguish between two different types of administrative decision; discretion (or policy) decisions, and operational (or implementation) decisions. The distinction is very inexact, but it makes the point that there is a difference between a decision to formulate a policy, and one to put it into effect. For some time it was thought that different rules applied to each of these stages of decision making. More recently, however, the view has sometimes been expressed that the same rules of negligence apply, but the more a decision is seen as one involving policy, the more difficult it becomes to challenge it.[26]

This explains why the application in *Kinnear* was not hopeless, but its chances of succeeding were small. However, there was another allegation in this case, namely that, quite apart from the decision to adopt the policy, the manner in which it was implemented was negligent. This met with more success. The claim was made on the basis that the DoH knew that certain categories of children were more prone to adverse reactions to the vaccine than others. Thus, it was argued, it ought to have taken proper steps to notify doctors and parents of the type of child at risk. In other words, the allegation was based on the failure to give adequate instructions and warnings about the product. This was held to be a serious allegation. The issue of liability, however, was left unsettled.[27]

The point of highlighting this case is to show that some decisions may be susceptible to challenge; for example, decisions relating to the type of condition for which a product is to be used, the category of patient for which the drug is suitable, the correct dose, the list of warnings and instructions to be included, and so on. It is true that the courts are sometimes reluctant to make central authorities responsible for the actions of those they are supposed to supervise.[28] This may be because Parliament has provided an alternative remedy for the individual,[29] or because it was not reasonable for the individual to have relied on the authority for a guarantee of safety,[30] or because the provision of such a remedy would hinder it in the exercise of its duty.[31] In all the circumstances it must be fair and just to impose liability on the authority.[32] On the other hand, if the authority exerts a close degree of control over an activity, liability may be imposed, particularly it if is concerned with the safety of the public.[33]

The licensing role of the DoH is designed specifically to promote safety in medicinal products.[34] In addition, the Medicines Act 1968 excludes the possibility of an action for breach of statutory duty in respect of contraventions of the Act or the regulations made under it. Only negligence or product liability laws, can give the individual a remedy in damages against the DoH, neither of which are affected by the licensing provisions of the 1968 Act.[35]

Unforeseen Damage and the Development Risk Defence

The foregoing has addressed the need to weigh the risks alongside the benefits of drugs and the extent to which warnings and other information affect the issue of liability. In each case it has been assumed that the manufacturer and the licensing authority have known about the dangerous aspects of the product in question. What is the position, however, with regard to the unforeseen harm caused by drugs? Under the law of negligence, unforeseeable loss is not recoverable. This is one of the reasons for the European Directive on Product Liability which aimed to introduce a more compassionate system of compensation. But the Directive is not wholly committed to liability without fault since it retains a development risk defence for undiscoverable defects.

There are a number of forceful arguments for saying that a no-fault scheme of compensation ought not to deny a remedy to those injured in unforeseen circumstances. Be that as it may, the Consumer Protection Act has included a development risk defence, but in a form which is not identical to the one in the Directive. What is the nature of the defects that will be excused by the development risk defence? The following considers: the difference between the EC and UK versions of the defence; whether the difference of wording is justified; and the position when larger numbers than expected suffer adverse reaction to a drug.

Difference between EC and UK Defences

The defence was made available by the Directive at the option of the member states of the European Community, in the following form:

> The producer shall not be liable as a result of this Directive if he proves ... that the state of scientific and technical knowledge at the time when he put the product into circulation was not such as to enable the existence of the defect to be discovered[36]

The Government is obliged to adhere to the terms of the defence and has intended to do so.[37] However, it included the defence in the 1987 Act in a form which differed from that in the Directive. Thus, Section 4(1)(e) provides that it will be a defence for the producer to show:

> ...that the state of scientific and technical knowledge at the relevant time was not such that a *producer of products of the same description as the product in question might be expected to have discovered the defect* if it had existed in his products while they were under his control....[38]

Is this qualification justified? The wording of the Directive is ambiguous. However, it carries a possible interpretation as follows: if scientific and technical knowledge existed somewhere in the world, or in some field of learning, in whatever language, which would have enabled the defect to be discovered, the defence is unavailable. It is entirely irrelevant that such knowledge could not reasonably have been expected to be available to the producer of the defective product. The fact that it existed somewhere is sufficient to disallow the defence. The Government considered that view to be mistaken. It argued that the defence must be understood in a wider sense to protect producers of defects that could not *reasonably* have been foreseen by them.

Which Defects are Protected under the Defence?

Is the Government correct in its interpretation? The following example seeks to explain which view is more likely to be right. A pharmaceutical manufacturer produces a drug designed to stabilise an arrhythmic heartbeat. It knows that the effective ingredient in the product is a molecule (molecule A) of certain shape and dimensions. It is also well aware of the danger that drugs may interact adversely with one another and that if that molecule were to change its characteristics in a particular way, by becoming a different shape, it would cause heart attacks and become fatally dangerous. It has tested the molecule against a large variety of agents for evidence of the possibility of molecular interaction. No test has suggested that the molecule is likely to react in this adverse way. The findings have been presented to the DoH which has examined them, found them satisfactory and approved the drug for marketing. A situation has been created where an allegation of insufficient or negligent research would certainly fail.

Molecule A is also used by a carpet manufacturer because of its capacity to bind fabric. In its laboratory it has noticed that, when exposed to a certain chemical (chemical B), the molecule does tend to change into the shape which the drug manufacturer has attempted to guard against. Naturally, it has no knowledge of the interest of the drug manufacturer in the question and takes no further action on the matter. This discovery is entirely unknown to the pharmaceutical industry when the product is supplied.

Chemical B is also used in the preparation of a fungicide. The fungicide is sprayed onto fruit. The fruit is eaten by patients taking the drug. Chemical B alters the characteristics of molecule A, which becomes dangerous. Many suffer cardiac failure as a result. Litigation proceeds against the drug producer, which concedes the product is defective and pleads the development risk defence. There was 'knowledge such as to enable the existence of the defect to be discovered', but not such that the producer ought to be expected to have known of it. Is the defence available?

A requirement that the producer show there to have been no such knowledge anywhere is effectively impossible to satisfy. A manufacturer would not be required to show that he had scoured every library and unpublished thesis in the world before proving an absence of knowledge at the relevant time. A court would probably be satisfied by the evidence of experts that they had no knowledge of the defect. Inevitably, the most relevant evidence would come from experts in the field in question (in the example above, pharmacology, pharmacokinetics, biology and so on.) From this point of view, the scope of the enquiry will often be confined to the area of learning with which the manufacturer would be expected to be familiar. To this extent the interpretation of the development risk defence by the Government represents the practical effect of the defence in most cases.

But what if evidence was adduced that an unpublished, internal, company memorandum from (say) a carpet manufacturer had noted the fact that the molecule in question would alter its characteristics in certain circumstances? Given that the drug company could not have known about it, should the defence be denied? The strict interpretation – of the EC Directive – says the defence is not available. There was 'knowledge which would have enabled the defect to be discovered'. The fact that no-one appreciated its significance is irrelevant.[39]

This is a possible interpretation but, it is submitted, an unlikely one. If such a view were to be adopted the availability of the defence will turn on nothing more than luck. Was the plaintiff lucky enough to turn up some piece of research, from whatever field of learning, or language, or country, which could have been used by the manufacturer to identify the defect in his product? The search for evidence would necessarily be random and the imposition of liability arbitrary. The majority without the luck to have stumbled across such 'undiscoverable' evidence might well criticise the fairness of such a system. Like cases should be treated alike. It seems unlikely that the defence can have been intended to depend on such a criterion, therefore.

For these reasons it is suggested that the Government is correct in its interpretation of the Defence. There is no doubt that it sits uneasily in a regime intended to introduce a system of strict liability for defective products. In effect it amounts to absolving the manufacturer from liability when he has taken reasonable care in the research and development of his product. There is no distinction in substance between the rule in product liability and in negligence.[40] Unattractive as this conclusion may appear to the consumer, it appears to follow inevitably from the inclusion of the possibility of a development risk defence in Article 7 of the EC Directive.

Unforeseen Numbers Suffer Adverse Reaction

The decision to make a drug available involves a value judgement. Do the benefits justify the anticipated costs? Let us assume that a drug is estimated to carry a danger of causing kidney damage in 5 per cent of its users and that this is considered justifiable in view of its overall benefits. After a year's use it is discovered that 40 per cent of all users have suffered kidney damage and that such a percentage makes the drug unsafe. That degree of danger could not have been foreseen before the product was released. Is the manufacturer liable for the additional suffering caused? Is the development risk defence available?

It could be argued that the product in its dangerous state gives rise to no right of action to private consumers. Each was subject to the risk of kidney damage and ought not to complain if that damage happened to materialize in their case. On the other hand, each was exposed to a much larger risk than was anticipated. If it could be shown that the drug would probably not have been taken by the patient had the true position been known (either because the doctor would not have prescribed it, or the patient would not have accepted it), and that the patient would therefore not have been exposed to the risk, then the product ought to be considered defective.

Is the development risk defence available? The danger of the adverse reaction was foreseen, it was the extent of it that was not. In the law of negligence, once a defendant has been shown to be in breach of his duty of care to the plaintiff and to have caused loss of a foreseeable *type*, he is liable for all the loss, notwithstanding that its full *extent* was not foreseeable.[41] In this way, the defendant is held responsible for loss that was unforeseeable. There is some force in the argument that, if the law of negligence is presently prepared to impose liability for this type of loss, the Consumer Protection Act ought to do the same – because it was passed with the intention of improving upon, not restricting, the law of negligence. On this analysis, the development risk defence ought not to protect producers in these circumstances.

Did the Drug Cause the Damage?

No-one disputes that drugs can cause damage, but proving the causal connection in a particular case can be extremely difficult. Occasionally the question is straightforward. The effects of Thalidomide were not denied because the damage it caused (phocomelia – a disruption of the growth of foetal limbs) was most uncommon and the scale of the damage became evident very quickly as a result of the way the drug was promoted and used. But if the disease in question also occurs naturally, and if the numbers alleged to suffer from the product are relatively small, the difficulties of showing that a particular drug caused the injury may be insurmountable.

Typically, the difficulties of establishing causation arise as follows. The producer may argue: first, it was not the drug that caused the disease, it was some other natural cause, such as the patient's illness. While conceding that the product is capable of creating a risk of the type in question, he denies that the risk from the drug has materialized into harm. Secondly, it may be said that it was another manufacturer's drug which caused the loss. This argument may arise in two forms. It may be said (a) we produce the type of drug that caused the injury, but so do many other producers. It was one of theirs that did it, not ours; or (b) our product is not capable of causing damage of that type. It was caused by a different drug altogether. Thirdly, the producer may admit his product was defective in failing to have a sufficient warning notice. But, says the producer, the patient would have taken the drug and suffered damage even if the warning had been attached. Therefore, it was not the failure to warn that caused the damage, which would have happened in any event.

As in all cases turning on the issue of causation the burden of proving the causal link is on the plaintiff, who must adduce some evidence of the capacity of the product to give rise to the damage. There is room for considerable disagreement between experts in this field. It is often impossible to say with certainty whether an illness is of natural or man-made origin. Given these intractable difficulties of proof, what is the plaintiff expected to show? Common law on causation does not require the impossible. There are some circumstances when it is prepared to infer causation despite the inevitable shortcomings of medical evidence. It is not at all clear, however, that these concessions benefit users of drugs.

When will Causation be Inferred?

The concessions were developed in the House of Lords in *Bonnington Castings* v *Wardlaw*[42] and *McGhee* v *National Coal Board*.[43] The circumstances of the cases were as follows. Workmen were employed to work in dangerous environments. The danger arose from noxious dust. The employers could not be criticised for that, the risk of damage was unavoidable and 'excusable'. However, they ought to have reduced the risk of damage so far as they reasonably could by installing better facilities in the factory, but they failed to do so.[44] Thus, to that extent, the employees were exposed to an additional 'blameworthy' risk of injury. Subsequently the employees developed the diseases expected from exposure to those risks, and sued for compensation. No-one knew whether the diseases had been caused by the 'excusable' or by the 'blameworthy' sources. Either, or both together, could have done so. The employers admitted behaving negligently toward their employees, but said that no-one had shown that their 'blameworthy' conduct was responsible for the injuries suffered. They could equally have been caused by the 'excusable' risk for which no compensation was payable. Therefore, they claimed, the plaintiffs had not satisfied the burden of proof as to causation and their actions had to fail.

In both cases the House of Lords rejected these arguments. A strictly logical approach to the requirement of proof was inappropriate. Medical and scientific knowledge was unable to say exactly which category of risk was responsible. But the question was not: 'Which source caused the damage?' It was: 'Did the blameworthy dust "materially contribute" to the loss?'[45] On a common sense basis it seemed probable that the blameworthy risk must have contributed, at least in some part, to causing the disease. That was sufficient to raise the presumption of causation in favour of the plaintiffs.

These cases had two features in common. First, the injury was caused by a known risk (factory dust). Secondly, the exposure to the risk was known to have been the responsibility of one defendant (the employer). Thirty years later an attempt was made to employ this reasoning in the context of the risks to patients in hospital. In *Wilsher* v *Essex Area Health Authority*,[46] the plaintiff was born three months premature. He survived but became blind. There were perhaps five explanations for the cause of his blindness. One involved the negligent treatment he received in the special baby care unit in hospital. He was wrongly given an excessive supply of oxygen which is known to cause retrolental fibroplasia and, thus, blindness. But it could also have been caused by four other agents which did not arise from the fault of the defendants and were of natural origin. At first instance and in the Court of Appeal, the plaintiff succeeded. Both courts treated the *McGhee* case as saying that once the defendant has been shown to have exposed the plaintiff to an unjustifiable risk of injury, and the plaintiff suffers damage of a sort to be expected from exposure to that risk, causation will be presumed. This is the case even though the damage could have arisen from a number of risks for which the defendant is not responsible.

Naturally, such a rule would give considerable benefit to drug users. Their disease might have developed naturally or from the drug. Nevertheless causation would be presumed provided the product was shown to be capable of causing damage of the type suffered. However, the House of Lords said that such an interpretation was wrong and reversed the ruling arrived at by the lower courts.[47] The Lords reaffirmed the principle that it is for the plaintiff to show causation. The plaintiff cannot succeed if there are a number of possible causes of which the defendant is only one, until it is proved, on the balance of probabilities, that the defendant is responsible.[48] Thus, the essential feature of *Bonnington* and *McGhee*, that a particular defendant be shown to have made a 'material contribution' to the injuries, is crucial to the rule which relaxes the burden of proof as to causation.[49] If that issue is in doubt, as it was in *Wilsher*, then causation will not be established.

Only against the background of these rulings of the House of Lords can we understand the position of those who suspect they have been injured by drugs.

Iatrogenic or Spontaneous Disease?

The problem of distinguishing drug-induced from natural illness is clearly illustrated by elderly patients. Not surprisingly, they absorb a large quantity of drugs on a *per capita* analysis. Equally, they suffer a disproportionate amount of natural illness.[50] How is the one to be separated from the other?

When there are two or more possible causes of injury, one the responsibility of the defendant and the other(s) of natural origin, the law is not particularly generous to the plaintiff. There is no presumption as to causation and the burden of proof rests with the plaintiff.[51] Thus, if the explanation as to iatrogenic causes is no more persuasive than that of natural causes, the plaintiff will fail on the issue of causation. This is the case, *a fortiori*, if there is a single iatrogenic explanation, but a number of spontaneous ones.[52]

This rule may be considered harsh, because it enables the defendant to behave negligently (by exposing the plaintiff to a risk of injury) but fails to subject him to any concomitant responsibility in damages. On the other hand it is also very imprecise. Whether or not the plaintiff's expert evidence is sufficient to satisfy a judge is entirely a matter of fact. This is largely a question of instinct, with which appeal courts are reluctant to interfere.[53] In a suitable case, there would be nothing to stop a judge from deciding in favour of the plaintiff's claim, even though the evidence was finely balanced.

However, in the few cases in which a quantification of the risk is possible, the same strict rule on the burden of proof applies. If it can be demonstrated that the plaintiff has been exposed to a risk of harm, but not, on the balance of probabilities, that the exposure to the risk actually caused the injury, causation is not proved. Proof of exposure to a *risk* of harm is not proof of the *harm itself*. There is a temptation to say that proof of a risk of 51 per cent must satisfy the burden of proof, and that anything less must fail. But each case must be judged on its own merits. Indeed, in some cases, proof of a risk below 50% may, as a matter of instinct, be sufficient.

Ultimately the plaintiff must show that it is more likely than not that the defendant's risk materially contributed to his damage.[54]

Which Manufacturer made the Drug?

The problem of deciding which manufacturer to blame arises in two forms. The first concerns the situation where the patient has taken a number of different drugs from different manufacturers, and suffers iatrogenic illness. However, there is doubt as to which of the drugs was responsible. The same type of damage could have been caused by more than one of them. The second arises when the patient has taken a drug which is made by a number of different manufacturers. The illness is attributed to the drug in question but no-one knows which manufacturer made the product(s) ingested by the patient.

Different drugs from different manufacturers Particular drugs are known to have the capacity to affect particular parts of the anatomy.[55] As the number of drugs taken by a patient increases, so does the potential number of adverse reactions. However, the science of attributing a particular reaction to a particular drug is still relatively crude and a number of products may attract suspicion. If it is impossible to say which one was responsible, what is the position?[56]

In principle the answer is straightforward. The plaintiff must lose until it can be shown, on the balance of probabilities, that one defendant rather than another caused the harm. The same rule applies as has been described above. If there are a number of possible causes of the damage, the plaintiff has the burden of proving which one (or ones) was responsible.

Same drug made by different manufacturers Doctors are encouraged to prescribe drugs in their generic, rather than proprietary form, because it is frequently less expensive to do so. Once the patent life of a product expires, a number of manufacturers copy the drug and sell it in competition with the original proprietary product. In this way, over a period of time, a patient may take one drug produced by a number of different manufacturers. The drug is dispensed from a chemist without identifying who made it. If injury results from taking the drug, how is the injured patient to know who made the ones he took?

The DES (diethylstilbestrol) litigation in the US gave rise to precisely this problem. In the late 1950s about 200 companies produced a generic drug designed to reduce the risk of miscarriage in pregnant women. The drug caused cervical and vaginal cancer in many of the daughters of those who took it. It has been impossible for plaintiffs to identify which manufacturer(s) was responsible for the particular drug ingested by their mothers. How have these evidential difficulties been tackled?

No uniform approach has been adopted throughout the States of the USA.[57] The most conservative have taken the view that the plaintiffs must fail. Until they can identify one party as being the probable cause of their injury, the action is incomplete. Though they are the innocent victims of harm, the injustice is not remedied by holding liable those who cannot be shown to have caused the loss. On the other hand, the most radical response to the problem has been the development of the 'market share' theory of liability. By this principle, all those who manufactured the generic product may be held responsible for the defect. The measure of their liability is the share of the market their product enjoyed at the relevant time. On this basis all those who made the defective product contribute to the plaintiff's compensation. They are not absolved from liability simply because a particular plaintiff cannot identify a particular defendant.

Which view would be adopted in the UK? It is extremely improbable that British judges would adhere to the market share theory of liability. Though it has some superficial attraction, there are considerable difficulties involved in its administration. If a manufacturer has (say) 80 per cent of the market, should he be liable for 80 per cent of the compensation, or should he be liable in full on the basis that it is more likely than not that the drug was his? Should the claim fail entirely if a less than 50 per cent share of the market can be identified, on the basis that it is more likely that a member of the unidentified share was responsible? On what basis is the share to be calculated – net or gross profits of the company generally, or from the drug alone? From which market is the share to be taken; regional, national or international? And should account be taken of the 'culpable' companies which have ceased trading? These difficulties, both theoretical and practical, would probably be sufficient to dissuade a court in the UK from adopting this approach.[58]

Inadequate Warnings – would the Plaintiff have Suffered the Damage Anyway?

Let us assume a drug manufacturer fails to supply sufficient information about its product, either to the patient, or to the doctor, such that it is unsafe and, therefore, defective. Now, a second question arises before the company can be held responsible for the damage. Would the patient have taken the drug even if the warning had been given? If so, the failure to warn did not cause the loss because the treatment would have been taken in any case. How can it be shown that the failure to inform caused the injury?

Two US cases illustrate the problem. Manufacturers of vaccines failed to warn of the rare incidence of brain damage from their products. They were defective for that reason. In one[59] there was a presumption in favour of the plaintiff, that if he had been warned properly of the danger, he would have chosen not to have been vaccinated. In the other[60] the presumption of causation was rebutted by evidence that a reasonable person with knowledge of the risk would have been vaccinated, because of a high risk, at that time, of polio. The failure to warn was not, therefore, the cause of the loss. What would be the position in the United Kingdom?

There is no suggestion, in the UK, that a presumption of causation would be introduced for the plaintiff's benefit. The burden of proof is on the patient. With non-prescription, over-the-counter medicines the risks are relatively minor and the numbers at risk from them relatively small. Warnings are few and short. Given the involvement of the licensing authority in determining the proper extent of such warnings, a plaintiff would have difficulty in showing the product to be defective.

The more serious problem arises in relation to prescription drugs, for which the patient normally relies on his doctor for information. If a doctor reasonably prescribes a course of treatment but fails to mention a particular risk of reaction, how can the patient prove that, armed with that information, he – the patient – would have refused the treatment? As a reasonable patient would he not accept and act on the doctor's recommendation, with or without the warning? If so the failure to warn cannot be said to have caused the loss.

There may be circumstances when patients refuse the reasonable advice of their doctor. In *Buchan* v *Ortho Pharmaceutical (Canada) Ltd.*,[61] for example, the plaintiff suffered a stroke after taking the defendant's contraceptive pill. No warning of such a risk was attached to the product. Would she have taken the pill in any case? The court was satisfied that she would not. She was particularly concerned about her health and the dangers presented by drugs in general. She would have chosen an alternative method of contraception had she known of the danger of a stroke.

The test of causation requires that the plaintiff persuade the court that with full knowledge of the risks he or she would not have undertaken the treatment. Sometimes it is said that this is an 'objective' test – what would a *reasonable* person have done? But reasonable people react in a large variety of ways to the prospects of medical treatment. Some will postpone a decision in order to take advantage of a career opportunity. Others would rather put up with their complaint than run the risk of being unable to enjoy a game of golf. These are all the reactions of reasonable people. A purely objective test, therefore, does not answer the question, would *that* plaintiff have accepted the risks or not? As a reasonable person he might have done either. This was acknowledged in *Buchan*:

> ...a proper test for the plaintiff to meet is, on the balance of probabilities, was there a reasonable likelihood that a reasonable person *in the plaintiff's position*, if fully informed, would not have taken the drug?[62]

It should not be assumed, however, that the plaintiff will only satisfy the test of causation if he or she is a reasonable person. No-one is obliged to accept medical treatment just because it could be considered reasonable to do so. A plaintiff who can show that he ought to have been informed of a risk attached to treatment, that a reasonable person would have accepted the risk, but that *he* would have refused it, ought still to succeed. The test of causation requires only that the plaintiff would not have had the treatment will full knowledge of the risks. It does *not* require that he must have acted as a reasonable plaintiff.

In theory a claim in these terms could succeed, but in practice it will be very difficult to prove, for two reasons. First, it will be difficult to persuade a court that the patient would have behaved unreasonably. After all, with the benefit of hindsight, many patients who have suffered injury from treatment without being informed of the danger will be strongly inclined to say they would have refused reasonable treatment had they known. The court must look at the evidence at the time the treatment was discussed, not after the damage has occurred. Secondly, if the risk of danger is so small that a reasonable person would be prepared to accept it, it may also be so small that a reasonable doctor would not consider it worth disclosing in the first place.[63] The plaintiff must also show that he has been wrongly deprived of information. This is the case even though the court believes that the patient would have refused treatment had he known about the risks.[64]

Mass Litigation and the Opren Action

Mass litigation for personal injury damages is often considered in two broad categories. The first concerns mass accidents in which large numbers are injured by the same event, for which the defendant is responsible, such as the Manchester air disaster, the fire and explosion on the Piper Alpha oil platform, the Zeebrugge ferry calamity and the fire at King's Cross underground rail station. The second relates to product liability, when a product is released by the defendant to the market and causes injury, often in differing circumstances, over a period of time, (such as with asbestos, intra-uterine devices and drugs). Both create difficulties of their own, but the more complex problems arise in the latter case, of which *Opren* is an example.

The present Rules of the UK Supreme Court provide no procedure capable of managing the problems posed by mass drug litigation. Although 'Representative' proceedings are available,[65] they are restricted to those actions in which it can be said that 'all the members of the alleged class have a common interest, that all have a common grievance, and that the relief is in its nature beneficial to them all.'[66] The Rules have in mind the form of action where all the members of the class have identical grounds for claiming the same remedy. The answer to the claim of one of the plaintiffs is the answer to the claim of them all.

Drugs and the Opren Case

Claimants against drug companies do not possess these characteristics. Although they may seek damages from the same defendant, their individual claims are different. Opren (chemical name *benoxaprofen*), for example, was a drug designed to relieve the symptoms of arthritis. It was released in 1980 and used by a large number of people, many of them elderly. Although it provided significant benefit to some users, it caused serious side-effects in others and was withdrawn by the company in 1982. Soon thereafter the 'Opren Action Group' was created to press for compensation for those who had been injured by the drug. Eventually, some 1 500 people joined the group, which was represented, in the main, by six firms of solicitors.[67]

From the outset it was clear that the action could never proceed on a 'class' basis. The drug was alleged to have caused a variety of side-effects. It was blamed, amongst other things, for photosensitivity of the skin, gastro-intestinal disorder, Stevens-Johnson syndrome, onycholisis (a loosening of the nails of the hands and feet) and death. In each of these separate categories, the question of damages was specific to the facts of each case. Some suffered transient side-effects; others, long-term injury. In addition, each case raised a separate issue of causation. Was the particular plaintiff prescribed the correct dosage by the doctor? Did the patient follow the dose regimen correctly? Were the injuries of natural, rather than iatrogenic origin? Was a sufficient warning given by the defendant against use by a certain category of user? Thus neither the claim, nor the defence, were sufficiently uniform to provide the basis of a representative action.

Although the litigation could not proceed on the basis of a class action, there was a powerful incentive not to have to litigate each case separately. From the point of view of individual plaintiffs, the expenses involved in attempting to do so would be prohibitive. Pharmacists, pharmacologists and other experts were required to assess and interpret the documents (about 1.3 million in all) made available by the defendant on discovery. Some of this assistance was relevant to all, or some, of the plaintiffs. It made no sense to conduct the assessment more than once. Similarly, both the court and the defendant faced the prospect of serious administrative difficulty unless the claims could be rationalised in some way.

In the absence of any established procedure for dealing with such a claim, how was the issue to be tried? The action was begun, with the agreement of the court, by the service of a 'master' statement of claim and 'master' defences, in which the claims of all the plaintiffs, and the defences to them, were combined into one set of pleadings. The hearing of the preliminary matters in the case was assigned to one judge and each issue was fought in the name of one plaintiff, on behalf of the group as a whole. For example, how were the costs of the action to be borne and the different issues arising under the claim to be heard? From the outset it was clear that a number of themes arose which were common to the entire group. Questions concerning the development of the drug, its testing and the evaluation of side-effects were common to each plaintiff. In addition, some categories of plaintiff could be separated from others to form sub-groups of common claims, for example those with differing types of adverse reaction. Thus it was agreed that some fifteen 'lead cases' would be selected for the purpose of giving to others in the same category an indication of the likelihood of their claim succeeding or not. They would be tried separately, and although their outcome would not be binding on the others, they would clearly be persuasive as to the result that might be expected.

In the event, the suitability of these arrangements was never put to the test because the case was settled out-of-court. After discussions with the plaintiff's lawyers, the defendant made available a lump sum to be distributed by the six lead solicitors as they thought fit, on the basis of medical reports and the seriousness of each case. A large majority accepted the sums awarded by the lead solicitors. A minority took advantage of an arbitration procedure made available by the court to review the cases of those who were dissatisfied with their award.[68]

The Future of Mass Litigation

Mass litigation will probably become a more prominent feature of the modern market place. Particularly in the case of drugs, some form of arrangement will be inevitable whenever large numbers claim compensation for damage. To what extent are the solutions devised in Opren an answer to the problem?

Mr. Justice Hirst, who supervised the Opren litigation, considered that the case could not provide a model on which other cases should proceed:

> What would be suitable for an Opren type case might well not work well in other types of relevant actions, for example large disaster claims where there are disputes as to liability... What is needed is an enabling rule, subject to very broadly drawn criteria, empowering the Court to set up a scheme to fit an individual case which falls under one or other of the relevant categories, and to do so by binding order if necessary if the parties cannot themselves agree.[69]

It is difficult to improve on this 'take each case as it comes' basis.[70] But even with this infinitely flexible approach, significant problems remain, most particularly in relation to the issue of costs. The basic rule relating to the costs incurred by individuals in a group is that they should be distributed equally amongst the class, without regard to legally aided and non-legally aided cases. The legal aid fund cannot be used to finance the actions of the privately funded cases.[71] Some plaintiffs, therefore, are likely to fall outside the legal aid limits and have to bear their own costs. How is the issue of funding to be resolved with regard to this group of claimants?

What if, amongst a group of claimants, some have claims of significantly higher value than others? Should they all incur a flat rate, or a pro rata fee? Others may have relatively small, but very difficult, claims. Consequently, disproportionate expenditure must be incurred in bringing them to court. Should they pay proportionately more costs than the others, or be forced to set up a separate group? What if a plaintiff seeks to join a group of litigants after it has spent large sums discovering documents and having experts assess their relevance. Should he or she be required to buy into the litigation before taking the fruits of the progress already made? How should costs be distributed 'equally' amongst these individuals?

There are a variety of answers to these questions, but the issue is the same in each. How far should a group of litigants be allowed to restrict the entry of others into its ranks? Presumably some control is appropriate. If this is right, what should become of the plaintiff refused entry to the group? Naturally, he or she can seek individual advice. But should there be entitlement to approach counsel, retained on behalf of the group, for separate, independent advice? On the one hand, counsel is supposed to be on the 'cab rank', and ought to be available to advise unless his impartiality is compromised by another case. On the other, if counsel's advice and expertise in the case has been obtained at great expense to the group of claimants, why should it be automatically available 'on the cheap' to the latecomer? If counsel were obliged to confer the benefits of work, paid for by others, on those outside the group, then the incentive to create such an arrangement would be seriously diminished.

One response to problems of this sort is to introduce a contingency fee system to group litigation. The plaintiff could agree with his solicitors to pay a percentage (perhaps between 25 and 50 per cent) of his damages on condition that his action succeeded, but nothing if it failed. At present contingency fees are void of legal effect and unenforceable,[72] but recent enquiries into the question have recommended that the case for introducing such a system be considered more seriously.[73] There is no guarantee that contingency fees would assist claimants in the Opren type of case. Solicitors would only commit their resources to such a claim if there were a reasonable likelihood of it succeeding, and thus of their retaining a percentage of their client's damages. But the cost of coordinating such a claim, of employing experts for guidance, and of establishing both defectiveness and causation, would be enormous – perhaps hundreds of thousands of pounds. One might think that, in the face of such an 'investment', solicitors would require a greater probability of a return on their money than the present system is able to offer.[74]

The most recent development in this field is contained in the Legal Aid Act 1988. With the group claim in mind, the Act permits the Legal Aid Board to enter into contracts with solicitors.[75] Contracts may be arranged when common issues arose from a single claim, which could be dealt with effectively by a particular firm, or firms. Those plaintiffs awarded legal aid would be directed to the firm in question. At the cost of depriving the plaintiff of an entirely free choice of solicitor, this will achieve some streamlining of actions for those on Legal Aid. But it leaves unchanged the complications created by those in the group who are not legally aided.

Conclusion

The problems associated with drug compensation are not unique to it. What is different is the way in which some of the most awkward questions of compensation are presented as a matter of routine by medicines. Patients are given no special rights against drug companies. In view of these difficulties, an understanding of the special problems which drugs create is important if there is to be a sensitive and systematic response to the claims we may expect in relation to them.

Notes

1 Committee on the Safety of Medicines (1988) Update, *British Medical Journal* **296,** 1319.

2 NSAIDS are amongst the most commonly prescribed drugs. See Spiers C.J., Prescription Related Adverse Reaction Profiles and Their Use in Risk-Benefit Analysis', in D'Arcy, P.S. and Griffin, J.P. (eds), *Iatrogenic Diseases* (3rd Ed) Oxford (OUP). The drug Opren (*benoxaprofen*) fell into this group and was associated with 61 deaths.

3 Committee on the Safety of Medicines (1986) Update, *British Medical Journal* **292,** 1190.

4 The true figure may be impossible to obtain, but could be ten or more times the official estimate. See discussion in Dukes, M and Swartz, B. (1988), *Responsibility for Drug-Induced Injury*, Holland, Elsevier, 1–10.

5 See Griffin, J.P. (1984), 'Adverse Reaction Monitoring', *The Lancet*, 10 November, in which it is estimated 16 per cent of doctors use the Yellow Card system.

6 See Ridout, S., Waters, W.E. and George, C.F. (1981), 'Knowledge of and Attitudes to Medicines in the Southampton Community', *Br. J. Clin. Pharmac.* **21**, 701, in which 72 per cent of those taking drugs appeared unaware of the potential dangers associated with their treatment.

7 Committee on the Safety of Medicines (1985), Update, 'Weighing the Risks', *British Medical Journal*, **290**, 383.

8 See Walker, S.R. and Asscher, A.W. (eds), *Medicines and Risk/Benefit Decisions,* M.T.P.

9 For example, the drug Roaccutane (*isotretinon*) is particularly effective in the treatment of serious and persistent acne. To this extent it might be said to be a cosmetic as much as a medicine. But it is also a powerful teratogen. Effective contraception is, therefore, essential to those at risk of becoming pregnant. Also see *Felix* v *Hoffman La Roche* 513 So.2d 1319 (1987), *Thomas* v *Hoffman La Roche* No. EC86/W/D. END MISS Nov 16 1989 in which allegations of defectiveness against the drug failed.

10 For those who have been given adequate warning of the dangers inherent in the product see Note 11. For general comments on information disclosure, see chapter 4.

11 See Drummond, Teeling-Smith, G., and Wells (1988), *Economic Evaluation in the Development of Medicines*, OHE, and Teeling-Smith, G. (1988) 'Economic Benefits', in Walker, S.R. and Asscher, A.W. (eds) *Medicines and Risk/Benefit Decisions.*

12 'We have considered the cases of transient side-effects common to most people and the small risk of catastrophic reaction to a minority. Is exposure to risk of damage justifiable, not for the benefit of the individual himself, but for the benefit of the next generation of children? Parents have been encouraged to have their children vaccinated against whooping cough and pertussis even when the risk of infection is very small. A justification for doing so is to prevent the incidence of the diseases rising in order to protect future generations of children'. See HMSO (1977), *Whooping Cough Vaccination.*

13 The case in favour of an insurance fund for this type of loss, set up by the manufacturers themselves is very strong. It has even been suggested that it could be in their commercial interests to do so, on the ground that consumers would be more prepared to use drugs produced by a company willing to pay compensation in the event of it causing undue damage. See Medawar, C. (1988), book review in Scrip No. 1340/1, 2 September, 22. The voluntary Swedish compensation scheme is discussed by Brahams, D. (1988), 'Swedish Medical Insurance Schemes', *The Lancet* 2/9 January, and Brahams, M. (1988), 'Swedish No-Fault Compensation', *N.L.J.* **138,** 14, 31.

14 Section 3(2)(a), 1987 Act.

15 See Newdick, C. (1987), 'The Future of Negligence in Product Liability', *L.Q.R.* **103,** 288, 307.

16 SI 1976 No. 1726, as amended by the Medicines (Labelling) Amendment Regulations 1977 (SI 1977 No. 996 and 2168) and SI 1978 No. 41.

17 SI 1977 No. 1055.

18 [1985] AC 871; for further discussion see Chapter 4.

19 *Davies* v *Wyeth Laboratories Inc.* 399 F.2d 121, 130 (1968).

20 SI 1972 No. 2076.

21 See O'Brien, B. (1986), *What Are My Chances Doctor? A Review Of Clinical Risks*', OHE.

22 See Green, D. (1987), *Medicines in the Marketplace* I.E.A. Health Unit, 43.

23 See O'Brien, *op. cit.*

24 Sections 7 and 8, Medicines Act 1968.

24[a] See Newdick, C. (1992), 'The Impact of Licensing Authority Approval on Pharmaceutical Product Liability', *Food and Drugs Law Journal* **47**, 41.

25 Reported briefly in *NLJ* **134** 886 (1984). The comments in the text are from the transcript.

26 *Rowling* v *Takaro Properties Ltd*, [1988] 1 All E.R. 163, 172 and Re HIV Haemophiliac Litigation (1990) 140 NLJ 1349. See also Bailey, S and Bowman, M. (1986) 'The Policy/Operational Dichotomy' *C.L.J.* 430.

27 The issue was never finally decided. In *Bonthrone* v *Secretary of State for Scotland* (1987) S.L.T. 34, decisions relating to the manner in which a vaccine was presented to doctors and parents were said to be a matter of discretion which was immune from attack provided it was exercised within the ambit of the statute and *bona fide*. See also Ross v Secretary of State for Scotland [1990] 1 Medical Law Report 235. This gives the Minister a huge measure of discretion. A narrower approach was taken in *Kinnear*, see Note 25.

28 *Rowling* v *Takaro Properties Ltd.* [1988] 1 All E.R. 163. 173; *Yuen Kun-yeu* v *Attorney-General of Hong Kong* [1987] 2 All E.R. 705, 713.

29 See *Yuen Kun-yeu ibid, D. and F. Estates Ltd.* v *Church Commissioners* [1988] 2 All E.R. 992, 1007.

30 See *Yuen Kun-yeu ibid., Hill* v *Chief Constable of West Yorkshire* [1987] 1 All E.R. 1173.

31 See *Rowling (supra), Yuen Kun-yeu, ibid.*

32 See *Peabody* v *Sir Lindsay Parkinson & Co.* [1984] 3 All E.R. 529, 534.

33 See *Home Office* v *Dorset Yacht Co. Ltd.* [1970] A.C. 1004.

34 Section 85(1) and (2), Medicines Act 1968. The DoH has the power to vary, suspend or revoke licences granted to pharmaceutical manufacturers and distributors, see ss. 28–30, Medicines Act 1968.

35 See S.133 (2)(c).

36 Article 7 of the European Directive.

37 Thus section 1(1) introduces the Act by providing that 'This Part shall have effect for the purpose of making such provision as is necessary in order to comply with the product liability Directive and shall be construed accordingly.'

38 Emphasis added by author.

39 It might be argued that the defence is unavailable when knowledge elsewhere appreciated that the product in question would be *defective*. But the wording of the Directive is against such a view.

40 This comment must be understood subject to the fact that the burden of proof is reversed. The producer will be presumed to have known of the defect until he can

prove the contrary. The effect of this provision should not be underestimated, see Newdick, C. (1988), 'The Development Risk Defence of the Consumer Protection Act 1987', *Camb. L.J.* **129**, 147.

41 See *Vacwell* v *BDH Chemicals Ltd.* [1971] 1 Q.B. 88, *Bradford* v *Robinson Rentals Ltd.* [1967] 1 W.L.R. 337, *Smith* v *Leech, Brain & Co.* [1962] 2 Q.B. 405.

42 [1956] 1 All E.R. 615.

43 [1973] 1 W.L.R. 1. See the general discussion of this and *Bonnington Castings* v *Wardlaw* in Stapleton, J. (1988), 'The Gist of Negligence' *L.Q.R.* **104** 389.

44 In *Bonnington, ibid* the risk (of pneumoconiosis) was caused by inadequate extraction of dust during employment. In *McGhee, ibid,* the risk (of dermatitis) was caused by a failure to provide adequate washing facilities after employment was ended.

45 See *Bonnington*, at p. 618; and McGhee at p. 4 (both per Lord Reid).

46 [1988] 1 Q.B. 730 (CA).

47 *Wilsher* v *Essex A.H.A.* [1988] 1 All E.R. 871. See also *Kay* v *Ayrshire and Arran Health Board* [1987] 2 All E.R. 917 (H.L.).

48 See *Brown* v *Rolls Royce Ltd.* [1960] 1 All E.R. 577 (H.L.).

49 The rule could operate against a number of defendants provided they can all be said to have made a material contribution to the risk of injury; see *Bryce* v *Swan Hunter and others* [1988] 1 All E.R. 829. The decision in this case appears now to be wrong, however, in the light of *Wilsher*, because there remained doubt whether the defendants had materially contributed to the plaintiffs' condition.

50 See generally, and particularly as regards the elderly, D'Arcy, P.F. 'Epidemiological aspects of iatrogenic disease', in D'Arcy P.F. and Griffin, J.P. (eds) *Iatrogenic Diseases* (3rd Ed), Oxford: OUP.

51 See *Wilsher* v *Essex AHA* (*supra*).

52 See *Loveday* v *Renton and Another* in 'The Times' 31 March 1988, on the evidence supporting the claim that pertussis vaccine could cause brain damage in children.

53 See the comments of Lord Bridge in *Wilsher*, 883.

54 See *Hotson* v *East Berkshire HA* [1988] 2 All E.R. 909 (H.L.). The risks in *McGhee* and *Bonnington* could not be quantified but causation was established nevertheless.

55 Brodie, M.J. and Feely, J. (1988) 'Adverse drug interactions', *British Medical Journal* **296,** 845.

56 For an example see *Basko* v *Sterling Drug Inc.* 416 F.2d 417 (1969).

57 See Fleming, S.G. (1988), *The American Tort Process*, Oxford: O.U.P., 1988, 252–66.

58 In *Fitzgerald* v *Lane* [1987] 2 All E.R. 455, two motorists negligently collided with a pedestrian, but only one of them actually caused the tetraplegia suffered by the victim. It was impossible to know which motorist was responsible. Liability was shared between the motorists. The ratio of the case is based on the discredited reasoning of the Court of Appeal in *Wilsher*, but is justifiable on the ground that both defendants were at fault and there were no other possible causes of the damage.

59 *Reyes* v *Wyeth Laboratories Inc.* 498 F.2d 1264 (1974).

60 *Cunningham* v *Charles Pfizer & Co.* 532 P 2d 739 (1975).

61 8 D.L.R. (4th) 373 (1984).

62 *Ibid.*, 406.

63 The requirement is discussed in *Sidaway* v *Royal Bethlem Hospital* [1985] AC 871. See section in this chapter on Warnings and Instructions for Use.

64 In *Videto* v *Kennedy* (1981) 125 D.L.R. (3d) 127, the plaintiff agreed to be sterilized without being informed of the risk of 0.3 per cent of scarring. The risk was significant to the plaintiff who wished to keep the fact of the operation from her Catholic

parents. The court held that a risk of that size did not have to be disclosed at all. Thus the issue of causation did not arise.

65 See Order 15, rule 12, Rules of the Supreme Court: 'Where numerous persons have the same interest in proceedings... the proceedings may be begun, and, unless the Court otherwise orders, continued, by or against any one or more of them as representing all or as representing all except one or more of them.'

66 *Smith* v *Cardiff Corporation* [1954] 1 Q.B. 210, 221, per Evershed M.R.

67 About 200 other firms of solicitors were involved, representing those who preferred not to join the larger group of solicitors.

68 See *Randall* v *Eli Lilly & Co.* (Q.B.D., 1988 3 February 1988 unreported).

69 See Rt. Hon. Mr Justice Hirst, 'Litigating Disasters', address to the 1988 Bar Conference.

70 The experience of product liability class actions in the US courts tends to support this view. A tiny number of cases have been certified as suitable for class litigation and, to the author's knowledge, all have been settled before coming to trial. See Bush, L.S. (1986) 'Some Observations on Federal Rule 23 and Mass Tort Class Actions in the United States', *C.L.Q.* **5** 109 and 201, and Fleming, J.G. (1988), *The American Tort Process*, Oxford: O.U.P., Ch. 7.

71 See *Davies* v *Eli Lilly & Co.* [1987] 1 All E.R. 801. For further discussion, see chapter 2.

72 An arrangement with the six lead solicitors, that they would waive the costs incurred by their non-legally aided clients if the action failed, was held to be a contingency fee and therefore bad. See *Davies* v *Eli Lilly & Co.* (Q.B.D., 8 May 1987, unreported) and Solicitors Act 1974, s. 59(2)(b). See also chapter 2.

73 See the Civil Justice Review (Cm.394, 1988, para. 384), and A Time For Change (the Marre Report on the Future of the Legal Profession, Law Society and the Bar Council, 1988) para. 10.22. The general issue of contingency fees is considered by Fleming in 'The American Tort Process', ch. 6.

74 If the action were lost, who would pay the costs incurred by the other side; the litigant himself, or his solicitors?

75 Legal Aid Act 1988, Section 4(2).

2 Litigating Disputes in Consent to Medical Treatment: The United Kingdom Position

Sheila A.M. McLean

The starting point of this discussion will be the assertion – now widely accepted in most circles – that patients have rights in the medical enterprise. These rights may relate to a wide variety of issues and have a variety of shapes, but for present purposes the crucial right is that to receive information about benefits, risks and alternatives in therapy, in order that a self-determining choice can be made by the patient as to whether or not the clinical recommendation should be followed. It will also be assumed that, given that patient decision-making is part of self-determination – a concept impliedly if not expressly protected by law – the law should offer a means of redressing legitimate grievances arising from a breach of that right. Three things will be concluded: that the law does currently recognise a right to receive information; that despite this the current form of action made available renders the task of the aggrieved patient extremely difficult; and that the test applied by the courts in the UK makes it effectively, perhaps even technically, impossible for the patient to succeed in suing in respect of being inadequately informed.[1]

It is important initially, and briefly, to assess the medical act itself, since it need not be perceived as one homogeneous enterprise. There is a level to the medical act which goes beyond the purely clinical or technical. What may be called the moral aspect of medicine – as with all human interactions – cannot be described solely in terms of the narrow discipline. The responsibilities to his or her client of the lawyer or the architect, as well as the doctor, share characteristics which make it difficult to describe the action under consideration as only 'medical' or 'legal' and so on. The manner in which professional groups deal with their clients in a principled way – using concepts like truth-telling, respect for persons, and so on – is not specific to any one discipline, but relates to the characteristics of the client as much as it does to the profession or professional involved. Thus, whilst the nature of the skill being sought may change, the essentials of a 'good' transaction do not.[2] A good act remains one which respects the client's moral autonomy and facilitates his or her capacity (and right) to make free and uncoerced decisions based on the honest provision of information.[3] The rights of the client generate the duty of the professional not to overstep authority in the name or the interests of professional skill or technical superiority. Thus, although the technical gap can seldom, if ever, be bridged, respect for the individual demands that relevant information is disclosed and an opportunity presented for individual or consensual decision making.[4]

In the case of medicine, this provision of information permits the patient to make choices about whether to run risks and/or which risks to run. Whilst information disclosure can easily be seen as an aspect of the doctor's professionalism, it is scarcely *only* this. Assessment of the doctor's behaviour in the provision of advice and recommendation is arguably less obviously susceptible of clinical judgement than are matters of an operational nature.[5] If the aim of disclosure is the protection and facilitation of individual autonomy, then the issue is far wider than the clinical and is not, and cannot be, defined by reference to standard medical practice. Respect for persons demands that the opportunity for free decision-making is made available and that the decision, albeit coupled with clinical recommendation, is that of the person who holds the right.

If medicine is to be a 'good', it must do more than merely demonstrate a high level of technical skills. It must also contain and foster this moral element which protects the integrity of the individual. When communities delegate to a professional group important decisions about health and illness, with all of the social, personal, financial and political consequences which can flow from them, then it is even more than usually important that participation is both free and knowing.[6]

The potential invasiveness of medicine and its social and political implications, make it an area ripe for rights discourse. More importantly, the inevitable personal impact of diagnosis and therapy places medical care at the forefront of concern for the individual. But rights are not protected merely by the payment of lip service to their conceptual soundness. Translation of rights into reality is also vital, and for this we generally turn to the law to provide both a statement of what rights are, and the machinery whereby they can be vindicated.[7]

It is not, therefore, sufficient to agree that patients have rights in the medical enterprise nor that doctors' duties flow from these rights. The willingness of the law to redress legitimate grievances, and the mechanisms available to do so, are of equal importance.

In sum, it will be argued that the significance of consent rules lies in their capacity to reflect and enhance the moral standing of the individual. The law has a major role to play in guiding professionals as to what is acceptable behaviour and what is not, whatever their professional colleagues may believe.[8] It also has a necessary commitment to disinterested decision-making and an interest in the provision of a viable method of redressing grievances. It will be assumed, therefore, that the law should reflect the rights of patients to give or withhold consent to medical treatment based on information disclosure, both by the form of action made available and through judicial decision-making.

Few would deny that a good medical act is an act in which the patient is a willing participant. In passing, it is worth noting that the Department of Health in its recent proposed amendments to consent forms felt constrained to point also to the *clinical* benefits of this.[9] Few would dispute that, in order to be willing, a patient has to make a choice based on the available relevant information. As the court said in *Bowater* v. *Rowley Regis B.C.*[10]

> A man cannot be said to be truly "willing" unless he is in a position to choose freely; and freedom of choice predicates...full knowledge of the circumstances upon which the exercise of the choice is conditioned...[11]

It will generally also be conceded that the law has a role to play in enforcing rights. As Weir notes, '[in] addition to its more obvious function of redressing harms the law of tort also indicates rights: it has a constitutional as well as a compensatory function.'[12] Nonetheless, as Walker points out, it is of course 'a policy decision for the law'[13] whether or not to recognise certain rights. If the law chose therefore not to recognise a right to receive information, then much of this case would collapse. However, despite an early reluctance to develop a theoretical position on information disclosure,[14] the right to receive information and to accept or reject therapy was firmly recognised in the case of *Chatterton* v *Gerson*,[15] the case which also settled the issue of the appropriate legal analysis to apply in such cases. Following from this case, British courts have presumed that – unless the failure to disclose is gross – allegations will be considered by the use of negligence analysis.[16]

So far, then, an attempt has been made to show the relevance of concern about information disclosure, and to indicate its status as a right which we can realistically expect the law to recognise and enforce. Further, it is clear that the currently appropriate form of action for resolving grievances is the negligence action. Many commentators have noted the difficulties of raising a successful action against a doctor, and these need not be rehearsed here.[17] Nor is it necessary to describe in detail the fundamental elements of proof in negligence analysis.[18] Rather, and assuming that the above assertion of a right to receive information is accepted, the nub of the question is: does the law actually fulfil the expectation that it will provide an appropriate decision-making ethos, applying rights based criteria, and an appropriate mechanism which offers the patient a realistic chance of success?

It must first of all be noted that, although a distinction has been made between the operational (clinical) aspects of a doctor's job and that which I have loosely called the moral, the courts have been unwilling to do the same. The most significant British case until recently was the case of *Bolam* v *Friern Hospital Management Committee*.[19] Whilst this case recognised the existence of a duty to make disclosure, the court chose to see its description not in terms of patients' rights but rather – and very specifically – in terms of doctors' duties. The obligation of the doctor was to act in a manner consistent with good medical practice and 'the issue of whether this duty encompasses the giving of information relating to risks inherent in the treatment is a question, not of law, but of reasonable medical judgement.'[20] In *Bolam*, therefore, there was no serious suggestion that medical evidence as to standard practice would be anything other than determinative of the issue. Montrose[21] states that:

> From the premises of McNair, J. [the judge in the *Bolam* case] it does indeed follow that in "a situation which involves the use of some special skill or competence", and where there are diverse practices followed by those possessed of that skill, then conformity with one of those practices cannot be negligent.[22]

The so called *Bolam Test* which emerged from this case is as follows: where a doctor acts in accordance with a school of thought accepted as reasonable by a responsible body of medical opinion, then he or she will not be negligent. The effect of this is that the assessment of sufficiency of evidence to establish the *legal* concept of negligence is essentially set by doctors themselves. This is problematic enough as an approach in allegations of operational negligence, but how much more problematic when it is not the doctor's technical skills which are under scrutiny, but rather his or her response to, and respect for, patients' rights?

The *Bolam Test* has been followed by subsequent courts. In *Thake* v *Maurice*,[23] the court openly held out the possibility that the surgeon in question could have provided himself with a legal excuse for his somewhat vague explanation had he claimed that it was not common practice to give any more clear an explanation. As Kerr, L.J. said:

> It would have been open to the defendant to qualify the answers which he gave either in cross-examination or re-examination, by saying that he did not believe that it was the general practice to give any such warning...He was given the opportunity of doing so in a later part of his cross-examination when it was suggested to him that he might not have given the warning because this might have caused worry or concern to the plaintiffs, but he did not accept this. Accordingly,...in the present case there was nothing to be placed in the balance against the need for the warning which the defendant himself recognised in his evidence.[24]

In sum, then, British courts made no pretence at setting anything other than a professional test for disclosure. The emphasis is on doctors' duties and not on patients' rights. The evidence of fellow practitioners, notoriously reluctant to criticise their colleagues, will determine the scope of the legal concept of negligence. As Robertson puts it:

> The doctor is under a duty to take reasonable care to avoid exposing his patient to any foreseeable risk of injury, and, as the decided cases indicate, "foreseeable risk" is equated with "real risk". Thus, it would follow that the source of the duty to inform the patient of the "real" risk inherent in the proposed treatment is simply the overall duty of care arising from the doctor-patient relationship.[25]

He continues:

> ...since the doctor's duty of care is defined in terms of acting as a reasonable doctor, there is a danger that...English courts will see the duty to disclose inherent risks as stemming from the fact that reasonable doctors disclose such risks (which may be subject to rebuttal by medical evidence) rather than from the fact that the patients' right to self-determination demands such disclosure.[26]

The impact of the *Bolam Test* on the development of a theoretical or judicial commitment to the protection of this right cannot be underestimated. It gives rise to the concern that the disinterested decision-making which can be expected in a court of law will be subverted by an interested professional group, and that the rights of patients will come a poor second to the interests of physicians in exercising clinical freedom and judgement. Whatever the motivation of the doctor, and however potentially beneficial the therapy, the outcome of the medical act is not solely clinical, the considerations which predict its acceptance or rejection are substantially non-medical and the choice is that of the patient.[27] It is for the law to set a test which takes account of these factors. In accepting the *Bolam Test* the courts reneged on the reasonable expectations of the consumer of health care. It was, however, open to a superior court to modify or overrule this test and substitute an alternative.

The House of Lords was recently given an opportunity to redress this apparent imbalance in the case of *Sidaway* v *Bethlem Royal Hospital Governors*.[28] Indeed, in the Court of Appeal, Sir John Donaldson had postulated a modification to the *Bolam Test* which would have rephrased it. A defence would, in his formulation, be available only if the practice was 'rightly' accepted by a responsible body of medical opinion.[29] Not perhaps a huge difference, but a chink through which the light of legal commitment to patients' rights could have shone.

The view of the majority in the House of Lords was, however, somewhat different. Hopefully without labouring the point, a brief consideration of the judgements in the Lords is necessary.

In his judgement, Lord Diplock, in the first few sentences, seems to take the professional test for granted. The presumption is that decisions will be taken *by* doctors *for* their patients. Accepting that there are risks associated with all therapies, he goes on:

> All these are matters which the doctor will have taken into consideration in determining, in the exercise of his professional skill and judgement, that it is in the patient's interests that he should take the risk involved and undergo the treatment recommended by the doctor.[30]

Lord Diplock accepted that it was not altogether clear in this case whether or not the doctor had weighed up the risks to his patient or whether or not he had passed them on to his patient. However, this was not seen by him as being of particular significance. What was important was the evidence of other doctors that they would not have disclosed the information of whose lack Mrs. Sidaway later complained. As he said, although the court did not know what actually had happened,

> What we do know...and this is in my view determinative of this appeal, is that all the expert witnesses specialising in neurology... agreed that there was a responsible body of medical opinion which would have undertaken the operation...without specific reference to risk of injury of the spinal cord.[31]

Lords Keith and Bridge concurred in this judgement, referring with approval to the case of *Hunter* v *Hanley*,[32] that 'in the realm of diagnosis and treatment there is ample scope for genuine difference of opinion and one man is clearly not negligent merely because his conclusion differs from that of other professional men.'[33] Lord Bridge noted that:

> It could be argued that if the patient's consent is to be fully informed, the doctor must specifically warn him of all the risks involved in the treatment offered, unless he has some sound clinical reason not to do so. Logically, this would seem to be the extreme to which a truly objective criterion of the doctor's duty would lead.[34]

He also noted, however, that this was not a feature of any jurisdiction to which the House of Lords had been referred and dismissed it as a possibility. In effect, Lord Bridge on the one hand agrees that the prime matter for consideration is patient autonomy, while on the other he considers its attainment to be best served by the clinical judgement of the doctor. The decision about which information to disclose in order to help the patient make a 'rational' choice is thereby adequately covered by the *Bolam Test.*

Lords Diplock, Keith and Bridge were in substantial agreement, therefore, that the *Bolam Test*, presuming as it does the supremacy of medical judgement and assuming the disclosure question to be simply an aspect of the doctor's overall duty of care, was the appropriate test to use. Lord Templeman reached substantially the same conclusion but by a somewhat different route. He placed considerable emphasis on the fact that the reasonable patient could be presumed to know that major surgery was potentially risky and also on the skill of the doctor in coming up with a recommendation which is in the patient's best interests. He accepted that the ultimate decision is that of the patient, but emphasised that this did not mean that the patient should be told of all of the risks. He concluded that:

> An obligation to give a patient all the information available to the doctor would often be inconsistent with the doctor's contractual obligation to have regard to the patient's best interests.[35]

Whilst Lord Templeman does not explicitly accept the *Bolam Test*, neither does he explicitly reject it, and in any event the application of his view would arguably have effectively the same result.

From the patient's perspective the most reassuring judgement was that of Lord Scarman, who, although agreeing with the final decision in this case, nonetheless took a radically different view of the fundamental issue. In urging his colleagues to the adoption of the so-called *Canterbury Test*[36] (that is the reasonable patient test) he seems to give primacy to the rights of the patient over the duties of the doctor – a priority which is at least logical. He started by questioning whether the professional test, used in operational matters, was the appropriate test to be applied in matters of disclosure. If it were, he argued, then:

> The implications of this view of the law are disturbing. It leaves the determination of a legal duty to the judgement of doctors. It would be a strange conclusion if courts should be led to conclude that our law, which undoubtedly recognises the right of the patient to decide whether he will accept or reject the treatment proposed, should permit the doctors to determine whether and in what circumstances a duty arises....[37]

Following the *Canterbury Test*, which he describes as '...a legal truth which too much judicial reliance on medical judgement tends to obscure'[38] it was, in his view, for the courts to decide, albeit with the assistance of medical opinion, the scope and extent of the legal duty which exists. This he regards as appropriate because there are 'factors other than the purely medical'[39] which may play a significant role in the patient's ultimate decision. Unfortunately, the impact of this apparently unequivocal commitment to patients' rights is somewhat diluted by his adoption from the *Canterbury Test* of the concept of 'therapeutic privilege' which permits withholding of information where the doctor deems disclosure not to be beneficial to the patient. The 'prudent patient' test itself is at least one step removed from the instant patient – this further exception takes it even further away.

This review of the *Sidaway* case admittedly ignores some of the finer details of the judgements, but it serves to highlight the most important features of the case. Three of the judges effectively endorsed the *Bolam Test*, one proffered an alternative which is not dissimilar and only one argued outright for patients' rights although even he was somewhat cautious in doing this. Each of the judges, however, conceded that patients do have a right to receive information on the basis of which to make decisions. Having reached this concensus, four of them still seemed to sense no tension between this assertion and the conclusion that doctors will decide which information should be disclosed. But at least we have cleared up one thing – there is, it would appear, a right to information, implying a corresponding duty on the doctor to make that information available. The doctor who fails in this duty may appropriately be sued. But what does this really mean?

For the patient to succeed, the nature of the duty must be established. Whether couched in terms of disclosure of 'material' risks or 'the general nature of the therapy' or whatever, it is clear that the duty *in fact* is to act in accordance with a responsible body of medical opinion. This, despite the fact that the rationale for decision-making may be partially or exclusively non-medical. And how do we know what is a 'responsible body of medical opinion'? Well, obviously we know this from the evidence of other doctors – not huge numbers of them, of course, but one or perhaps two in a court of law. As the Pearson Commission[40] noted, it is notoriously difficult to find a doctor who is willing in a court of law to criticise a colleague.[41] Moreover, since – as the court in *Hunter* v *Hanley*[42] noted – there is ample room for disagreement in medicine, even if one doctor disagrees it is likely that others will not. And since the *Bolam Test* is to be applied to information as well as clinical matters, it matters not how many disagree, so long as one (responsible doctor) agrees. Given that the doctor's defence organisation or hospital board or authority will generally attempt an out-of-court settlement unless they think they have a case, it is pretty well inevitable, if the case gets as far as a court of law, that this crucial witness (or witnesses) will be available to the defence. Effectively, therefore, only in cases where the failure to disclose is gross – for example performing surgery other than that which was agreed to – will the doctor's duty not be met.[43] In any event in these cases the patient can still use assault analysis – which is effectively easier for the patient[44] – rather than negligence analysis.

Even if it were possible to establish a breach of duty – admittedly unlikely, if not impossible – the claimant would still require to show that, if the information *had* been disclosed, he or she would not have gone ahead with the therapy. This, of course proves the element of causation which is essential to the negligence action. Two problems present themselves here. First, the patient must show legally recognised harm if he or she is to have an action. This requires the law to recognise the insult to integrity as a harm,[45] since if the crucial factor were the protection of patient autonomy, a right of action should lie even if the risks which were not disclosed do not in fact occur. The patient who has sustained physical harm will at least be able to point to this as a basis for compensation – it is measurable and evidently equates to legal harm. However, the patient who complains of an insult to integrity is claiming compensation for a harm which will only be recognised if self-determination in medicine is accepted as a legally vindicable interest. Winfield and Jolowicz[46] note that there is a growing body of case law recognising liability even where the defendant has not injured the plaintiff by a positive act, and where 'their conduct seems most naturally expressed in terms of failure to ensure the receipt of expected benefits.'[47] However, they go on to point to the advantages of actions such as that in trespass which do not require proof of actual damage.[48] In Scots Law the *actio injuriarum* provides an ancient, albeit substantially obsolete, remedy for invasions of integrity.[49] However, the negligence action raises more problems.

The second problem posed here relates to cases where a known, but undisclosed, risk actually occurs. In this case, the patient may have a less arguable claim but also requires to prove that the therapy would not have been undertaken had the risk been disclosed. In addition the link between the non-disclosure and the occurrence of the risk may be somewhat tenuous, given that there is generally a presumption in favour of therapy. If a risk is inherent in a given diagnostic or therapeutic act then its disclosure to the patient may render the doctor non-negligent, but by definition the risk could not be avoided. Conversely, the negligence of the doctor who does not disclose the risk is less clearly capable of correlation to the harm which occurred – again given the preference for clinical judgement demonstrated by the courts – since it could have occurred in any event.

The patient, therefore, must show that he or she *would* have rejected therapy had the risk been made known to them. This can of course be extremely difficult to do. The patient will evidently claim this, when the risk occurs, but the courts perceive considerable difficulties in deciding what kind of test they should apply to such an assertion. It is thought to be too easy for the patient to claim with hindsight that therapy would have been rejected. So one more test is invoked – not merely, and unobjectionably, to test the credibility of the witness – but rather to conclude on whether or not the risk *should* have deterred the patient. Despite the fact that courts are well used to determining witness credibility, this is thought to be insufficient in cases of this sort. Courts will not therefore address themselves to whether or not the patient in question is reliably stating that he or she would not have undertaken this risk, but will rather ask whether or not the 'reasonable patient' would have done so.

This presents a clear paradox. On the one hand, courts will allow that doctors can, in the exercise of clinical judgement, decide – without being negligent – that a particular risk may deter a patient from therapy or cause unnecessary distress. These are reasons for legally sanctioned non-disclosure. On the other hand, courts purport to set themselves the task of deciding on an objective basis whether or not the reasonable patient *would* have been deterred by disclosure of risk. In other words, if the doctor acted in good faith and in line with a responsible body of medical opinion, how *can* the court subsequently conclude that the risk *should* have been disclosed, without defeating the test which they themselves have chosen to apply to cases of this sort? Effectively, therefore, it can be argued that the patient is incapable of suing successfully on the basis of lack of information unless the shortfall was so gross as in any event to merit the use of assault based actions rather than those based in negligence.

Of course, not everyone would agree with this viewpoint. In what could be regarded as a somewhat optimistic argument, Brazier[50] suggests that all that the *Sidaway* case tells us is that the transatlantic doctrine of informed consent is no part of our law. This we already knew from *Hills* v *Potter*,[51] and with respect the adoption of the *Bolam Test* by the majority of judges at the highest level implies much more than this.

Indeed, in *Gold* v *Haringey Health Authority*,[52] an attempt was made to take advantage of the loophole which Brazier foresees. It was argued here that the *Bolam Test* applied only to operational matters and not to matters of advice and information. The court however regarded themselves as bound by the *Sidaway* judgement and therefore by the *Bolam Test* itself.

The mess into which the law has got itself in these cases is amply illustrated by a series of other cases. The position seems to be that the law claims to recognise a right to receive information, whilst effectively making it impossible for the patient to succeed in suing on this basis. This is one paradox. The second however is that *some* patients may have their right vindicated on grounds which seem not to stand up to scrutiny. These are the so-called 'enquiring patients'. In *Blyth* v *Bloomsbury Health Authority*, [53] the judge indicated that since the patient was asking for information, and since she was someone with nursing training who could be trusted not to act 'irrationally', she should have been given the information for which she asked. Thus, the patient who asks a direct question seems to acquire rights which other patients do not have (particularly if the patient can be trusted not to act 'irrationally').

Now it may seem morally satisfying that a patient who asks questions should be told the truth and not a lie, (unlike the decision in *Hatcher* v *Black*[54]) but this merely begs a rather fundamental question. If courts would otherwise have upheld non-disclosure, as seems almost certain, then there must presumably be good reason for this. This good reason is generally conceded by the law to be that it is not in the patient's interest to have the information. On what grounds then does it become in the patient's interest to receive it merely because the question occurs to him or her, perhaps fortuitously? In truth, of course, the patient consults the doctor because he or she lacks certain information. In view of this it is unlikely that patients will know what questions to ask the doctor, and yet if they stumble on the right question there is an immediate attribution of rights.

It could of course be argued that the fact that a patient asks a certain question is not dependent on medical knowledge, since the argument presented here is that the impact of receiving information is personal and not technical. Thus, it could be said, if it is true that the patient should be told of risks, and that these risks are not merely technical risks, then the patient *will* ask the right questions because no technical knowledge is necessary to frame them. This is somewhat disingenuous, however, since the patient is arguing only that the *outcome* of the risk may be personal, and does not dispute that *knowledge* of the potential for the risk to occur is technically based. In any event, the patient is under no obligation to question. As the court put it in *Canterbury* v *Spence*,[55] *caveat emptor*[56] is not a relevant concept in cases of this sort.

Patient distress, so convenient a reason for non-disclosure, is more validly applicable here. Patients will likely have no medical background and may well be anxious and distressed about what is wrong with them. Should they also be expected – if their rights are to be vindicated – to ask the right question? To hold to such a position would be to attribute important rights only to the patient with some medical knowledge, to the lucky patient who stumbles upon the right question or to the assertive patient who is – unusually, some might say – not cowed by his or her involvement in the medical enterprise. Verbal acuity or personal confidence scarcely seem sound reasons for the attribution of rights.

Yet not only did *Sidaway*[57] approve this distinction, but so have a number of other cases. Indeed the Canadian case of *Lepp* v *Hopp*[58] goes one step further and argues that even where a direct question is asked the doctor may still rely on therapeutic privilege to withhold information. In any event, as Robertson[59] argues, this and other similar decisions rely on an arguable interpretation of the rule in *Hedley Byrne* v *Heller*[60] which permits the person who is asked questions the option of silence. He argues that the doctor/patient relationship differs from the standard contractual one in a significant and determinative manner – namely that there is a pre-existing duty of care on the doctor which 'deprives the doctor of the "option of silence" and which requires him to answer the question with reasonable care'.[61]

It is, therefore, a highly dubious proposition that the patient who asks relevant questions is entitled by this mere fact to additional, autonomy-enhancing information. If the issue were solely the truth telling of the doctor then this would, of course, be of considerable significance, and it is not argued that the enquiring patient should *not* receive information. If the issue is the question of patients' rights, however, then truth telling should extend to all patients. Only in this way is the doctor entitled to use the defence of *volenti non fit injuria*.

It can be concluded, therefore, that at present the negligence action in British courts, as restricted by the *Bolam Test*, offers little – if any – chance for the patient to succeed. The action itself apparently lacks the capacity for subjectivity which adherence to individual rights might demand, and the attitude of the judiciary serves to increase the distance between the individual litigant and possible compensation. One can only agree with Skegg[62] when he says that it would be:

> ...regrettable if in future the English courts did not play a more important role in protecting the interests of patients who wish to be able to reach an informed decision about whether to consent to medical procedures.[63]

even if one cannot necessarily agree that it would be 'surprising'.[64] Indeed, not only have English courts continued to adopt this approach but in Scotland, where the issue was arguably still open to different interpretation, the courts in *Moyes* v *Lothian Health Board*[65] and *Goorkani* v *Tayside Health Board*[66] seem to have adopted the Bolam Test and the Sidaway judgement as being expressive of Scots as well as English law.

Conclusions

Can this position be resolved? The US commentator Marjorie Shultz[67] argues that assault, negligence and contract analysis have been ineffectual in dealing with matters of this sort. None of them have supplied a decision-making framework which concentrates on the rights at stake. What she calls a 'new protected interest' is required. If UK courts are to continue – as seems likely – to use the negligence framework in matters of this sort, then the patient would be somewhat better protected were they prepared to distinguish between the technical and the moral aspects of the doctor's job. As the court said in *Canterbury* v *Spence*[68] it is for the law to set standards which protect patients' rights and not for medicine. And as Lord Scarman said in *Sidaway*,

> In a medical negligence case where the issue is as to the advice and information given to the patient as to the treatment proposed, the available options and the risk, the court is concerned primarily with the patient's rights. The doctor's duty arises from the patient's right. If one considers the scope of the doctor's duty by beginning with the right of the patient to make his own decision...the right to be informed of significant risks and the doctor's corresponding duty are easy to understand.[69]

In *Accidents, Compensation and the Law*,[70] Atiyah suggests that 'the duty of care concept has largely been used for the purpose of restricting liability for cases of proved fault, rather than as a means of expanding liability.'[71] There can be few cases where this is so clearly demonstrated as this one.

I have tried in this essay to establish, first that the language of rights is appropriately used within the doctor/patient relationship; secondly, that the right to self-determination incorporates the right of the patient to receive information on which to base a personally satisfactory decision; and third that legal process and judicial discretion play a highly important part in whether or not such a right is in fact attributed. Analysis of the complex and important values which characterize the patient's involvement with medicine cannot help but demonstrate and reinforce the view that medicine is scarcely a value-free discipline. Important issues of personal integrity demand disinterested decision-making, free from the professional or therapeutic imperative – the kind of decision-making which we have come to expect of the law. The question posed here has been deliberately couched in the language of rights in order to disentangle it from the current analytical framework which fails to make an adequate distinction between the separable issues of patients' rights and professional competence. Just as the status of patients is enhanced by this, so doctors are not threatened by it. The aim of medical practitioners should be, and generally is, not just a professionally competent act but also a morally appropriate one.

What is needed therefore is an assertion of the values which can be enhanced or threatened by being a patient. For the moment questions of autonomy predominate neither in medical nor apparently in legal thinking. In a rights-conscious society, the sporadic and equivocal protection of patients' rights can no longer be tolerated and a new formula for the allocation of responsibility is urgently required. Giving serious weight to the values identified here may provide a starting point for the law to seek an appropriate allocation of rights and obligations in medicine.

Notes

1 For further discussion, see McLean, S.A.M. (1989), *A Patient's Right to Know: Information Disclosure, the Doctor and the Law*, Aldershot: Dartmouth.
2 For an excellent discussion of a 'good' medical act, see Pellegrino, E. and Thomasma, D. (1981), *A Philosophical Basis of Medical Practice*, Oxford: OUP.
3 For discussion, see Robertson, G. (1981), 'Informed Consent to Medical Treatment' *LQR* **97** 102; Mason, J.K. (1986), 'Consent to Medical Treatment' *Scolag Bulletin* **110** 73; McLean, S.A.M. (1986), 'The Right to Consent to Medical Treatment' in Campbell, *et al.* (eds), *Human Rights: From Rhetoric to Reality*, Oxford, Basil Blackwell; Strong, C. (1979), 'Informed Consent: Theory and Policy' *Journal of Medical Ethics* **5**, 196.
4 See Brazier, M. (1992), *Medicine, Patients and the Law* (2nd Edn), Harmondsworth, Pelican; Mason, J.K. and McCall Smith, R.A. (1991), *Law and Medical Ethics* (3rd Edn), London: Butterworths; McLean, *op. cit.*
5 A point noted by Lord Scarman in *Sidaway* v *Bethlem Royal Hospital Governors & Ors.* [1985] 1 All E.R. 643 (H.L.) This distinction, however, was subsequently dismissed as inappropriate in *Gold* v *Haringey Health Authority*, 'The Times' 17 June 1986.
6 For an argument that, amongst other things, the delegation of such important decisions to medicine is inherently dangerous, see Illich, I., *Limits to Medicine. Medical Nemesis: The Expropriation of Health*, (1988 Edn) Harmondsworth, Penguin.

7 See Campbell, T., 'Realizing Human Rights' in Campbell, *et. al*, *op. cit.*
8 See Skegg, P.D.G. (1984), *Law, Ethics and Medicine*, Oxford: OUP, at p. 83 '...by no means all decisions taken by doctors concern matters within the exclusive competence of the medical profession, and with these matters the court should not act as if evidence of any approved practice was determinative.'
9 Reported and discussed in *I.M.E. Bulletin*, no. 44, November 1988, pp 5–6.
10 [1944] 1 K.B. 476.
11 *Ibid.*, at p 479.
12 Weir, T. (1983), *A Casebook on Tort*, (5th Edn) London: Sweet and Maxwell, 5.
13 Walker, D.M. (1981) *The Law of Delict in Scotland*, (2nd Edn. revised), Edinburgh: W. Green & Son Ltd., 9.
14 For discussion, see Robertson, loc. cit.
15 [1981] 1 All E.R. 257.
16 For a discussion of negligence analysis and its alternatives, see Shultz, M.M. (1985) 'From Informed Consent to Patient Choice: A New Protected Interest' *Yale Law Journal* **95**, 219.
17 See *Report of the Royal Commission on Civil Liability and Compensation for Personal Injury* (Pearson Commission) Cmnd.7054/1978.
18 For an explanation of these elements, see Weir, *A Casebook on Tort*; Walker, *The Law of Delict*; McLean, *A Patient's Right to Know.*
19 [1957] 2 All E.R. 118.
20 Robertson, 'Informed Consent', 115.
21 Montrose, J.L. (1958), 'Is Negligence an Ethical or a Sociological Concept?' *Modern Law Review*, **21** 259.
22 *Ibid.*, 261.
23 [1984] 2 All E.R. 513; [1986] 1 All E.R. 497.
24 *Ibid.*, [1986], 506–507.
25 Robertson, 'Informed Consent', 117.
26 *Id.*
27 For discussion, see Shultz, 'From Informed Consent to Patient Choice'; McLean, *A Patient's Right to Know.*
28 *Supra cit.*
29 [1984] 1 All E.R. 1018, at p. 1028.
30 *Ibid.*, 656.
31 *Id.*
32 1955 S.C. 200.
33 *Ibid.*, at p 217.
34 [1985] 1 All E.R. 643 (H.L.), at pp 660–1.
35 *Ibid.*, at p 665.
36 From the US case of *Canterbury* v *Spence* 464 F. 2d. 772 (1972).
37 *Supra cit.*, at p 649.
38 *Ibid.*, at p 654.
39 *Ibid.*, at p 652.
40 *Supra cit.*
41 *Report of the Royal Commission*, para 1327.
42 *Supra cit.*
43 See *Chatterton* v *Gerson*, *supra cit.*; *Devi* v *West Midlands Regional Health Authority* [1980] 7 C.L. 22.
44 For discussion, see Shultz, 'From Informed Consent to Patient Choice'; McLean, *A Patient's Right to Know.*

45 As for example in the ancient Scottish action, the *actio injuriarum*; for discussion, see Walker, *The Law of Delict*, particularly at p 20, and McKechnie, H. (1958), 'Delict and Quasi-Delict', in *An Introduction to Scottish Legal History*, Edinburgh: The Stair Society.
46 Rogers, W.V.H. (1984), *Winfield and Jolowicz on Tort*, (12th Edn), London: Sweet & Maxwell.
47 *Ibid.*, 7.
48 *Ibid.*, 43.
49 See Walker, *op. cit.*; McKechnie, *loc. cit.*
50 Brazier, *Medicine, Patients and the Law.*
51 [1983] 3 All E.R. 716.
52 *Supra cit.*
53 'The Times' 24 May 1985.
54 'The Times' 2 July 1954.
55 *Supra cit.*
56 Usually translated as 'let the buyer beware'.
57 *Supra cit.*
58 (1979) 98 D.L.R. (3d) 464.
59 Robertson, 'Informed Consent'.
60 [1963] 2 All E.R. 575.
61 'Informed Consent' p 119.
62 Skegg, *Law, Ethics and Medicine.*
63 *Ibid.*, 86.
64 *Id.*
65 (1990) S.L.T. 444.
66 [1991] *Medical Law Review*, **3**, 33.
67 Schultz, 'From Informed Consent to Patient Choice'.
68 *Supra cit.*
69 [1984] 1 All E.R. 1018, at p 654.
70 Atiyah, P.S. (1980), *Accidents, Compensation and the Law*, (3rd Edn) (reprinted 1984) London: Weidenfeld & Nicolson.
71 *Ibid.*, 38.

3 The Case for a No-Fault Compensation Scheme for Medical Accidents

Margaret Brazier

In 1978, when the Royal Commission on Civil Liability and Compensation for Personal Injury[1] (the Pearson Commission) reported, proposals for a no-fault compensation scheme for medical accidents were regarded with disfavour by the leaders of the medical profession, and attracted little interest from the practitioner on the wards or in the surgery. Indeed, no-fault compensation was seen as heralding the erosion of professional freedom.[2] Individual liability for individual error reinforced the concept of medical autonomy. The medical practitioner was at liberty to exercise his clinical judgement in the 'best interests' of the patient. Should doctors, in the judgement of their peers, fall below the required professional standard in so doing, they were rightly accountable to their patients and to their profession. Moreover in 1978 doctors feared that, should a state funded compensation scheme for medical accidents be introduced, then the state – via the medium of the health authorities – would want to assert a greater degree of control over medical practice. If the state had to pay for medical mishaps then obviously the state would do all that was feasible to reduce the number of such mishaps.

A decade later the medical profession appeared to have undergone a radical change of heart. The BMA[3] and many senior members of the profession declared their support for a change from negligence liability to no-fault compensation. Discussions were held with the DHSS and its successor the Department of Health (DoH) about the merits, demerits, and difficulties of implementing a no-fault scheme. So far the DoH remains sympathetic to the doctors' dilemma, but has been unresponsive to their plea for radical reform. The DoH prefers to pursue tentative proposals for a voluntary

NHS arbitration scheme to adjudicate on medical negligence claims. The cynical observer will no doubt express little surprise at the medical *volte face*. After all nearly every day the newspapers carry stories of the alarming rise in the rate of medical litigation. In 1978 medical negligence actions were comparatively rare, and medical law, as we know and teach it in British universities today, barely existed.[4] Fears of a malpractice explosion in the UK are, as a recent report from the King's Fund Institute in 1988 establishes,[5] much exaggerated. Litigation against doctors has increased both in the number of claims brought and the amounts of damages awarded,[6] but it has not reached crisis level. And it should not be overlooked that a considerable number of the recent court cases involving medical practitioners are *not* claims for compensation for medical mishap. They are rather attempts to define patients' rights and doctors' obligations including, for example, such matters as challenging the criteria as to who should receive infertility treatment,[7] attempts to safeguard an unborn child by making it a ward of court,[8] and asking the courts to define patients' rights to autonomy in relation to both questions of competence and consent to treatment.[9]

The full picture of the state of medical litigation in 1989 was understandably obscured for the individual practitioner by its *apparent* effect on his or her pocket. In 1978 the annual subscription to the Medical Defence Union (MDU) cost £40. The standard rate for 1989 was £1350.[10] And in 1989 two disturbing developments in the debate on medical indemnity took place. The Medical Protection Society (MPS) threatened to introduce differential subscriptions making practitioners in 'high risk' specialties, such as obstetrics, pay more for cover and reducing the cost to general practitioners and to doctors practising in such specialties as psychiatry.[11] Commercial insurers too began to consider entry into the arena of medical indemnity cover previously occupied by the established medical defence organisations. The prospect for a young obstetrician of having to pay £4,500 each year for indemnity cover might appear pretty horrendous. The spectre of young doctors avoiding 'high risk', but essential, specialties was vigorously canvassed in medical journals. The Department of Health responded, not as the MPS might have hoped with a no-fault scheme for birth injuries, but with the introduction in January 1990 of its proposals for NHS indemnity. From January 1 1990 health authorities have indemnified NHS hospital doctors directly just as they already do all other NHS employees.[12]

The cynical observer who has always perceived medical support for no-fault compensation for medical accidents as motivated exclusively by pressure on doctors' pockets will now confidently expect that support to evaporate. And he may well be proved right. This chapter, however, attempts to examine why, whatever provision may be made for indemnifying individual doctors against tort liability, there are sound reasons for giving serious consideration to the case for a no-fault compensation scheme for medical accidents. The case for such a scheme arises from an analysis of the interests of patients and their carers, and of the underlying interests of our community. The faults with no-fault are admirably highlighted by Sheila McLean in chapter 4. Thus no apology is made for a degree of partiality in this chapter.

Indemnity Cover for Doctors

The financial cost to the individual NHS practitioner was never of itself a sound reason for relieving doctors of a tort liability which all other professionals share. Also the extent of that cost was often exaggerated. Indemnity cover for doctors has remained relatively inexpensive in comparison to its cost to other professionals.[13] Moreover the health service itself was, even prior to 1990, making a substantial contribution to the cost of medical indemnity cover. Subscriptions paid by general practitioners are reimbursed as expenses by the Family Health Service Authority.[14] Indeed, from 1988 two thirds of the subscription paid by any whole time or part time practitioner working wholly in NHS hospitals was reimbursed to him or her by the health authority. The maximum real cost then to an NHS doctor was *less* than £500. The MPS proposals for differential subscriptions, and fears that commercial insurers would seduce 'low risk' practitioners away from the defence organisations – so starting an escalation of costs to hospital doctors in 'high risk' specialties – triggered a crisis. The Department of Health's response was the introduction of NHS indemnity.

A hospital doctor who does no private work will now be indemnified directly by his or her employing authority. The DoH circular advises that doctors should nonetheless retain membership of a defence organisation to cover matters excluded from the scheme – for example, legal advice and representation in disciplinary proceedings[15]. The total cost in 1992 of such limited membership of the MDU is £195 at the full rate with a discount for the first six years in practice. A consultant undertaking considerable private work will be charged £1,495.

The practitioner wholly committed to the NHS can thus no longer complain of the financial burden of indemnity cover.[16] The spectre of young men and women shunning obstetrics or surgery because of the cost of cover should have been exorcised, if indeed it ever had substance. But NHS indemnity is open to much the same criticism as regards tort liability and individual practitioners as were the earlier indemnity provisions. The possible impact of NHS indemnity on health authorities is considered at the end of this chapter.

Tort liability is designed to serve three functions. It should provide a framework within which one person's obligations to another can be properly defined. The tort of negligence has manifestly failed to fulfil that function in the context of consent to treatment.[17] It should operate as a fair and effective compensation system; that it does not do so for patients is amply illustrated by later sections of this chapter. It should also operate as a deterrent to negligence; in many cases the deterrent impact of tort liability on individuals operates via indemnity provisions. The careless driver will see his premiums rise. The careless doctor is subject to no similar financial deterrent. Even had differential subscriptions been implemented, the differentials would have operated between specialties, not individuals. Nor is there any concrete evidence that the differentials would have operated against 'careless' specialties or specialists. Obstetrics is not a 'high risk' specialty because obstetricians are more careless or less skilled than general practitioners or geriatricians. Childbirth is hazardous and when a child survives with extensive brain damage the cost of compensation is high. General practitioners and geriatricians may just not be worth suing. Tort liability, to have had direct deterrent impact, would need to have been backed by individually-rated premiums.

Commercial medical indemnity cover might of course have resulted in a pattern of indemnity cover for practitioners more closely related to a deterrent model. For that reason some commentators took a relatively favourable view of the prospect of commercial insurers entering the health care arena. As the King's Fund Institute report put it

> ...the positive collaborative response of the profession, the hospitals and the insurers through improved physician and risk management programmes suggests that the quality promoting aspects of the tort system should not be lightly dismissed.[18]

A greater degree of medical audit would indeed be a welcome prospect. But commercially driven audit of a public and underfunded health service might be less welcome. Medicine is a hazardous art. A good outcome can never be guaranteed. Commercial insurers would operate an audit in which commercial and financial considerations predominated and risk taking was kept to a minimum. Yet risk taking is the essence of good health care. And judgements on risks, are, or should be, shared between doctors and patients. Minimising liability risks indicates that a troublesome labour be resolved by Caesarean section. The mother and her obstetrician may prefer to accept the risk of letting labour take its course. Do patients want health care judgements to be directed by commercial insurers? Moreover, the experience of commercial insurance in the USA suggests even less desirable outcomes for health care. There is evidence that the much debated US malpractice crisis was, at least in part, the result of business strategies by the insurers to increase their profits.

Commercial indemnity cover, at least for public medicine, now seems an unlikely prospect for the United Kingdom. The role of the defence organizations has been taken over by the health authorities. The deterrent impact of individual liability cover is thus altogether absent from medical litigation. Deterrence will have to be via the medium of the health authority, now the indemnity provider. It remains to be seen whether the introduction of NHS indemnity will motivate health authorities and their employees to adopt more effective means of monitoring and eliminating poor practice. Viewed at the start of the 1990s, neither current nor immediately past arrangements for medical indemnity constitute a case for or against a no-fault scheme.

Why a Medical Accidents Scheme?[19]

The case *for* a no-fault medical accidents scheme rests on the manifold and adverse effects of the current tort system on patients and on health care. It is these adverse effects and the inequities of the system which justify radical reform. But, as will become apparent, much of the criticism that can properly be levelled at medical litigation is equally valid in the context of compensation for personal injuries generally. So, can a scheme which favours only one group of injured plaintiffs be justified? Would it not be preferable to see a universal scheme of compensation for disability introduced in this country? Under such a scheme compensation would be provided for disability regardless of the cause of that disability and regardless of whether disability results from accident or disease. There are no rational or humane grounds for providing that X who is injured by a medical accident receives compensation, while that compensation is denied to Y who is injured in a road accident or Z who is crippled by disease. But that ideal is currently unlikely to be attainable. The question therefore becomes whether, in the absence of a fully comprehensive and humane compensation system, a no-fault scheme limited to medical accidents can be justified. It is no argument against such a scheme that it falls short of the optimum compensation scheme, nor that it is unfair to other accident victims or those who succumb to disease. If true equity is at present unattainable, reducing the level of inequity is defensible, unless such a step will prejudice the long term aims of comprehensive compensation provision. And were a medical accidents scheme to be established, and be seen to be both effective and economically feasible, the prospects of persuading the government of the benefits of a wider scheme become considerably rosier.

What, then, are the grounds for pressing for a medical accidents scheme now? They stem largely from the damage which results from an adversarial and fault based system of medical litigation. This damage has several aspects.

The Cost of Litigation

The first derives from the cost of the present system. Cost is a problem common to all tort liability, but is acute in the context of medical litigation which tends to be prolonged and to rely heavily on expert opinion. In personal injuries litigation generally, it has been estimated that for every £1 awarded in damages at least 85p is eaten up by costs.[20] In New Zealand, by contrast, the Accident Compensation Corporation[21] pays out in compensation 93p of every £1 of its income.

In the instructive case of *Wilsher* v *Essex AHA*[22] the ludicrous expense of the current British system is highlighted. In 1978, Martin Wilsher was born nearly 3 months premature. He was admitted to a neo-natal unit where staff saved his life, but sadly he succumbed to retrolental fibroplasia (RLF) and is now nearly blind. RLF may be caused by excess oxygen, and it was established that doctors caring for Martin failed to monitor the oxygen in his bloodstream accurately, thus exposing him to what may have been dangerous levels of oxygen. Mrs Wilsher sought compensation for her son's disability. In February 1988 the case reached the House of Lords who held that the trial judge and the Court of Appeal applied the wrong test on causation and ordered a retrial. The agreed quantum of damages if negligence is proved to be the cause of Martin's disability is £116,119. Costs before any retrial already exceeded £200,000.

Nor is it simply the overall cost of medical litigation which is difficult to defend. The cost of litigation militates against many victims of medical accidents who might well be able to prove fault if they had the opportunity. Very many plaintiffs in medical claims are legally aided. Many others are excluded from the system because they are too rich for legal aid and too poor to fund an action unaided. Such persons might of course benefit from the proposed introduction of contingency fees. But, as will hopefully be demonstrated later, contingency fees would have only a marginally beneficial effect on a few patients who allege medical negligence and a detrimental effect on medical litigation overall.

The impact of the cost of medical litigation on the health service itself is considerable. The fact that many plaintiffs are legally aided means that not only does a defendant health authority bear the cost of litigation and the award of damages where a claim succeeds, but must often also bear the cost of successfully defended litigation.[23] Health authorities do not insure themselves on the commercial market. Money to meet the costs of litigation and damages awards is money taken from patient care. Moreover the burden – being unrelated to the quality of the service provided – rests unequally on the various authorities. Consider a health authority in a large city responsible for teaching hospitals. High risk surgical and obstetric cases from throughout the region may be referred to those hospitals. Thus the risk of litigation against that authority rises without the provision of additional funds to meet that risk, save for limited provision for 'pooling' risks within regional health authorities. The National Health Service and Community Care Act 1990 has implemented the proposals made in the National Health Service Review[24] to allow hospitals to opt for NHS trust status. The first wave of NHS trusts were approved in April 1991. The Conservative Party's election victory a year later looks set to trigger further wholesale creation of trust hospitals free of district health authority control and competing with each other and the private sector for business. Many leading teaching hospitals have already acquired trust status. Such hospitals have traditionally been national centres of excellence operating at the cutting edge of modern medicine. Inevitably that involves a high risk of litigation. Each NHS trust hospital is responsible for its own litigation costs in the first instance. May our 'best' hospitals now be tempted to opt for low-risk profitable enterprise rather than risk escalating litigation costs?

Of course, one of the arguments for the introduction of NHS indemnity was that by eliminating the medical defence organisations from any direct role in medical litigation, the overall cost of litigation will be cut and the disgraceful delays in resolving such litigation significantly reduced. Some reduction in cost should be achieved. Any NHS hospital doctor seeking separate legal representation will be obliged to fund that representation personally and must thus retain membership of a defence organisation against that eventuality. It remains to be seen how many will do so. Should separate representation become the norm – because doctors are unhappy to leave their professional fate in the hands of health service managers – then the perceived cost benefit of NHS indemnity will not materialise. In a year or two the spiral of increasing indemnity costs and total litigation costs will begin to turn upwards again. As to delay, the Department of Health has apparently produced no evidence which identifies the defence organisations, as opposed to the health authorities, as the principal culprits. Faced with a vastly increased workload, will overstretched regional health authority legal departments be able to cope without increasing delays? And if they elect to contract work out, as the circular permits, what will that cost?

Unfair to Patients and Doctors

The second ground for introducing *now* a no-fault medical accidents scheme is that the inequity in the fault-based system, again common to all tort actions, is acute in medical litigation and actually detracts from good relations between patients and their doctors. Judicial recognition of the inadequacy of the system as it affects patients was made explicit in *Ashcroft* v *Mersey RHA*.[25] Mrs Ashcroft consented to surgery on her left ear. In the course of that surgery her facial nerve was damaged and she was left with partial paralysis of the left side of her face. The expert witnesses were divided as to whether such damage could occur without negligence on the part of the surgeon. The evidence was equally divided between plaintiff and defendant. So Mrs Ashcroft's claim failed. Kilner Brown J commented:

> Where an injury is caused which never should have been caused common sense and natural justice indicate that some degree of compensation ought to be paid by someone.[26]

Martin Wilsher's case illustrates the potential unfairness of the fault based system for health care professionals.[27] The staff who cared for him saved his life. The unit where he was admitted was under-staffed. A house officer inserted the catheter to monitor his oxygen levels in the umbilical artery rather than the umbilical vein. He and the senior registrar failed to notice their error for some 24 hours. The senior registrar was held to be negligent. His error is patent, and he fell below the required standard of professional skill and competence on that occasion. Yet his skill had helped to save the baby. As Mustill LJ put it:

> They safely brought the baby through the perilous shoals of its early life. For all that we know, they surpassed on numerous occasions the standard of reasonable care. Yet it is said that for one lapse they ... are to be found to have committed a breach of duty. Nobody could criticise the mother for doing her best to secure her son's financial future. But has not the law taken a wrong turning if an action of this kind is to succeed?[28]

The reply to this question might well be (and indeed Mustill LJ's answer to his own rhetorical question in part was), that such a burden of liability for a single error is shared by all professionals. Medical practitioners are not unique in being penalised for one lapse from professional competence – so too are solicitors and architects. Culpability in the sense of moral blameworthiness is not the basis of civil liability for negligence. But nonetheless, there comes a stage when legal and moral concepts of fault become so far divorced as to make it indefensible to retain a fault based system of liability.

The position of health care professionals is distinguishable from that of their colleagues in law, accountancy and architecture. The solicitor will normally have an opportunity to check and correct a faulty contract or inadequate instructions to counsel. A surgeon rarely gets a second chance to put right surgery which has gone awry. Few professionals outside medicine are compelled to work over 24 hours without sleep. Few of them are backed up in their work by a shifting population of agency staff and creaking equipment.

It was suggested in *Wilsher*[29] in the Court of Appeal that allowance might properly be made for 'battle conditions'. That is, in ascertaining the standard of care demanded of a doctor or nurse, any evidence that they were acting in an emergency, without time for reflection, or that they were unavoidably distracted by the demands of other patients, would be taken into account. It is doubtful that this concession deals with the 'doctors' dilemma', for it appears that it covers only the obvious emergencies such as the patient rushed into Casualty with a cardiac arrest. It does not take account of the impossible hours worked by 'junior' doctors or the inadequate facilities with which they must too often manage. The 'battle conditions' reference in *Wilsher* may only add another pawn to the litigation game. Defendant authorities may seek to invoke 'battle conditions', prolonging litigation while their Lordships consider and define Mustill LJ's *obiter dictum.*

Accountability and Deterrence

Health care professionals are subject to pressures which influence both arguments in the debate on no-fault compensation. It may validly be contended that if the circumstances in which medicine is practised in the public sector are difficult, an incentive to good practice and an effective deterrent against carelessness is much needed. But is the medical negligence action an effective deterrent and/or means of ensuring professional accountability? The deterrent effect of the tort action in this context is in reality minimal, and the existence of the tort remedy in fact obscures the issue of accountability.

Consider the following (hypothetical) example. Dr A is somewhat lazy and rather out of touch with current medical developments. Nevertheless he is popular with patients and certainly he considers that he has their interests at heart. To what extent does the continued existence of the action for medical negligence deter him from sloppy practice and/or offer him an incentive to mend his ways? Unless Dr A is an anaesthetist, obstetrician, paediatrician or surgeon the risk of being sued remains very low. In certain disciplines, even if there is blatant evidence of negligence causing injury, a lawsuit may be unrealistic. If Dr A were a geriatrician whose negligence caused a patient of 86 to receive the wrong medication or an overdose of medication, what damages would be payable in respect of her shortened lifespan, or disability, or pain and suffering? The minimal payments made to elderly British Opren victims illustrate that at present the tort action has little to offer to elderly patients and little to make their doctors quail.

Even if Dr A is sued successfully for negligence, the judgement may have little impact on him. The damages will not come out of his pocket nor will his 'premiums' be increased. Tort has a deterrent effect on employers and car drivers because bad practice will mean a higher cost for indemnity cover. Dr A will not be monitored and charged extra because he is a 'bad risk'. If the financial penalty attached to litigation is not a deterrent to bad practice then surely the adverse publicity is? A headline 'Dr A let granny die" *will* affect the doctor both personally and professionally. But cases of gross or indefensible error do not attract such adverse publicity. They never reach the courtroom. Such cases are settled quietly out of court.

It is the disputed cases which hit the headlines. And those cases usually involve doctors and nurses who may have made a single error. The deterrent function of the action for negligence is nil in certain specialities and dubious in others. 'Good' doctors may make an error actionable in negligence. 'Bad' doctors too often escape scot free.

In 1988 a horrifying tale of medical malpractice reached British newspapers. A New Zealand gynaecologist had conducted a trial over several years to test his theory that an abnormal smear result was no indication that the affected woman would develop cancer itself. Several women were unknowingly entered into the trial and denied conventional treatment to remove the abnormal cervical cells. Some died and many suffered years of painful and unnecessary treatment as their condition progressed. It was alleged that the existence in New Zealand of no-fault compensation for medical accidents was in part responsible for this dreadful state of affairs. But the trial began in 1966 six years *before* the introduction of the Accidents Compensation Scheme and, in the judicial inquiry which investigated the trial, no evidence was found to justify any contention that the abolition of the action for medical negligence encouraged the prolongation of the trial.[30] What did emerge was the need for the law to define with precision patients' rights to information and to ensure that medical practitioners are fully accountable for their actions. At the heart of the cervical cancer scandal in New Zealand is the shame that for so long well-intentioned doctors, becoming aware of what was happening, were afraid to speak out against a powerful colleague. The continued existence of the tort action for medical negligence will not encourage greater openness.

The alleged deterrent function of the action for medical negligence obscures the necessity for ensuring that effective means of investigating poor practice and incompetence are introduced to safeguard patients. What is required are inquisitorial procedures which investigate the cause of any medical mishap. Health service employees should be obliged to comply with such procedures. At present, all too often medical practitioners may refuse point blank to co-operate with certain internal inquiries and are in any case reluctant to give evidence which may expose them or their colleagues to legal action.[31] Investigation of medical accidents will enable poor practice to be identified, and incompetent doctors and nurses can be adequately and appropriately dealt with. Such a system of rigorous investigation of medical accidents necessarily means some erosion of clinical freedom. But that is the inevitable price for removing from health care professionals liability for professional negligence. What must not be contemplated is succumbing to special pleading from the medical profession and introducing a no-fault scheme for medical accidents without ensuring that the tort of negligence is replaced by an effective deterrent against bad practice and incompetence.

Perhaps the preferred means by which medical accidents should be investigated would be to empower the National Health Services Ombudsman to investigate all complaints relating to medical mishaps[32] including matters of clinical judgement, at present excluded from his jurisdiction. Obviously the Ombudsman's staff would have to be increased and steps taken to ensure that he has adequately qualified and experienced clinicians to assist him. The Ombudsman would and could not, of course, investigate every misadventure. Primarily, responsibility for inquiring into the cause of an unhappy outcome of treatment, or a patient's complaint, would remain with the health authority. But authorising the Ombudsman to review clinical judgement places the ultimate authority to investigate medical accidents with him, and empowers him to lay down the criteria by which health authorities conducting their own investigations should act.

Supporting such formal structures for considering patients' complaints, regulation and monitoring of practice by medical audit and peer review must be actively encouraged and has rightly been made mandatory.[33] Where provision for internal audit exists, as in certain Manchester teaching hospitals, the review of patient care is rigorous and critical. An adverse result is taken as an opportunity to discover why it occurred and to design measures to prevent repetition. What is sad is that the frankness with which doctors will criticise each other in private is not translated into information available to the public. The risk of litigation is one of the reasons for an unwillingness to admit errors outside the staff common room. Its removal may enable the benefits of medical audit to be fully realised. The impact of the UK Government's proposals for medical audit which came into effect in April 1991 will be crucial.[34]

Additionally, consideration must be given to the provision of greater regulation of practice in the private sector, and to the institution of a statutory and independent complaints procedure for private patients. The expansion of private medicine in the United Kingdom looks set to continue with, for example, tax incentives for elderly patients to take out private health insurance. Difficulties of proof where the consultant is not the employee of the private clinic may mean that the private patient seeking redress for a medical mishap via the tort of negligence is at a significant disadvantage to a NHS patient. It would be irresponsible to encourage the growth of private medicine without affording adequate safeguards for those urged to 'opt out' of the National Health Service.

Finally, once procedures for the thorough investigation of medical accidents have been settled, the role of the General Medical Council (GMC) must be evaluated.[35] At present, only the most gross incompetence and disregard of the patient constitutes serious professional misconduct. No-one would contend that the GMC should discipline a doctor responsible for a single error. What is required is that the GMC, if necessary via statutory extension of its powers,[36] should act to punish culpable incompetence and to safeguard patients against incompetence or poor practice ensuing from inadequacies in training, or experience, or a failure to keep up to date with current practice. Ultimately only the GMC can safeguard the patient. Proceedings exist within the NHS to remove a doctor from practice in the public sector. Only the GMC can prevent that doctor resuming practice in the private sector. The jurisdiction of the GMC, unlike the reach of the tort of negligence, is not capricious. The lazy general practitioner and the incompetent geriatrician are as much at risk as the careless obstetrician. The GMC has in the past shown reluctance to extend its remit to incompetence and poor practice. There was, no doubt, something of a feeling that 'There, but for the grace of God, go I'. And judgements demarcating the culpable from the non-culpable error are far more difficult and controversial than judgements as to whether Dr X sleeps with his patient. The GMC is however potentially the most effective deterrent against bad practice. The hypothetical Dr A is much more likely to mend his lax ways once a more activist approach to incompetence is displayed by the GMC, than by the speculative danger of an action in negligence. The current GMC proposals to introduce 'performance review procedures' are, in principle, to be welcomed wholeheartedly.

The priority in reform of the law relating to medical accidents must thus be to establish a system whereby every aggrieved patient has a right to know what has gone wrong, and why. And every prospective patient should be reassured that, wherever humanly possible, inadequate practice will be identified and corrected. Only then should the second stage – the creation of a no-fault compensation scheme which will in general remove doctors from the perils of medical litigation for error – be attempted. Within such a scheme, should patients retain the right to elect to sue in negligence, rather than claim under the scheme? Or should they be restricted solely to compensation under the scheme? This aspect needs careful consideration. *Prima facie*, perhaps access to the courts should be restricted to cases of 'gross negligence' with the preliminary leave of the court.

Defensive Medicine

Before examining the possible framework of a no-fault compensation scheme for the UK, brief attention must be paid to the spectre of defensive medicine. Defensive medicine is frequently invoked as a key part of the case for the introduction of no-fault compensation. The increased likelihood of litigation, it is asserted, results in doctors deciding on the course of action least likely to result in litigation rather than that which is best for the patient. Doctors will subject patients to a battery of tests which may be unnecessary and unpleasant for the patient and will in any case be an 'alarming waste of resources.'[37]

There is little objective evidence that defensive medicine is currently practised in the UK even in 'high risk' specialties. Michael Jones[38] and others[39] have argued that even where a practice might superficially be regarded as defensive medicine, for example ordering additional tests, this may in fact be good medicine and for the patient's benefit. Analysis of the Caesarian rates over six countries reveals no conclusive evidence for the much vaunted theory that a high level of obstetric litigation increases the Caesarian rate.[40]

The absence of hard evidence of defensive medicine should be of little surprise to lawyers. As Jones puts it, '...medical negligence is a failure to measure up to proper medical standards, and those standards are set by doctors'.[41] Defensive medicine should thus be a phenomenon without substance. If a practitioner should be liable in negligence only if he is responsible for an occurrence which is unacceptable to any body of responsible medical opinion; thus rationally there should not be practices which are seen as dictated by litigation. The relevant practice is dictated by 'responsible medical opinion'. Consider the controversy over intervention in childbirth.

It would seem that a patient alleging a high degree of intervention causing her unnecessary suffering must fail in an action for negligence because there is a considerable body of opinion that such intervention is justifiable. And a patient alleging that intervention should have been planned to safeguard her and her child may also fail because another body of opinion among obstetricians backs a policy of minimum intervention. So why do doctors complain that the law 'forces' them to practise defensive medicine?

The answer is two-fold. First, the proper medical standards by which the doctor will be judged will be ascertained in our adversarial system of trial by expert. This puts a premium on the establishment stance. The party contending that responsible medical opinion is that supported by the senior members of the profession will be able to summon more impressive sounding expert witnesses. Remember the cohorts lined up to attack Wendy Savage at the inquiry into her practice.[42] Secondly, defensive medicine operates on doctors' minds. They believe litigation to be a threat to them, and that their clinical freedom is thereby eroded. This leads, if not to defensive medicine, to *defensiveness in medicine*. Doctors are less open with their patients, less willing to admit the possibility of mishap and terrified to admit to error. Defensive medicine is only a spectre, but like the rest of its kind it is a spectre which does harm to both doctors and patients. The spectre of defensive medicine is not a ground for introducing no-fault compensation, but exorcising that spectre would be another welcome side-effect of such an introduction.

A Scheme for the United Kingdom

It is impossible here to outline in detail a compensation scheme for the United Kingdom. Broad guidelines only can be suggested. The categories of patients entitled to compensation should be as comprehensive as possible, and should cover patients injured by a failure to treat as well as those injured by treatment errors. Neither the Accident Compensation Scheme in New Zealand nor the Swedish Patient Insurance Scheme offers a model which can simply be copied and transplanted to this country. Both schemes, in practice, retain too high a degree a negligence-oriented definition of medical accident, and neither has a method of funding which corresponds to the reality of what would be needed for a British scheme. Sheila McLean's criticisms of aspects of the New Zealand scheme are well founded. We should learn from their experience.[43]

In New Zealand the Accident Compensation Act 1972 provided for compensation for 'personal injury by accident'[44]. Personal injury by accident was further defined to include 'medical, surgical, dental or first aid misadventure'. It is the further interpretation of medical misadventure which has restricted the range of patients who are eligible for compensation under the original New Zealand scheme. Medical misadventure is described as arising when

> (a) a person suffers bodily or mental injury or damage in the course of, and as part of, the administering to that person of medical aid, care or attention, and (b) such injury or damage is caused by mischance or accident, unexpected and undesigned, in the nature of a medical *error* or medical *mishap*.[45]

What constitutes medical error or mishap? Error has been held to be a failure to observe 'a standard of care and skill reasonably to be expected of' a practitioner.[46] Mishap was defined as 'an intervention or intrusion into the administration of medical aid, care or attention of some unexpected or undesigned incident, event or circumstances of a medical nature which has harmful consequences for the patient'.[47] The criteria determining what counts as medical misadventure do not necessarily coincide with the elements of the tort of negligence, and patients denied a remedy in Britain would in some cases recover compensation in New Zealand. But, as Sheila McLean has demonstrated,[48] eligibility for compensation under the New Zealand no-fault scheme retained, to an undesirable degree, some of the problems of the fault based system.[49] It is ironic that in a compensation system where doctors seemed to be very ready to classify non-medical incidents as 'personal injury by accident', proving that a medical mishap falls into that category remains problematical. Moreover, it is increasingly becoming the practice for a patient to have to commence disciplinary proceedings against the doctor if he or she is to establish a successful case before the Accident Compensation Corporation. If one of the aims of no-fault provision is to sever the link between culpability and compensation, such a practice can only be counterproductive.[50] The overall cost of New Zealand's universal accident scheme has led to substantial changes being introduced in the Accident Rehabilitation and Compensation Insurance Act 1992[51]. This Act significantly affects compensation for medical mishap. Claims will be allowed only where the mishap is severe and a rare occurrence. It appears that all medical practitioners will now have to pay a flat rate fee (estimated at £150 in the first year after the Act) towards the operation of the scheme. General reforms of the scheme have abolished lump sum payments to claimants and limited loss of income compensation to 80% of lost earnings. The impact of the New Zealand reforms on medical claims is impossible as yet to evaluate but the New Zealand experience of the difficulties in operating a no-fault compensation scheme must obviously weigh heavily on any Briton advocating following the New Zealand model.

The Swedish Patient Insurance Scheme[52] is in one sense a more useful model for a United Kingdom scheme, in that it is expressly designed as a medical accidents scheme. Compensation is payable in respect of injury or illness resulting from medical treatment subject to three crucial provisos. The injury must be shown not to be an inevitable consequence of the original sickness; injury resulting from a risk taken to avert permanent disability or death is excluded; and the procedure causing injury must be a procedure not *medically justified*. This last proviso reintroduces, to some extent, criteria from a negligence based test. And the scheme, like the New Zealand scheme, excludes patients such as Mrs Sidaway[53] whose complaint is not that their surgeon caused the relevant injury but that he failed to warn of the risk of injury and so offer the patient the opportunity to avert injury.[54]

The provision made in Sweden for the reporting and audit of medical accidents has much to commend it. The pattern for funding the scheme is perhaps closer to what might be envisaged for the United Kingdom. The County Councils responsible in Sweden for health care, together with all those engaged in private practice, assume liability under the scheme and are themselves backed by a private group of insurers. In the United Kingdom similar arrangements would require contributions from health authorities, family health service authorities, private medical organisations and, without doubt, from individual practitioners. Payments made to a patient in the United Kingdom would undoubtedly require more ample funds than in Sweden. This is not only because of our larger population but also because in Sweden compensation payments to disabled patients 'top up' an already generous social security system. Medical practitioners who are solely interested in a no-fault scheme believing that it will reduce the cost of indemnity cover delude themselves. Substantial contributions will be required from them to fund a no-fault scheme. What they may expect is that contributions will remain relatively stable once the scheme is in operation.

The target for the United Kingdom needs to be a comprehensive no-fault scheme which covers failure to treat and failure to warn as well as treatment mishaps. There should be two categories of eligibility.[55]

(a) A patient who can establish that injury or illness resulted from an absence of treatment or delay in appropriate treatment should be eligible for compensation providing that:
   (i) treatment would have been likely to prevent or substantially alleviate the relevant injury or illness *and*

(ii) a reasonable request for treatment was made of a person or authority under a duty to provide treatment.

(b) A patient suffering injury or illness in the course of medical treatment shall be eligible for compensation providing that:

(i) the relevant injury or illness did not result from natural progression of disease or the ageing process

and

(ii) the relevant injury is not an inevitable consequence of an unavoidable risk *of which the patient had been given proper warning*.

Such a scheme would offer compensation to a wide group of patients currently denied a remedy in tort. It is an almost inevitable consequence of such a scheme that, for it to be economically feasible, restrictions must, at least initially, be put on the amounts paid out to patients. In New Zealand the maximum payments to claimants in 1987 were set at 80 per cent of weekly earnings to a maximum of $976. Relatively small payments are made for pain and suffering, and the New Zealand Law Commission review of the scheme proposes total abolition of such payments.[56] Consideration would have to be given to both minimum and maximum payments. Claims of less than £500 might be excluded. In such cases what the victim seeks is not money but accountability. The new system for investigating medical accidents should provide this remedy. Moreover, effective investigating and disciplinary procedures may, in practice, mean that certain patients forego larger claims. Their desire to know why they suffered injury and for a culpable practitioner to be brought to book will be satisfied elsewhere.[57] The levels of compensation for non-financial losses will have to be limited; and it is doubtful whether the option of unlimited private care could be maintained unless necessary treatment was unavailable within the NHS. Limiting compensation payments runs counter to current trends.[58] CITCOM (The Citizens' Compensation Campaign) has proposed that damages for bereavement be made available to a wider range of claimants and raised from £7500 to at least £10000 and advocates much more generous payments for pain and suffering. Yet such recompense does not of itself alleviate bereavement or physical pain. It may serve two functions. First, a significant award marks society's recognition of the injury done to the victim and disapprobation of its cause. Other means of accountability could and should fulfil that function. Second, it offers the victim money to pursue alternative pleasures to compensate for those of which they are now deprived. Perhaps that good will have to be sacrificed for the benefit of those who now receive nothing from the fault system. The thorniest issue revolves around the cost of continuing care. A no-fault scheme must be structured to provide sufficient moneys to enable patients to rehabilitate themselves. Money to convert accommodation, to provide the best wheelchair and proper nursing care and help at home is essential if compensation is to be meaningful. By contrast some limitation on loss of earnings may have to be accepted. To offer a decent existence to all victims, former high earners whose compensation is 'capped' by a maximum earnings limit may indeed suffer. The governing policy consideration becomes: should we seek to compensate as many injured patients as possible for their loss of income and provide for the additional costs of disability fully? Or do we pay larger and larger amounts to the lucky few who win in the tort lottery?

Causation

At the end of the day Martin Wilsher's claim was sent for retrial because of problems of causation. The trial judge had adopted an erroneous test of causation. A number of other recent judgements on medical negligence also revolve around the thorny problem of proving whether a condition results from an admitted medical accident or is a consequence of the original injury or disease.[59] Where – as may often be the case – proof of causation is the plaintiff's major problem, does a no-fault scheme help at all? Martin Wilsher, it has been said, would not have recovered under a no-fault scheme either![60]

A no-fault scheme, embracing injury or illness resulting from medical treatment or failure to provide it, but excluding the victims of disease, will not, of course, solve problems of causation. But it will alleviate them. The expert evidence presented in *Wilsher* v *Essex A.H.A.*[61] was highly contradictory. Like the expert evidence in *Whitehouse* v *Jordan*[62] it gave the impression that the medical profession itself was deeply divided on the cause of the relevant damage. Without minimising the real conflict of informed opinion on such issues as the cause of RLF and the relationship between obstetric mishap and brain damage, the adversarial system aggravates that conflict. A lawyer acting for the plaintiff has a duty to select the most eminent and articulate expert available to assert that the cause of X is Y. Were the same lawyer to act for the defendant instead, he would have an equal duty towards the opposite outcome.

Within a no-fault scheme matters of causation would be investigated. The tribunal adjudicating on disputed claims could appoint distinguished and impartial experts to examine the patient, question the health care staff and scrutinise the records. Moreover, in such cases as the controversial link or absence thereof between obstetric mismanagement and brain damage, inquiries could be put in place in advance of individual claims. Research could and should be commissioned into the cause of brain damage at birth, and into similar questions of causation which arise again and again in medical negligence claims.

Additionally, within a no-fault scheme, proposals to alleviate the burden of proof have a greater validity. It has been suggested that the plaintiff-patient should recover compensation when he or she can establish 'a reasonable possibility'[63] that the relevant *negligence* caused his injuries. Within a fault based system where a link, however tenuous, remains between culpability and liability, such a proposal will be vigorously resisted. Finding a doctor or a nurse negligent on the basis of a *possibility* that that negligence caused injury will be seen as manifestly unfair.[64] But where the aim of the compensation provision is to afford some degree of recompense for the injury itself, and acknowledging the manifest difficulties of proving cause and effect within the human body, such a proposal seems simple common sense.

The Future of Medical Litigation

There is a consensus that the present system of medical litigation requires reform. The King's Fund Institute report concludes that *in the short term* the aim should be to modify the existing system and strengthen accountability.[65] Thus, *inter alia*, steps should be taken to ensure that patients can identify solicitors with the necessary expertise, fee-splitting arrangements should be modified to allow easier access to specialists and access to legal aid should be made easier. Such measures would improve the options open to patients seeking to prove negligence. The report's recommendations on accountability included developing medical audit and extending and simplifying the GMC's disciplinary procedures. Consideration of a no-fault compensation scheme should be a *longer term* aim of policy makers. The report's proposals are welcome. Implementation of procedures to ensure greater accountability must in any case precede implementation of no-fault compensation. The risk inherent in the report's strategy is that 'longer term' becomes 'never'.

The short term proposals of the report, concentrating on improving access to the tort system, will be backed by many plaintiffs' lawyers. The problem is that one of those proposals – extending legal aid – is most unlikely to be met. In its place could be substituted improved access to the tort system via contingency fees. Would contingency fees on the US model help patients? The only beneficiaries might be a limited number of patients presently denied access to the tort system. Their claims would have to be a good risk for the lawyer, and be substantial in nature. And, most undesirably, the lawyer acting for the patient would have a direct financial interest in the amount of damages awarded. The patient resorting to litigation to find out why he or she suffered injury, or to assert his or her autonomy rather than claim massive damages, will be no better off. The patient seeking to assert a right to know why she has been denied infertility treatment, or the father trying to prevent the abortion of his unborn child, would not benefit from contingency fees. Section 58 of the Courts and Legal Services Act 1990 does now make provision for 'conditional fee agreements' enabling the Lord Chancellor to approve arrangements for an amended form of contingency fees in England and Wales. In effect lawyers and clients will be permitted to agree that the lawyer may act for the client on the basis that his fee, or part thereof, is only payable if the litigation in question is successful. Lawyers will not be permitted to charge on the basis of a direct percentage of the damages awarded thus eliminating one of the most pernicious features of the US model. The impact of section 58 on medical litigation will take some years to assess but like US style contingency fees is unlikely to be of use other than to plaintiffs making substantial personal injury claims.

The prominence of the action for medical negligence has bedevilled the development of a proper relationship between law and medicine. It has concentrated attention on *wrongs* done to patients. The legal and moral concepts of wrong have too often become far divorced, and the alleged deterrent effect of tort has diverted attention from the proper regulation of health care. Once compensation for accident is assumed as a collective responsibility of the health care professions and providers, attention can be re-focussed on patients' rights and on the rights and obligations of their carers. What does the right to autonomy involve in the context of health care?[66] Do doctors have a right to refuse treatment which they believe to be morally wrong? Who decides if X or Y gets treatment when resources are scarce? While the tort of negligence reigns, such questions are either buried by its weight or attempts are made to litigate them within the very inappropriate straitjacket of that tort. When I gave the paper on which this chapter is based, in 1988, I was convinced that the case for a no-fault compensation scheme was well founded. Once compensation for medical accident was provided within such a scheme, competence and culpability could be properly investigated, and I foresaw a unique opportunity to start afresh to define patients' rights and devise effective means to enforce such rights. Some four years on, I have less conviction that no-fault compensation should be introduced.

Second Thoughts: Towards a 'Privatised' NHS

Much of the case for no fault compensation for medical accident alone, as opposed to for personal injuries generally, rests on the assumptions (i) that in medical litigation the tort action fails lamentably as an effective and fair means of loss distribution, *and* (ii) that this failure is no way mitigated by its operation as a deterrent to bad practice. As the NHS changes character as a result of the enactment of the National Health Service and Community Care Act it may be that any evaluation of the deterrent impact of tort will need to be revised. GP 'budgets', competition between hospitals and health authorities, and NHS Trust hospitals are measures designed to encourage efficiency and economic discipline. Is there a risk that economic pressures will tempt health providers to cut corners and endanger patients? Might a GP who knows that drug X costing £500 is the optimum treatment for a patient succumb to pressure from the practice manager to 'make do' with drug Y costing £350? Is it possible that a health authority or NHS trust anxious to offer the lowest cost appendectomy in the region will provide a less than safe service? Should it prove to be the case that NHS reforms do in fact provide an incentive to cut corners then it may well be that the continued existence of tort liability would act as a deterrent to cost cutting measures which endanger patient care.

Nor is it only the provisions of the National Health Service and Community Care Act itself which may alter evaluation of deterrence in medical litigation. The introduction of NHS indemnity was designed at least in part to shift the focus of medical litigation from the individual practitioner to the health authority. Deterrence via the tort system may have a greater impact on hard pressed health service management. If managers perceive that the cost of liability will exceed the cost of avoiding the risk of medical accident arising from inadequate provision of care, they will take steps to avoid the risk of accident. Moreover the threat of litigation could be a powerful weapon in the hands of health care professionals seeking to combat management attempts to cut costs. Yes, the consultant might say, it would be cheaper to operate without a first surgical assistant, but what will it cost if something goes wrong?

It is impossible to predict how the revolution in the NHS will in practice affect medical litigation. Can a no-fault compensation scheme for medical accident be acceptable in a more cost conscious and cost cutting public health service? The prospects of greater competition in the service and its domination by economic constraints induce doubts in some, at least. No-fault compensation would be fairer to actual victims of medical accidents, and to doctors, and would prompt initiation of more rigorous means of investigating accidents and ensuring accountability. Of those merits of the case for no-fault compensation I remain convinced. But would such a scheme remove a degree of protection for potential victims, not from individual negligence, but from negligent management?

Notes

1 Cmnd 7045–1 (1978). See Ch 24, *Medical Injury.*
2 *Ibid.*, at paras 1342–4.
3 *Report of the BMA Working Party on No-Fault Compensation* (1987), London. Note however the exclusions from such a scheme proposed by the BMA. See Bolt, D. (1989), 'Compensating for medical mishaps – a model no-fault scheme', *New Law Journal*, **139** 109 and Mildred, M. (1989), 'Reforming the tort system', *New Law Journal*, **139** 124.
4 See the Report of the Pearson Commission, para 1318.
5 *Medical Negligence – Compensation and Accountability*; Ham, C., Dingwall, R., Fenn, P., Harris, D. (1988), London: King's Fund Institute.
6 *Ibid.*, Figs 2 and 3 at p 11.
7 *R* v *Ethical Committee for Infertility Services of St Mary's Hospital ex p Harriott* [1988] 1 FLR 512.
8 *In re F (In Utero)* [1988] 2 All ER 193 CA.
9 For example, *F* v *Berkshire HA* [1989] 2 All ER 545 HL, *Sidaway* v *Royal Bethlem Hospital* [1985] 1 All ER 577 HL; *Blyth* v *Bloomsbury HA*, *The Times* 11 February 1987; *Gold* v *Haringey HA* [1987] 2 All ER 888 CA; For further discussion see chapter 2.
10 For analysis of the steep rise in defence organisation subscriptions from 1978 to 1988 see Ham *et al.*, *Medical Negligence*, Table 3 at p 8.
11 The proposals from the MPS for differentials were overtaken by the Department of Health's own proposals, first made public in March 1989, for NHS indemnity. Interim rates were agreed by the MPS from April 1989 to the end of that year which only partially implemented differentials.
12 See Health Circular (89) 34.
13 See 293 BMJ 512 (1986); Jones, M. (1987), 'The rising cost of medical malpractice' PN **3**, 43: Ham, *et al*, *Medical Negligence*, pp 12–14.
14 General practitioners are not covered by the new scheme for NHS indemnity. The MDU subscription for general practitioners in 1992 was set at £1095 and arrangements for reimbursement of such subscriptions as expenses remain in force.
15 See Health Circular (89) 34 Annex A. For discussion of and commentary on the circular see Brazier, M. (1990) 'NHS Indemnity: The Implications for Medical Litigation' *Professional Negligence* **6**, 88.
16 Those engaged in substantial private practice will continue to face increased costs of cover if medical litigation continues to increase. Presumably such costs will be passed on to the patient via higher charges for private treatment.
17 See Brazier, M. (1987), 'Patient Autonomy and Consent to Medical Treatment: The Role of the Law?' *Legal Studies*, **7** 169.
18 Ham *et al.*, *Medical Negligence* at p 19.
19 For further discussion see Brazier, M. (1992), *Medicine, Patients and the Law,* 2nd ed., London: Pelican, Ch 10.
20 *Ibid.*, at p 143.

21 See *Unintentional Injury – New Zealand's Accident Compensation Scheme* (1987) New Zealand; Ham *et al., op cit* at pp 21–5.
22 [1987] QB 730, (CA); [1988] 1 All ER 871 (HL).
23 See Bowles, R. and Jones, P. (1989), 'A Health Authority's Experience', *New Law Journal*, **139** 119; Ham *et al., op. cit.* propose that health authorities should develop a system to pool risks.
24 See the White Paper 'Working for Patients' Cm 555 (1989).
25 [1988] 2 All ER 245.
26 *Ibid.*, p 246.
27 *Wilsher* v *Essex AHA* [1987] QB 730; [1988] 1 All ER 871, HL.
28 [1987] QB 730, at p 746.
29 *Per* Mustill LJ, at p 749.
30 *Report of the Cervical Cancer Inquiry*: Government Printing Office, Auckland, New Zealand (1988).
31 See Brazier *Medicine, Patients and the Law*, at pp 136–9.
32 *Ibid.*, at pp 134–4 and 330–1.
33 See Hoffenberg, R. (1987), *Clinical Freedom*, Nuffield Provincial Hospitals Trust.
34 See *Working for Patients* (Cm 555) and Working Paper 6 *Medical Audit* (1989) HMSO.
35 See generally Rosenthal, M. (1987), *Dealing with Medical Malpractice*, London: Tavistock.
36 See the attempt by Nigel Spearing MP to introduce a Medical Act (Amendment) Bill introducing a new category of unacceptable conduct, discussed in Brazier, *op. cit.* at pp 11–13 and 'Doctors and Discipline I and II' (1985) *1 PN* 122 and 175.
37 House of Lords Debates Vol. cols. 1350–1 (1987).
38 Jones 'The Rising Cost of Medical Malpractice' at p 45.
39 See generally Danzon, P. (1985), *Medical Malpractice*, Cambridge USA: Harvard University Press.
40 See Macfarlane, A., and Mugford, R. (1986), 'An Epidemic of Caesarians', *Journal of Maternal and Child Health*, Vol 11, 38.
41 *loc cit.*, at p 46.
42 See Savage, W. (1986), *The Savage Inquiry*, London: Virago.
43 See Chapter 4.
44 See Giesen, D. (1988), *International Medical Malpractice Law*, Dordrecht, Boston, London: Mohr Tubingen, 532–41.
45 Review No. 77 (R1352).
46 *Id.*, and see *Accident Compensation Commission* v *Auckland Hospital Board* [1981] NZACR 9.
47 *Id.*, and see *Re Munday* [1984] NZACR 339; *Re Stopford* [1984] NZACR 783.
48 Sheila McLean (1988) 'No Fault Liability and Medical Responsibility' in Freeman, M.D.A. (ed.) *Medicine Ethics and the Law*, London: Stevens, 147.
49 *Id.*, and see Mahoney, R. (1985), 'Informed Consent and Breach of the Medical Contract to Achieve a Particular Result', *Otago Law Review*, **6**, No.1, 103.
50 Vennell, M. (May 1988), Address to *Medical Litigation – Malpractice Crisis*? Manchester University.
51 See (1992) 304 BMJ 1203–4.
52 See Giesen, D., *op. cit.* at p 541; Brahams, D. (1988), 'The Swedish Medical Insurance Schemes', *Lancet*, **1**, 43; Oldertz, C. (1984), 'The Swedish Patient Insurance Scheme – 8 years of experience' *Medico-Legal Journal*, **52**, 43; Oldertz, C. (1986), 'Security Insurance, Patient Insurance and Pharmaceutical Insurance in Sweden', *Am J Comp. L.* **34**, 635.

53 [1985] 1 All ER 577; patients who complain of inadequate information on which to base a valid consent may still be able to resort to a tort action in New Zealand: see McLean, S. *loc cit.*, at pp. 159–60; see also McLean, S.A.M. (1989), *A Patient's Right to Know: Information Disclosure, the Doctor and the Law*, Aldershot: Dartmouth.

54 For an analysis of which British plaintiffs, who failed to recover in tort, might have been eligible for compensation in New Zealand or Sweden, see Brazier, *Medicine, Patients and the Law*, 149–50.

55 See further *ibid.*, at 151–2.

56 New Zealand Law Commission, (1988), *Personal Injury – Prevention and Recovery*, Wellington, fully discussed by Sheila McLean in Ch 4.

57 See *Kralj* v *McGrath* [1986] 1 All ER 54; the plaintiffs expressly declared that they went to court not for monetary compensation but to find out why their baby died as a result of a nightmare delivery in a private hospital; see *The Times* 28 June 1985.

58 As exemplified by the CITCOM proposals; discussed in *The Lancet*, **2**, 1088, (1988).

59 *Hotson* v *East Berkshire* AHA [1987] AC 750 HL; *Kay* v *Ayrshire and Arran Health Board* [1987] 2 All ER 917 (HL).

60 See Mildred, 'Reforming the Tort Systém'.

61 *Supra cit.*

62 [1981] 1 WLR 246 HL; and see Brazier, M. *Medicine, Patients and the Law*, Ch 7.

63 See Mildred, *loc. cit.*

64 '... to award compensation against the doctor or midwife in circumstances where causation is not clearly established may simply replace one injustice by another' (1989) *The Lancet*, **1**, 248.

65 Ham *et al.*, *Medical Negligence*, at pp 33–34.

66 For discussion see Chap. 2 *supra.*

4 Can No-Fault Analysis Ease the Problems of Medical Injury Litigation?

Sheila A.M. McLean

The recent revival in popularity of the concept of liability without fault owes much to the apparent frequency with which litigation is undertaken to obtain compensation for serious accidents. An overburdened legal process often seems unable to meet the demands of those who are hurt – particularly where they are hurt through no fault of their own. Increasingly, the notion of fault is seen as irrelevant when genuine and sometimes major needs are apparently unmet, or at best are met only after long delays and expensive proceedings.

In particular, however, pressure for change in the current system of liability has come in the wake of major disasters.[1] Litigation in such matters can be both problematic and protracted, with no guarantee of success. In addition, of course, the nature of the incident can create its own problems, and this is particularly true where the event is medical or associated with medicine. The cases of Thalidomide,[2] Opren[3] and the long-term problems associated with tranquillisers[4] qualify in their own way as disasters, but are notoriously difficult to resolve. A number of years ago, the British Medical Association (BMA) expressed reservations about a no-fault system of liability to the Royal Commission on Civil Liability and Compensation for Personal Injury (Pearson Commission).[5] Perhaps for the reasons above, and doubtless alarmed by the increased frequency of litigation, the BMA has now become a firm supporter of a no fault system of liability.[6]

There are a number of models of liability without fault currently available for comparison and analysis. In addition, of course, there are jurisdictions where compensation for personal injury is awarded at least in part under strict liability, rather than the traditional tort model based on fault.

Indeed, it is true to say that most countries no longer rely merely on one dominating tradition in such cases. It can be said therefore that to tackle the fault model is generally to tackle merely a small part of the law in respect of personal injury in developed jurisdictions. Nonetheless, it is the application of fault-based analysis which engenders the majority of interest and which attracts the bulk of criticism.

It can be criticised at a number of levels. Litigation demanding proof of fault is notoriously protracted and complex, particularly where the behaviour being challenged is that of a professional. Fault based analysis is not, and never was, designed to cover the more common cause of personal injury, namely accident.[7] The outcome is always remarkably uncertain – what has been called the 'forensic lottery'.[8] The rationale for fault-based analysis has generally been that the person who causes the harm should pay for its consequences. Increasingly, however, this personal attribution of fault has little relevance to contemporary life. Most professionals and companies are adequately covered by insurance-type schemes and therefore are not personally made to pay more than the monthly or annual subscription to them. This rationale, therefore, no longer holds water as a justification for maintaining fault analysis. In addition, the award of compensation is designed to put the person back in the situation he or she would have been in but for the fault. Manifestly, this was always unlikely, since the compensation awarded is inevitably financial; there is also increasing concern that the sums being given are spiralling out of control.[9]

Moreover, the purpose of litigating is not always the desire of the victim to punish the perpetrator by making him or her pay. It seems clear that many people simply want to know what has gone wrong. However, if the only avenue available is expensive and uncertain, recourse to the law is less likely. And yet, arguably, the law should be providing appropriate remedies, whether in order to provide compensation or to require disclosure of relevant facts. Moreover, since many cases of personal injury are resolved without recourse to litigation,[10] the fault principle can also be said to be becoming increasingly marginalised. Yet it is tenacious, and continues to be resorted to out of necessity even in those countries where alternative schemes go hand in hand with the traditional.[11]

These criticisms of fault analysis are heard with increasing frequency, not least because there now are models available for comparison. Countries such as New Zealand and Sweden have led the way in demonstrating that alternatives can be found, and it is to those jurisdictions that converts in the United Kingdom most often turn for support. Yet it should be remembered that – despite the flaws in fault analysis – major legal change should not be undertaken in ignorance of the problems which the alternatives may also have.

This essay will concentrate on the now well-established New Zealand system, both because it is the most comprehensive no-fault system in the world and because the legal tradition in New Zealand is sufficiently close to that of the United Kingdom as to make it valuable for comparative purposes. In particular, attention will be paid to the extent to which this no-fault model has or has not resolved the problems highlighted earlier, in respect of the negligence action and medical litigation.

What is Wrong with Negligence?

The major criticisms of the negligence action can thus be summarised: it is too expensive, it is too uncertain, it takes too long and it is inaccessible. The Report of the Review Body on Civil Justice[12] gave three main reasons for considering personal injury litigation:

> (i) It is one of the largest items of civil litigation which proceeds to full trial before a judge.
> (ii) Negligence claims, and the litigation they give rise to, constitute a major system of loss adjustment.
> (iii) This branch of civil litigation has aroused most public concern on the score of cost and delay.[13]

Under the heading of uncertainty, a further point might be made in respect of medical litigation. Each litigant, in order to obtain compensation, has to establish that there was a duty of care, that the duty was breached and that the harm complained of was a foreseeable consequence of that breach of duty. It has been said that, in medical cases, proving the breach of duty element can be every bit as difficult as establishing causation.[14] The patient, therefore, has a real burden to shift before any litigation is likely to be successful. In addition, the defence organisations and Health Boards/Authorities screen out indefensible cases before litigation, thus ensuring that those cases which do reach a court of law are ones where there seems to be a reasonable argument that the physician was not negligent.[15] Litigation, therefore, represents a genuine and real debate between the parties, the outcome of which will be dependent on the weight given by the court to the professional and expert evidence which is available to them.[16]

If no-fault analysis is to be a better way forward in medical cases, then each of these four difficulties will have to be met. And the question must be asked whether or not change is merited if only some of the problems are solved, or whether there would need to be clear benefits in each case.

No-Fault in New Zealand

The characteristics of the New Zealand Scheme are that it is a true no-fault system in the sense that it is essentially centrally funded, but with contributions drawn from employers, road users and so on. Contributions are made by employers, not necessarily on the basis of risk, but rather on the basis of numbers of employees. Its funding is therefore potentially flexible, although recent dramatic rises in the contribution expected have caused some concern.[17] Administration of the fault based system in the United Kingdom is notoriously expensive, with substantial percentages of all awards going simply to take care of the costs of litigating in the first place. In New Zealand, however, the costs are said to be dramatically lower. For example, in their review of the New Zealand System,[18] the Law Commission of New Zealand note that:

> The expenditure for 1987/88 was $693 million or 1.2 per cent of gross domestic product. For that outlay it provides 24 hour protection for the whole population. Considered in another way it costs only 60c per person per day for protection against every kind of accident.[19]

Indeed, the Law Commission points out that the contribution remains small compared with those operating in other countries which have a more limited no-fault system.[20]

It can be seen, therefore, that if expense were a major consideration in any comparison between the two systems, then the no-fault approach has traditionally been thought to be at a considerable and undeniable advantage. However, at least part of this advantage stems from the fact that the sums of money awarded are much lower than those which could be awarded in a successful action for personal injury in negligence. Assessment of the total costing of any system is not merely an assessment of the administrative costs, but must take account of the totality of the scheme. Recent increasing awards[21] in the United Kingdom have been the subject of some concern. In New Zealand on the other hand the compensation offered is calculated on a different basis:

> This scheme is not in any sense an insurance system. Its benefits are provided as of right without reference to cause and regardless of risk. It is simply one component of the general social welfare provisions of the country.[22]

The claim is that the no-fault system provides a relevant and appropriate cushion for lost earnings and that it meets the needs of those damaged. These assertions can usefully be looked at in turn.

First, the provision of a cushion for lost earnings. The New Zealander damaged by accident is entitled at present to 80 per cent of lost earnings up to a maximum amount, to retirement or 5 years beyond the age of 60. This entitlement currently commences after the end of the first week of disability – the employer being required to pick up the bill in the first week (assuming the person to be employed). The review, on quite frankly financial grounds, proposes that this entitlement should commence after the end of the second week,[23] leaving at least some people in a rather more vulnerable position. Default by the employer *may, but only may*, be picked up by the Accident Compensation Corporation. But even assuming that all duties are fulfilled, the question remains whether or not 80 per cent of lost earnings is an adequate cushion. For many it would seem not to be, and indeed a system of social security which replaces all lost earnings, at least for a period of time, might seem preferable.

In addition, lump sum payments of $10 000 or $17 000 can be made. Now these are particularly interesting figures. The scheme, like the court action which it effectively replaced, claims to have major concern for the most serious injuries. For this reason, those cases which reach a court of law in countries which continue to use fault-based analysis can result in very substantial awards of damages – awards which give grist to the mill of those who would abolish the current system. Health authorities, for example, may quite rightly point to the impact on medical care of their joint liability to pay such awards. On the other hand, the sum of money available in New Zealand is derisory, particularly when it is only awarded where damage is extremely severe. In other words, the replacement of the fault system may effectively spread the compensation net wider, but those whom it most overtly seeks to benefit – that is, those with the most serious handicaps – may lack the funding necessary to rehabilitate themselves by, for example, restructuring their house or modifying a car. So, arguably, the scheme does not provide an appropriate cushion, nor does it in fact meet the needs of the most seriously disabled. Having said this, it is interesting to note that the review of the New Zealand system suggests, not that these sums should be increased, but rather that they should be abolished.[24] This seems therefore to deal both with the claim that an appropriate cushion is provided and with the assertion that needs are met.

The second problem identified with the fault-based system is that its outcome is uncertain. As the Woodhouse Commission[25] put it:

> The moral basis for the application of the fault principle cannot be explained in terms of the legal conception of negligence because the test of negligence is objective and impersonal...Nobody can predict with any assurance the outcome of a damages action.[26]

This is certainly the case, since it is never clear what witnesses will actually say in a court (in medical cases it may even be difficult if not impossible to obtain relevant witnesses[27]) it is also seldom clear what the court will make of the evidence which is heard. Where juries are involved, the outcome is arguably even more uncertain. However, the New Zealand system hopes, by providing a statement of eligibility for compensation, to ensure ease of decision making. The problem is that it does not in fact achieve this, seemingly for two reasons. First, the distinction initially drawn between sickness and disease – a distinction which has shown itself to be extremely difficult to make – and secondly, in medical cases, as a result of what seems to be a hangover from fault-based analysis.

The universality of the New Zealand system is endangered by the distinction made between accident and sickness, drawn by the legislature on the recommendation of the Woodhouse Commission.[28] Few tort lawyers have failed to note this, and to attack it as logically inconsistent, if not an insurmoutable condemnation of the scheme.[29] And, of course, this is a serious attack if validated because one of the major benefits of no-fault analysis is its potential for universality. As one of the major criticisms of the fault-based system is the inevitable differentiation of people with equal needs, an alternative which is truly comprehensive has clear advantages.

However, the definition of eligibility – 'personal injury by accident'[30] – inevitably ensured that the claim of the system to 'protect the whole population against the consequences of personal injury'[31] can only be described as somewhat exaggerated. As Cripps points out:

> The meaning of 'accident' for the purposes of the Act has been a fundamental problem which has not been simplified by legislative definition. However, it is clear that merely because an injury is unexpected and caused by negligence it will not necessarily be covered by the Act.[32]

Further, Geoffrey Palmer[33] noted in the early stages of the scheme's operation that:

> To begin with the idea was to spell everything out so people would know their rights. The trend of the amendments [to the 1972 Accident Compensation Act] has been to give more and more discretion to the Commission so that certainty is lost but the obscurity remains. At present neither clarity nor predictability exist.[34]

In their review of the Accident Compensation Scheme, Mr Justice Woodhouse and Geoffrey Palmer recommend changes in elegibility which will go some of the way, but by no means all of the way, towards rectifying this problem. Their proposed legislation talks only of personal injury, since in their view the terminology of 'accident' creates problems.[35] In view of their belief that the right to benefits should, as soon as possible, cover sickness as well as accident, they seek to incorporate as a decision making tool the International Classification of Diseases formulated by the World Health Organisation.[36] This move would incorporate some disease which is currently excluded, but would still leave some cases uncompensated. Nonetheless, it must be seen as a step in the right direction.

The second aspect to this problem relates in particular to medical claims. Increasingly, patients in the United Kingdom are prepared to challenge the amount and quality of information given to them about possible risks and alternatives in therapy. In this, they have been singularly unsuccessful in the courts, but nonetheless each court has emphasized the importance of information disclosure even whilst holding that it was adequate in the instant case.[37] If nothing else, this provides an incentive to develop better patient care by reminding doctors that they have an obligation to provide such information. In the New Zealand scheme, however, this is not the case.

The system is designed so that there is precisely no incentive for the medical profession to make disclosure of known or inherent risk in advance of a medically selected therapy.[38] As one Review Tribunal put it:

> ...if adverse developments or results are known to reasonably informed medical opinion to constitute a known risk of the treatment, and that risk then materialises, can it be said that those adverse risks are personal injury by accident? In my view a person who accepts (*or in some cases is deemed to accept*) medical treatment is to be regarded as accepting the possibility that the known risks may eventuate. It is not to be considered as an 'accident' to him if the consequences that are at risk do in fact occur.[39]

The right to receive relevant information about one's treatment is thereby significantly affected. A risk which is known to the doctor and which eventuates (whether or not the patient has been told about it) is not an 'accident' for the purposes of the scheme and therefore can attract no compensation.

This, the Review of the scheme argues (and it is not alone in this argument) is inconsistent, since foreknowledge of risks, for example on the road, does not defeat a claim.[40] Foreknowledge should not, therefore, be a criterion for eligibility. However, although this modification would include some patients who were previously excluded, it still provides no incentive for the development of a theoretical position on the rights of patients. Arguably, this principle carries equal weight to that of ultimately meeting needs, especially since the creation of these needs might well have been averted had the principle of information disclosure been conceded in the first place.

Medical examples are particularly useful in highlighting the significant problems of the no-fault system in New Zealand, just as they are in challenging the fault principle. Interestingly, and perhaps even paradoxically, the difficulties have been parallel if not identical in both approaches. The fundamental difficulties relate partly to the attitudes of decision makers, but in some cases are also structural and probably inevitable.

It is currently the case that, both by those in the medical profession and patients themselves, a shift to liability without fault is seen as enhancing the prospect of compensation. Medical cases are notoriously hard to win in courts of law, for a number of reasons. Causation can be acutely difficult in these cases, but equally the professional reluctance to criticise colleagues, and therefore to attribute fault, plays a large part in their lack of success.[41]

In New Zealand, medical cases qualify for compensation if they can be described as 'medical misadventure'.[42] If 'medical misadventure' is very broadly defined, then obviously more people would be included in the compensation net than is feasible where the criterion is 'medical negligence'. It was said, for example, that:

> It is plain that 'medical misadventure' is broader in meaning than medical negligence and that to qualify for compensation...it is sufficient for a claimant to show a causal relationship between a medical mishap amounting to medical misadventure and his injury.[43]

This statement is somewhat convoluted since part of the definition of what one has to show is related back to the original concept. If we do not know what 'medical misadventure' is, then how can we know that a medical mishap amounted to misadventure. The tribunals' views on what amounts to medical misadventure are enlightening.

Misadventure has been defined as incorporating the injury (physical or mental) caused when a person is harmed by medical error or medical mishap.[44] Medical error is defined thus:

> ...the failure of a person involved in the administering of medical aid, care or attention to observe a standard of care and skill reasonably to be expected of him in the circumstances.[45]

Medical mishap, on the other hand:

> ...as a generalisation, but not as a definition...normally describes the situation when there is the intervention or intrusion into the administration of medical

aid, care or attention of some unexpected and undesigned incident, event or circumstance, of a medical nature, that has harmful consequences to the patient.[46]

Although, therefore, 'medical misadventure' was designed to be 'broader in meaning than medical negligence'[47] at one level it clearly is not. On the other level, what it encapsulates would seem to include, for example, instrument failures, which are equally covered in fault-based analysis. Indeed, Hughes[48] has claimed that there has been an 'unfortunate tendency to restrict the concept of "medical misadventure"...,[49] a tendency which leaves the New Zealand patient relatively no better off than his or her counterpart in other jurisdictions. Indeed, arguably, the tests established for 'medical misadventure' are almost exactly parallel to those used in fault-based jurisdictions, with the additional problem that some behaviour which *could* result in compensation awards in negligence (for example, failure to attend) *cannot* attract compensation in a system which does not compensate for illness. The reason for this is that the harm caused to the patient by a failure to offer treatment is a harm which is deemed to result from the original illness and not from medical misadventure. Although the review of the system would include some illness within the scope of no-fault liability, this is not universal and problems may still remain in assessing eligibility in these circumstances.

The third problem identified with the fault approach was that proceedings could be extremely protracted. This is without doubt a serious difficulty, and the Report of the Review Body on Civil Justice aims to make some inroads into the length of time it can take to complete an action.[50] Certainly, Mrs Sidaway[51] would not have been obliged to wait for some eleven years under the New Zealand system, but neither would she have been compensated. She would therefore have been forced – if she wished to pursue her claim – to go through the process of raising her case through the Accident Compensation Scheme (since courts will not entertain cases unless the Accident Compensation Corporation has agreed that they are not 'personal injury by accident') and then begin again in a civil action based on negligence. This, of course, could ultimately take even longer than it did in the United Kingdom unless reform also takes place in the processing of such cases.

Finally, it was alleged that the fault-based system is inaccessible. Most particularly this is true because of the complexities involved and because of the cost of litigating whilst uncertain of the outcome. There is no doubt that the New Zealand approach scores a clear victory over negligence here. Cases can be, and often are, dealt with by local officials who can make a decision and render an award in a matter of days or weeks from the claim being formally received. In fact, so simple is the process that there seems nothing left to say on this point.

What Other Claims Does No-Fault Liability Make?

It is, of course, the case that the alleged benefits of no-fault analysis are not necessarily confined to a strict comparison with the alleged drawbacks of the negligence action. The system can, and does, purport to achieve more than just this. For example, for many, the scheme has the additional benefit of reflecting an ideological position which satisfies their intuitive views of the interdependence of members of a community. Moreover, the scheme claims not just to offer compensation, but to offer *meaningful* compensation, regularly reviewed and paid in a manageable (that is, instalment) form.

Of course, a major criticism of no-fault schemes is the lack of large compensation payments. The benefits, however, are the periodic nature of awards in New Zealand and the capacity for regular review. It is, however, unarguable that where damage is severe, neither the estimated loss of earnings payment nor the rather small lump sums which can presently be awarded would satisfy those reared in the fault-based system.[52] Nor, indeed, do such awards provide for the potential expense associated with such major disabilities. This, it is submitted, is not merely a fine academic point. Awards of damages in fault based systems may well be reaching the point of being unreasonably high, with, in medical cases at least, all of the potential implications associated with meeting the required payment. On the other hand, this could equally be said to be a function of the way in which damages are currently calculated, rather than an essential component of the fault system itself. Perhaps the current popularity of structured payments may help to alleviate this problem.

In addition, and unlike a fault-based system which is essentially *post facto*, the New Zealand scheme was inherently concerned to minimise harm, not just by the award of damages after an accident, but by encouraging an awareness of accident prevention and rehabilitation, both of which could serve to dilute the problems associated with lower damages awards. Many of the proposed changes to the scheme are designed to re-emphasize these elements which sadly seem to have been given little, or at least insufficient, attention. Indeed, the draft legislation contained in the report is to be called the *Safety, Rehabilitation and Compensation Act*, effectively re-emphasizing the capacity of the scheme to do much more than merely provide financial compensation. The conclusion that insufficient attention had previously been paid to accident prevention and rehabilitation was inescapable,[53] but this Bill is designed to change that, and if it succeeds an enduring criticism of the scheme is at least partially answered.

Conclusions

In sum, the arguments for no-fault liability can be summarised as being that the scheme facilitates a more equitable distribution of resources. This is, of course, a very strong argument. However, proponents of no-fault arguably fail to take sufficient account of the baby who is being thrown out with the bathwater. Merely redistributing resources *in se* is no resolution of the issues in personal injury claims. It is also imperative that the resources can and do meet the needs for which the system claims to cater. The fact that lump sum payments characterize fault based systems should not blind the proponents of no-fault to the situations in which they also have genuine value.

Equally, whilst theoretically appealing, it seems most unlikely that the current political climate in the United Kingdom is suited to the development of what is effectively a grander – and expensive – social security safety net for the population. This last cannot of course stand as a reason for not seeking improvement, but it points to the harsh realities of political life.

For a system not based on fault to be truly comprehensive and for it genuinely to meet needs, not only the political will but also the financial commitment has to be available. Moreover, for as long as it is seen as a system of *liability*, as opposed to a duty of the state to support its injured or otherwise damaged citizens, eligibility will need to be defined, inevitably leading to exclusions. It is most likely that these exclusions will continue to relate to those disabled by the consequences of disease, whilst those damaged in other ways are more likely to be included. Such differentiation will still exist, albeit in a much more limited form, even under the new proposals for New Zealand, and would almost certainly exist were a similar system to be established in the UK. No-fault liability is not the panacea that it is sometimes claimed to be, and clearly other reforms are possible which would ease the situation somewhat. If the complaints about the fault-based system are genuinely based on its randomness, its expense and its delays, then we have the imagination to resolve these, and a genuine commitment to adequate, but not extortionate, compensation would seem to suggest that this is at least an option.

In addition to these general points about liability, there are particular problems associated with medical cases. The trend in New Zealand has been to introduce what Palmer has called 'a ring of the old tort law'[54] into cases concerning medicine. This is doubtless a hangover from the traditional legal response to medical negligence claims, and therefore may change, but it is just as likely that decision-makers in a United Kingdom scheme would behave in the same way. The extra-legal considerations which seem to affect the judiciary in medical cases[55] will not inevitably vanish in a no-fault system. In addition, legislators would need to bear in mind the complexities of definition. Arguably, at least some of the problems confronting the patient in New Zealand are due to the capacity for interpretation which is inherent in the definition of 'medical misadventure'. Thus, whilst some cases are excluded by the nature of the definition itself, others are excluded on interpretation.

This is significant in United Kingdom terms, since – although no-fault liability is widely perceived as a better system – it is most often appealed to in medical cases. Whilst some of the difficulties of medical litigation could be resolved under such a scheme, the New Zealand experience would tend to suggest that by no means all of them will disappear. If decisions are taken narrowly, the patient will continue to be aggrieved and will continue to require to have resort to the civil courts. Yet, as Mahoney[56] points out:

> The very existence of the Accident Compensation Act must have a negative effect on the public's recognition of the possibility of these claims. A public that has been told for a decade that the drunk driver and the rapist are immune from civil suit can hardly be expected to learn by osmosis from a few legal journals the possibility of suing a doctor where medical treatment does not turn out as expected or promised.[57]

Even if a residual right of action were left to the patient who is unable to demonstrate eligibility for compensation under the no-fault scheme, it is unlikely that many would be aware of this. Even those who *were* aware, might be reluctant to raise an action through the courts where they had already been turned down by a scheme which is supposed to give compensation more easily. Despite the relative success rates of claims under the New Zealand scheme, medical cases represent a particular problem, and this should be borne in mind when radical reform is proposed.[58]

Both in the United Kingdom and in New Zealand emphasis is firmly placed on the appropriate compensation of major injuries. Arguably the no-fault scheme is too mean and in some cases too limited, and the fault-based system too open handed and too exclusive. The first of these is an inevitable consequence of the nature of the no-fault system, whereas the second is potentially rectifiable within the traditional fault-based system. In other words, it should not be forgotten that the fault-based system may have within it the seeds of reform which would lead to a satisfactory resolution of its own problems, whereas the no-fault approach may always confront problems, substantially shaped by the use of limited public funding, which seem more difficult to rectify.[59]

In addition, the flexibility of personal injury litigation has much to commend it, at least at a theoretical level. Particular examples are its capacity to recognise new wrongs and to maintain important claims such as the right of a patient to receive adequate information about risks and benefits in therapy. The fault system can serve to maintain the integrity of the rights which it is designed to vindicate by keeping them in the forefront of decision making. This is not an apologia for fault analysis. Indeed, the social commitment of a comprehensive no-fault system is one which has more to commend it, in this writer's view, than does the traditional model. Merely, it is a caution against too ready an acceptance of the benefits of liability without fault, at least on the New Zealand model.

What the above discussion shows is that there are undoubted benefits inherent in the New Zealand no-fault model, but that there remain difficulties – perhaps even situations where the negligence action is preferable. In particular, this may be true in respect of the size of awards. Of course, this criticism of no-fault will remain only for as long as the system is a compensation scheme rather than a social security provision, and for as long as the type of award made is limited in the way it currently is. Are we then entitled to share the enthusiasm which no-fault analysis currently generates in the United Kingdom?

At the beginning, it was said that a question would remain – namely, must the no-fault system be better on *all* counts or merely on some? Since it *is* better only in some, should we nonetheless pursue it? Arguably, the question of damages (which is where the system does fall down) is a significant one and should not be ignored. If this problem is to be rectified it would require that a British no-fault system took a fundamentally different approach to the aims of damages and to their funding. Evidently, this could be done, but presently it seems unlikely that this would be a central aim of government. Cost-effectiveness is one important aspect of a compensation scheme, but it should not be pursued at the expense of those for whom the system is designed. If we are to move to such a system, then we must be alert to the problems already experienced by radical jurisdictions, conscious of the benefits – however slim – that might be lost by such a change, and prepared unequivocally to meet the challenge of adequate funding head on. Without this, little will be achieved.

Notes

* This Chapter and Brazier's Chapter were written before the passing of the (NZ) Accident Rehabilitation and Compensation Insurance Act 1992. Reference to this legislation can be found in the Introduction.

1 Disasters such as Zeebrugge, for example, result in immediate concern about compensation and reopen the debate.

2 For discussion, see Teff, H. and Munro, C. (1976), *Thalidomide: The Legal Aftermath*, London: Saxon House.

3 This case has received massive publicity over the years. For example, *The Guardian* 30 June 1987 reported that 'Around 100 people died in Britain and another 4 000 were injured by Opren before the drug was withdrawn in 1982.' Not only the effects of the drug but also the fight for compensation were widely reported – see *The Guardian* 10 November 1987; 10 December 1987: 11 December 1987: 14 December 1987: 16 December 1987: 15 January 1988.

4 For discussion, see *The Observer* 14 February 1988; see also *The Observer* 21 February 1988, under the headline 'Facing up to the Bitter Pill of Addiction'.

5 Royal Commission on Civil Liability and Compensation for Personal Injury Cmnd 7054/1978.

6 Indeed, they recently proposed their own no-fault liability scheme, at approximately the same time as a Bill was introduced (unsuccessfully) to the UK Parliament.

7 The Pearson Commission, *supra cit.*, for example, suggested at para 1348 that 'Changes made to improve the prospects of getting compensation in the cases of negligence could have no effect on the very much greater number of medical accidents where nobody is at fault.'

8 Ison, T. (1967), *The Forensic Lottery*, London: Staples Press.

9 See, for example, comments in the case of *Lim Poh Choo* v *Camden and Islington A.H.A.* [1979] 1 All E.R. 332. Recent press coverage reports sums awarded in medical cases of £500 000 to a brain damaged child (*The Guardian* 15 March 1988), £490 000 to a brain damaged man (*The Guardian* 2 August 1988), and £750 000 to a brain damaged boy (*The Guardian* 13 June 1989).

10 In medical cases by the defence organisations, and new Crown Indemnity Scheme for hospital claims.

11 For example, the Swedish no-fault scheme is only a partial one, and in New Zealand (see *infra*) claims which do not qualify for compensation under the Accident Compensation Scheme may still result in litigation.

12 Cm 394/1988.

13 *Ibid.*, p 73, para 390.

14 See Pearson Commission, *supra cit.*, paras 1326 and 1327. See also, Gamble, A.J. (1981), 'Professional Liability' in McLean, S.A.M. (ed.), *Legal Issues in Medicine*, Aldershot: Gower.

15 This function has now been taken over by Health Authorities/Boards under the Crown Indemnity Scheme for doctors employed by these organisations, although not for General Practitioners.

16 The role played by the expert witness in the United Kingdom is most significant, particularly given the test laid down in *Bolam* v *Friern Hospital Management Committee* [1957] 2 All E.R. 118. The setting of a so-called 'professional test' by the UK courts can be contrasted with the 'prudent patient' test applied in a minority of US States, following the decision in *Canterbury* v *Spence* 464 F 2d. 772 (1972). For further discussion, see McLean, S.A.M. (1989), *A Patient's Right to Know: Information Disclosure, The Doctor and the Law*, Aldershot: Dartmouth.

17 New Zealand Law Commission, Report no. 4 (1988), *Personal Injury: Prevention and Recovery*, Wellington, especially at para 16 – 'There have been complaints of escalating and unexpected cost increases in the operation of the scheme. Indeed the Officials

Committee Report of 1986 states bluntly that a "massive cost blow-out in compensation has occurred."'

18 New Zealand Law Commission, Report No. 4, *supra cit.*
19 *Ibid.*, para 16.
20 *Id.*
21 See note 8, *supra*.
22 New Zealand Law Commission, Report no. 4, *supra cit.*, para 2.
23 *Ibid.*, para 185.
24 *Ibid.*, para 194.
25 *Compensation for Personal Injury in New Zealand*, Report of the Committee of Inquiry, Wellington, 1967.
26 *Ibid.*, p 48, para 82.
27 As the Pearson Commission, *supra cit.*, noted at para 1327: 'When a doctor was accused of negligence, his colleagues might naturally be reluctant to give evidence.'
28 Woodhouse Report, *supra cit.*, p 113, para 289. Accident Compensation Act 1982 s 2.
29 See Klar, L.N. (1983), 'New Zealand's Accident Compensation Scheme: A Tort Lawyer's Perspective', *University of Toronto Law Journal*, **33**, 80.
30 Accident Compensation Act 1982 s 2.
31 New Zealand Law Commission, Report no. 4, *supra cit.*, para 2.
32 Cripps, C.R. (1978), 'Medical Practitioners' Liability for Personal Injury Caused by Negligence' *New Zealand Law Journal* 83, 84.
33 Palmer. G.W.R. (1977), 'Accident Compensation in New Zealand: The First Two Years' *American Journal of Comparative Law*, **25** 1.
34 *Ibid.*, p 9.
35 Woodhouse Report, *supra cit.*, para 165.
36 *Ibid.*, paras 165 and 166.
37 See *Hills* v *Potter* [1983] 3 All E.R. 716; *Sidaway* v *Bethlem Royal Hospital Board of Governors & Ors.* [1984] 1 All E.R. 1018 (C.A.); [1985] 1 All E.R. 643 (H.L.)
38 For discussion, see McLean, *A Patient's Right to Know*.
39 Review No 74/R00408 (1974), p 3 (emphasis added by author).
40 *Ibid.*, para 165.
41 See, for example, Pearson Commission, *supra Cit.*, paras 1326 and 1327.
42 Accident Compensation Act 1982 s 2 (ii).
43 Blair, A.P. (1978), *Accident Compensation in New Zealand*, Wellington: Butterworths.
44 Review no. 77/R1352 (1977).
45 *Ibid.*, at p 7.
46 *Ibid.*, at pp 7–8.
47 Blair, *op. cit.*, at p 43.
48 Hughes, J. (1981), 'Accident Compensation and Childbirth' *New Zealand Law Journal* 79.
49 *Loc. cit.*, at p 85.
50 *Supra cit.*, Note 12. See particularly chapter 7.
51 *Sidaway, supra cit.*, Note 37.
52 This may, of course, be a transient phenomenon. See, for discussion, Lloyd-Bostock, S. (1980), 'Common Sense Morality and Accident Compensation' *Insurance Law Journal*, 331.
53 New Zealand Law Commission, Report no. 4, *supra cit.*, paras 150-60.
54 Palmer, 'Accident Compensation in New Zealand' at p 39.
55 See McLean, S.A.M. (1981), 'Negligence – A Dagger at the Doctor's Back?' in

Robson, P. and Watchman, P. (eds), *Justice, Lord Denning and the Constitution*, Aldershot: Gower.

56 Mahoney, R. (1985), 'Informed Consent and Breach of the Medical Contract to Achieve a Particular Result: Opportunities for New Zealand's Latent Personal Injury Litigators to Peek out of the Accident Compensation Closet', *Otago Law Review*, **6** No. 1., 103.

57 *Ibid.*, at p 137.

58 For further discussion, and an alternative view, see Ch. 3 in this book.

59 Indeed, the New Zealand scheme has already run into financial difficulties, which have resulted from 1st July 1992, in doctors being required to pay premiums (over and above their subscriptions) to Defence Organisations, to help meet the costs of medical misadventure cases. For further discussion, see 'Introduction', infra.

PART II

5 The European Convention on Human Rights and Compensation for Personal Injury

Françoise J. Hampson

Introduction

Most legal practitioners probably assume that the European Convention on Human Rights deals with issues traditionally regarded as part of civil liberties. Its relevance to the British system of compensation for personal injury is not obvious. The proportion of cases dealing with such issues is not high. It is a matter of evaluating as yet unproven potential. This chapter attempts to deal with both of these issues. In other words, the lines of reasoning used by both the European Commission and Court of Human Rights in interpreting the Convention will be examined with a view to establishing, however tentatively, the usefulness of that procedure for a person seeking compensation for personal injury.[1]

It needs to be made quite clear at the outset that the Convention was not designed as a compensation scheme. It was designed to protect[2] what are usually known as civil and political rights[3], or civil liberties in British legal parlance. This does not mean that it is of no value in relation to issues arising out of personal injury. It does mean that the Treaty's usefulness will not immediately be apparent from the text. Familiarity with the case-law and the lines of reasoning which that reveals are essential to any appraisal. Furthermore, since the Convention deals with the responsibility of the State, it cuts across the legal boundaries familiar to the British legal practitioner. Questions such as alternative liability in contract or in tort, or of strict liability versus liability based on fault will not be relevant *as such.*[4] As will be seen, they may however be incidentally relevant.

The need for familiarity with the case-law cannot be over-emphasized. Who, on a first reading of Article 6(1),[5] which provides for fair trial procedures, would realise that the legitimacy of a bar to legal action contained in a statute can be called into question under that provision?[6] Or again, does the text of Article 2,[7] which prohibits arbitrary deprivation of life, immediately call to mind the case of vaccine-damaged children?[8] On the basis of a cursory reading of the text, British lawyers whose practice and experience does not lie in the civil liberties field may simply dismiss the relevance of the Convention to cases of compensation for personal injury; or, whilst admitting its possible usefulness, they may be daunted by the prospect of having to keep abreast of developments in yet another field of law, and never make the attempt. They should be warned that, in some areas at least, the case-law of the Commission and Court is so well-established that they might be liable in negligence if they failed to consider their client's remedy under the Convention. That might also be of interest to their insurers. This does not mean that every solicitor should necessarily be able to take a case to Strasbourg himself; there are organisations[9] and individuals[10] who are often willing and able to do so. It does mean that every legal practitioner needs to be able to *recognise* a Convention issue and to evaluate his client's chance of success.

This analysis will consider the Convention procedures in the barest outline, before examining the basis of admissibility of an individual complaint. This is one of the areas of greatest difficulty in relation to personal injury claims. Finally, the relevant substantive Convention rights will be examined to establish whether they may, in certain cases, afford redress. The emphasis throughout will be practical; in other words, the difficulties likely to be faced in practice will be emphasized.

Procedure[11]

A form is available on which to submit a complaint, but it is sufficient if an application discloses the name, age and address of the applicant, together with the facts forming the basis of his complaint. If the applicant is assisted by a lawyer or other adviser, he must give his authorisation in a signed document. At this stage, neither British nor Council of Europe legal aid is available. If the chances of success are to be maximised, however, it is at this stage that most of the work has to be done. This is particularly important where the applicability of the Convention is not immediately obvious. The overwhelming majority of applications are rejected at the admissibility stage. If the case is to be examined in depth by the Commission, it must be clear from the outset that the facts do raise an issue under the Convention. The application should therefore present the legal arguments as to why, on the basis of case-law, the facts reveal a possible breach of the Convention. Applicants can be assisted by academics, and it may be in the financial interest of a client for his solicitor to involve an academic or an organisation which will make no, or only a nominal, charge for services.

The application will be registered and assigned both to a member of the Commission's Secretariat and to a member of the Commission, who acts as Rapporteur. Where the case is clearly inadmissible, a committee of three members of the Commission can find it to be inadmissible at once. If the case cannot be disposed of in this way, it is referred to the government complained against. Where the case gives rise to no problems of interpretation of the Convention, it can be referred to a Chamber of at least seven members of the Commission, following consultation with the parties. The government's response is sent to the applicant or his representative for comments, and at this stage he becomes eligible for means-tested Council of Europe legal aid. The levels are not high and cannot be equated with costs. The plenary Commission or a Chamber again has the opportunity to declare the application inadmissible. Where that does not happen, the Commission or Chamber commonly proceed to hold an oral hearing, usually on both the admissibility and the merits combined. This is particularly likely to be the case where the possible ground for inadmissibility is that the application is 'manifestly ill-founded'.[12] The hearing is *in camera*. The proceedings before the Commission or Chamber are confidential because the object of the proceedings is to secure a friendly settlement of the case. After the hearing, the Commission or Chamber indicates its tentative thinking to the government. The object, presumably, is to concentrate the mind of the government on the friendly settlement negotiations, which now ensue. The carrot lies in the fact that, if the negotiations result in a settlement, there is no finding as to whether or not the facts disclose a violation of the Convention. The more likely it is that a breach will be found, the more a government may be tempted to offer. This is particularly true where financial compensation is sought by a victim. Where a change in the law would be required to remedy the situation, the government may prefer to risk an adverse finding. If the negotiations are successful, the Commission produces a Report, which outlines the facts and the solution agreed upon. If unsuccessful, the Commission's Report establishes the facts, the arguments of the parties and indicates the *opinion* of the Commission as to whether the facts disclose a violation of the Convention.

The Report is transmitted to the Committee of Ministers of the Council of Europe. If the case is not referred to the European Court of Human

Rights within a three month period, the Committee of Ministers *decides* whether there has been a violation of the Convention. Such a decision requires a two thirds majority. The Committee of Ministers generally follows the opinion of the majority of the Commission, but there have been instances where the requisite majority could not be obtained but where there was not a bare majority for the finding of no violation.[13] It is not necessary for the Commission to have found a violation of the Convention for a case to be referred to the Court. The Commission, a State party or, following the entry into force of the ninth protocol, the applicant can refer the case to the Court. The Court will have available to it the Report of the Commission, which becomes public at this stage. The applicant and the government may submit further written observations. On occasion, evidence has been accepted from interested third parties, whether organisations or states.[14] A public hearing is held and the Court then deliberates *in camera* and delivers a judgement binding on the parties. The applicant or his representative will be able to address the Court. The Commission does not 'represent' the applicant before the Court. The Court's judgement will declare whether a violation of the Convention has been found but it has no power to strike down the offending measure. The applicant may be awarded 'just satisfaction', but he is usually expected to be satisfied with the finding! Only in the event of winning before the Court is the applicant entitled to costs, provided they were actually and necessarily incurred and reasonable as to quantum. Any legal aid received is deducted from the costs awarded. The judgement is transmitted to the Committee of Ministers, which supervises its execution. Court judgements often give rise to a need for a government to amend its legislation but there is no subsequent check on whether the changes introduced actually meet the need revealed by the judgement.[15] From first submission to the final judgement of the Court takes on average seven years, five before the Commission and two before the Court. It is not uncommon for cases to take even longer. Because of the unacceptable delay in the determination of cases, the procedures of the Commission and Court are currently undergoing fundamental review.

Admissibility

The overwhelming majority of cases are rejected by the Commission for failing to satisfy the admissibility requirements.[16] Some of the criteria do not usually pose a problem; thus, anonymous petitions and abuses of the right of petition are unusual. There are likely to be four major areas of difficulty in establishing the admissibility of compensation cases. First, the applicant must be a "victim"; second, the application must not be incompatible with the Convention either *ratione materiae* or *ratione personae*. The third condition is that domestic remedies must have been exhausted, which co-exists with the requirement that the application must be brought within six months of the date of the final domestic decision in the case. Finally, applications may be declared inadmissible on the grounds that they are 'manifestly ill-founded'. These criteria will be examined in turn.

Applicant to be a 'Victim'

The requirement that the applicant be a 'victim' precludes the bringing of class actions or applications in which the compatibility of legislation with the Convention is challenged *in abstracto*. This is not an insuperable difficulty. For example, in the case of a group of claimants with the same grievance, the group should select a specimen case. Should it be successful, it will not as a matter of law provide redress in the other cases but the government will be on notice as to the likely result in other similar cases. Alternatively, all the members of the group can submit individual cases at the same time. These will then be joined by the Commission for the purpose of forming its opinion on the issue, but each case will generate a separate report. What the group can not do, is to submit an application in the name of the group. If, for example, the complaint is that the government has failed adequately to protect the right to life, it is unlikely that the right to life of the *organisation* has been jeopardised. Similarly, an organisation can not complain of nuisance caused by noise levels since it does not have ears.[17] Confusion as to this requirement has often been responsible for the delay experienced in proceedings before the Commission. The nationality of the applicant is irrelevant. The government is responsible for actions within its jurisdiction. This includes extra-territorial actions performed by those for whom it is responsible, such as diplomats,[18] members of the armed forces[19] and immigration officers.

A person may bring an application on behalf of a 'victim' where the latter is unable to do so himself. So, for example, applications have been brought by the parents of children and mentally handicapped persons and by close family members of those who have died as a result of the alleged violation. Commonly, the parent or other close relative will also be making a complaint in his own right.[20]

This raises the question of whether an application can be brought in the name of a foetus in, for example, the case of pre-natal injury. Article 1 guarantees the Convention rights to 'everyone' in the jurisdiction. Article 25 provides that applications must be submitted by a 'person'. These terms are not without difficulty in this context. The attitude of the Commission appears to be to consider each case on its facts and in the light of the Article being invoked.[21] Where an applicant wishes to complain that a pre-natal injury was occasioned as a result of a violation of the Convention, he would perhaps be best advised to plead in the alternative. He could complain both of the pre-natal injury itself and also of being born handicapped, which could only arise at the moment of birth. It may be possible, depending on the facts, for the parent to allege a violation of his own rights on account of the injury caused to his or her unborn child. The pre-natal injury may also give rise to a situation of continuing violation.[22] Whilst an individual cannot, for example, generally challenge legislation *in abstracto*, it is not always necessary to wait for the legislation to be applied to him. The legislation may create a situation of continuing violation of rights merely by virtue of its presence on the statute book. So, in the *Dudgeon* case,[23] the fact that legislation made all homosexual relations illegal in Northern Ireland was sufficient to make the applicant a victim and to violate Article 8, even though he had never been prosecuted. Again, in *Bruggemann and Scheuten*,[24] the female applicants were the 'victims' of German abortion legislation, even though they were not pregnant at the time. The concept of a 'continuing violation' is not confined to legislation; it relates to a state of affairs, however caused. It is also important in the context of the time limit in which to submit an application. This will be considered again in relation to the obligation to exhaust domestic remedies.

Incompatibility

The second admissibility criterion which can cause difficulties in practice is that, under Article 27.2, the Commission must reject applications 'incompatible with the provisions' of the Convention. It is unfortunate that the term 'incompatible' suggests 'inconsistent with' or in some sense 'opposed to'. It implies that an application should be rejected only if it is somehow destructive of rights recognised in the Convention. That situation is dealt with by a different provision.[25] The Commission has interpreted the admissibility requirement to mean that the complaint must come within the scope of a convention right. Two examples should illustrate this. If an applicant wishes to complain of discrimination in the field of employment, the application will be declared inadmissible *ratione materiae* because the non-discrimination provision (Article 14) relates only to discrimination regarding a right protected by the Convention. There is no provision directly relating to employment in the Convention. If, however, the father of a child born out of wedlock complains that he is denied access to the child, his complaint concerns his right to respect for his family life (Article 8). This involves questions of construction (does 'family life' include the relationship of a father and a child born out of wedlock) and questions of fact (has the particular father sufficient connection with the child to constitute 'family life'). If there is no *prima facie* violation of Article 8, the application must be declared 'manifestly ill-founded' but it will not be declared incompatible *ratione materiae*, since the complaint came within the scope of Article 8. Whilst this distinction seems straightforward, in some cases the Commission appears to have confused these two separate grounds of inadmissibility.

An application may also be declared inadmissible *ratione personae*. This is likely to pose very real problems in the context of personal injury litigation. The complaint must allege that the violation of a Convention right was at the hands of a High Contracting Party, in other words the State. The Convention does not directly protect a private citizen from a violation of his rights by another private citizen.[26] At first sight, this might be thought to exclude almost every personal injury claim. That, however, is an oversimplification. Firstly, in some situations the injury may have resulted from a violation of a Convention right by a body which is regarded as part of the State. Secondly, where the injury is caused by the fault of a non-State entity, the State may independently have violated the applicant's rights. These will be examined in turn.

The State does not consist simply of the organs of central government. The activities of other bodies may be attributable to the State. Following their consistent approach to analogous Convention provisions, the Commission and Court would determine the issue, not the State. So, for example, in the 'closed shop' case,[27] the Convention organs held that they did not need to establish whether the British Government was responsible for the acts of British Rail. The Government was held responsible for its legislation which allowed employers to breach applicants' rights. The implication is that, had it been necessary for the Commission and Court to determine whether the Government was responsible for the acts of British Rail, it would have been for those bodies to decide the issue.

A government would be held responsible for the acts of regional and district health authorities and the medical staff in their employment. This, together with its responsibility for the police, armed forces and the legal system may be the most important area of 'direct' state responsibility in the context of personal injury litigation.

In some cases, the applicant may be tempted to argue that the State has 'directly' violated his rights when, in fact, it would be more appropriate to argue that the State's independent violation of those rights made possible the injury caused by a non-governmental entity. So, for example, if a group of people were injured on a Sealink 'Ro-Ro' ferry, the applicants might seek to argue that the British Government was responsible for the actions of Sealink. They would be better advised either to plead in the alternative or else to rely only on the alternative argument. That involves the independent violation by the State of the applicants' rights.

Their complaint is either that the activity in question was hazardous and the State failed to regulate it, or else the stronger argument that the State in fact recognised that passenger safety required regulations, statutory regulations were in force, but the government failed effectively to enforce them. The substantive issue will be examined later in this chapter. The admissibility argument must be carefully framed. The applicants are not saying that the government is responsible for the body whose alleged negligence caused their injuries. *Independently* of that cause of action, the State is responsible for failing to protect the right to life of the applicants either by enforcing the safety legislation it considered necessary (as evidenced by the fact that the regulations were already in place), or alternatively by introducing and enforcing the safety regulations it ought to have made. In other words, in some cases the Convention obliges States to take measures in relation to third parties in order to protect potential victims. To that very limited extent, the Convention has an indirect third-party effect. The applicants must, however, be able to show that the State itself has violated their rights.

An example will illustrate the operation of this principle. In *Baggs, Rayner & Powell* v *United Kingdom*,[28] the applicants complained of the noise levels around Heathrow Airport. This raises an issue under Article 8 of the Convention. Those causing the noise nuisance are the airlines. An action in nuisance would avoid the practical problems this causes by attributing responsibility to the occupier of the land, at the time the British Airports Authority (BAA). The Government, at the time of the submission of the application, was responsible for the acts of BAA. Legal action was, however, barred under a statutory provision. Independently of that basis of responsibility, the government set maximum noise levels for day-time and night-time arrivals and departures from the airport. It appears, however, that the Government fails to enforce those levels, which it presumably regards as the limits of reasonable use. If the failure to enforce its own regulations caused a violation of the applicants' rights under Article 8, the State could be held responsible for that failure. The application could not be declared inadmissible *ratione personae*.

What was seen as a tremendous impediment to the bringing of a case based on personal injury – the need to establish the responsibility of the *State* – is therefore a significant but not insuperable barrier. The application must be carefully drafted to make it clear whether the State is being held responsible for the injury or for a failure to protect the applicant from the injury.

Exhaustion of Domestic Remedies

The third condition of admissibility is that the applicant must have exhausted domestic remedies. This reflects a rule of customary international law. It should be examined in tandem with the requirement that the case must be brought 'within a period of six months from the date on which the final decision was taken'[29]. The applicant must provide sufficient information to show that the requirements of Article 26 have been satisfied; if not, the Commission will examine the issue *ex officio*. If the objection of non-exhaustion is raised by the respondent government, it is for the government to prove the existence of remedies in municipal law which have not been exhausted. In the case of those States before whose courts the Convention can be pleaded,[30] it is relatively easy to identify potential remedies and hence to establish whether they have been exhausted. It is often much more difficult in the British context. It must be remembered that it is remedies relating to the alleged breach of the Convention which must be invoked, not necessarily those relating to the injury suffered. For example, where the complaint concerns the non-enforcement of safety regulations, it may be necessary to seek damages for breach of statutory duty, if that is available to individuals, or to seek *mandamus* by way of judicial review. It would not be necessary to exhaust remedies relating to the injury itself, where that action lies against a non-governmental entity. If the complaint concerns the procedures or avenues of redress available to the applicant, then a refusal to grant legal aid must be appealed and disclosure sought of any inspectors' reports on which the applicant wishes to rely.

To qualify as a remedy, the procedure invoked must be both effective and sufficient to redress the wrong suffered. It must also be available as of right. The availability of a remedy is a matter of substance and not of form. Where a remedy is subject to time limits, the applicant's case will be declared inadmissible for non-exhaustion if he sought the remedy in municipal law out of time.

The prospect of having to exhaust every channel of appeal and review is daunting. There are, however, limits to the scope of the obligation. If there are no prospects of success, the alleged avenue of redress is no remedy at all. So, for example, if the complaint alleges that an Act of Parliament itself violates the applicant's rights, he has no remedy in British law. Or again, if appeal formally or in effect only lies on questions of law, and it is the application of the law on the facts by the first instance judge that has caused the alleged violation, there is no need to appeal the decision. In the *Handyside Case*,[31] the judge at first instance found that the 'little red schoolbook' came within the Obscene Publications Acts. There was no dispute as to the law; the dispute concerned a finding of fact which would not be overturned by an appeal court. The Commission and Court did not require the applicant to appeal the case but accepted counsel's opinion to the effect that such a course of action would have been pointless. By way of contrast, the *Sunday Times* had to appeal its objection to the issue of an injunction preventing it from publishing an article on the thalidomide controversy, since what was at issue was the scope of the law regarding contempt of court.[32]

A further limit to the requirement of exhaustion of domestic remedies concerns the allegation that the violation in question formed part of an administrative practice. If that can be proved, then remedies formally available are clearly not effective. That is unlikely to arise in 'normal' personal injury litigation; it usually concerns allegations of ill-treatment at the hands of the police or armed forces where there is evidence that the practice is condoned by those in authority and nothing has been done to prevent its recurrence.[33]

The obligation to exhaust domestic remedies coexists with a requirement that the application be brought within six months of the final decision. In many cases it has not occurred to applicants that they may have a remedy under the Convention until the six months have elapsed. Where a case is in the hands of legal advisers and they fail to consider such a remedy, they may be liable in negligence, at least where the Convention case-law is settled. It is therefore imperative that the question of a Convention remedy be considered even during the period in which domestic remedies are being exhausted. There is an obvious potential difficulty; if the applicant does not submit his case until he has invoked a procedure which may not be regarded as a remedy by the Commission, it might well be out of time. On the other hand, if he fails to use the procedure and it is subsequently held to constitute a remedy, the case will be inadmissible for non-exhaustion. The solution is for the applicant to submit the case to the Commission as soon as he has exhausted what are indisputably remedies in municipal law, and at the same time, to seek the questionable remedy, notifying the Commission of the fact. In that way the case will be registered within the six month period but a consideration of it can be deferred until the outcome of the municipal proceedings is known.

In one situation, the six months rule causes no difficulty. Where there is alleged to be a continuing violation of the Convention, the complaint arises afresh each day. It is not an exception to the six month rule. It can be difficult to distinguish between a breach of the Convention which gives rise to long-term effects and a continuing violation of the Convention. Where a case concerns the non-enforcement of safety standards, it may represent a violation of the State's obligation to protect the right to life irrespective of the occurrence of any injury. Such a complaint could be made by potential victims. Where, on the other hand, the case concerns the medical treatment afforded the applicant, the complaint is of a specific violation with long-term effects. In the former case, the complaint may be brought at any time whereas, in the latter, it must be brought within six months of the final domestic decision arising out of an alleged violation of the Convention.

'Manifestly Ill-Founded'

The final admissibility criterion is that an application must be rejected if it is 'manifestly ill-founded'. This has been interpreted as meaning that the applicant must establish a *prima facie* case of a violation of a Convention right.[34] This necessarily involves at least a cursory examination of the merits at the admissibility stage and explains why so many oral hearings deal with both admissibility and merits. It also makes it all the more important that the application be submitted in as complete a form as possible. In particular, the arguments on the merits need to be set out in the original submission. The applicant must argue that, on the basis of existing case-law and the lines of reasoning which that reveals, his case comes within the terms of certain Articles. Again, this explains the need for familiarity with the case-law on the part of practitioners. In effect, it is the only guide, together with the text, as to what constitutes a *prima facie* violation of the Convention.

A particular difficulty arises in the context of Articles 8 to 11, which in a first paragraph establish a right, and in a second, set limitations on its exercise. If the two paragraphs were viewed as separate provisions, the applicant would have established a *prima facie* violation by proving an interference in the right protected. In that case – however likely it was that the government could successfully invoke one of the grounds of limitation of the exercise of the right – the application could not be declared 'manifestly ill-founded'.

In practice, the Commission appears to view the two paragraphs together as defining the scope of the right. Thus, where there is an obvious interference in the exercise of a right protected by the Convention, but it is equally obviously justified by a limitation inherent in the right, the case will be declared 'manifestly ill-founded'. The clearer the interference in the right, the clearer will have to be the justification for it. Where there is considerable, but not overwhelming, evidence of an interference in the right, but it is open to question whether that interference is in fact necessary, as opposed to administratively convenient, the application will probably be declared admissible. The phrase 'manifestly ill-founded' also causes a 'knock-on' problem in the interpretation of one of the substantive rights, Article 13.[35]

It is now possible to turn to a consideration of the substantive Convention rights most likely to be at issue in a case concerning personal injury.

Merits

The three most relevant Convention issues appear to be: first, that the government is responsible for the injury sustained by virtue of its responsibility for the actions of medical and para-medical personnel; second, that its non-enforcement or lack of provision of safety regulations violated its obligation to protect the right to life; and third, that the procedures available in the field of personal injury litigation violate the fair trial guarantees of Article 6.

Article 2 of the Convention protects not life but the right to life.[36] It imposes both a positive and a negative obligation on States. The use of lethal force is prohibited except in the circumstances defined in the second paragraph of the Article and with regard to the lawful use of the death penalty. The first sentence of Article 2, however, states a positive obligation – 'Everyone's right to life shall be protected by law'. The scope of the right was considered in the 'vaccine – damaged children' case.[37] The Commission recognised that Article 2 requires States '... to take appropriate steps to safeguard life.'[38]

In the case of injury or death caused by medical or para-medical staff whose actions are attributable to the State, it should be possible to obtain a domestic remedy. The difficulties in practice concern the need to prove negligence and the related question of medical judgement and the cost of such an action, if contested. The Convention right is of no assistance since an effective domestic remedy exists and must be exhausted. Where the applicant has failed to prove negligence before the domestic courts, Article 2 is not likely to be of much assistance. Whilst the Article does not lay down the basis of liability, it appears to be targeted at intentional and arbitrary deprivations of life.[39] This suggests that the State must be in some sense to blame for the death. No liability arises merely by virtue of the death of the victim whilst in the care of a doctor. This is further confirmed by an examination of the reasoning in the case referred to above. The Commission did not simply rely on the proposition that vaccination is for the greatest good of the greatest number. It examined what measures the British Government had taken to safeguard against the known risk of an adverse reaction. It drew attention to weaknesses in the scheme but considered that:

> ... although proper liaison and informed health visitors are desirable precautionary measures, the system of control and supervision established by the State ... [was] sufficient to comply with its obligation to protect life under Article 2 of the Convention.[40]

This suggests that *some* system for dealing with the risk was required and that, if none had existed, there might have been a violation of Article 2, notwithstanding that vaccination is given for the general good in an attempt to protect life. It also suggests that the Commission was trying to determine whether the State was at fault. The applicant is, then, apparently no better off under Article 2 than under domestic law, in those cases which involve treatment given by persons for whose actions the State is responsible. At best, the Commission may draw the boundary line in a different place from the national authorities in borderline cases. The applicant's complaint that the domestic remedies are unduly expensive to pursue will be examined below, in the context of Article 6.

Article 2 may also be of relevance in a different type of case, where the injury or death is caused by a person or body whose actions are not attributable to the State but where it is alleged that the State failed to prevent the injury pursuant to its obligation to protect the right to life. Professor Fawcett suggests that the phrase 'protected by law' in Article 2 is

> ... the kind of expression which provokes broad and sometimes extravagant constructions. It might be argued, for example, that failure to impose speed limits on the roads, or to enact safety legislation for industrial work engaged the responsibility of a contracting State under Article 2 for accidental deaths on the road or in factories. But this argument ignores the fact that it is not life, but the right to life which is to be protected by law.[41]

It is submitted that this construction is too narrow. It would, in effect, mean that the first sentence of Article 2 is otiose; it merely expresses the same notion as the rest of the Article but in different words. It is also contrary to the Commission's opinion in the 'vaccine – damaged children' case, in which the Commission expressly stated '... that the first sentence of Article 2 imposes a broader obligation on the State than that contained in the second sentence.'[42] The scope of that obligation is uncertain but it would appear from the case that where an activity carries known risk of injury then, even if the activity is for the public benefit, the government must take certain measures to reduce the incidence of the risk. The case concerned an activity *designed* to protect life. *A fortiori*, where an activity is for public economic benefit, but not in the interest of public health as such, the Commission might be expected to demand more of States by way of measures to reduce known or foreseeable risk of injury. To that extent, Article 2 may well oblige States to enact and enforce safety legislation.

There would appear to be two stages to the argument. Where no such regulations have been made, the applicant would have to show that the activity carried known or foreseeable risk of death or serious injury. The State's breach of Article 2 would consist of its failure to do that which it ought to have done. Where such regulations already exist, on the other hand, the applicant may be able simply to rely on that as evidence of the need, without having to prove the known or foreseeable risk. In other words, a form of estoppel would be invoked. In such a case, the complaint would be of the non-enforcement of the regulations recognised by the State to be necessary. Such an argument appears to fall squarely within the principle of the 'vaccine – damaged children' case and would therefore appear to afford some chance of success.

It must be remembered that the relevant domestic remedies would need to be exhausted before submitting an application under the Convention. In this context, the remedy would presumably be in damages for breach of statutory duty, where a minister was under a statutory obligation to make regulations and had failed to do so, and the applicant's injury had resulted from such a failure. There might be difficulty in establishing a right to damages on the part of an aggrieved individual. It is not clear what, if any, remedy exists where the minister has not made any safety regulations and is not under a statutory obligation to do so. That in itself might provide ground for a complaint under Article 13. This requires States to provide some means by which individuals can raise alleged violations of their rights under the Convention before a domestic authority.[43] Such a situation would appear to be unusual. The more common problem seems to be of ineffectively or erratically enforced safety standards and regulations. A second remedy would be judicial review by way of *mandamus* where the minister has made regulations but has failed to enforce them effectively. This could be used as a preventive measure; the applicant would not need to show that he or she had been injured. The claim is rather of a continuing violation of the State's obligation to protect the applicant's right to life.

Article 2 would, therefore, appear to afford applicants a useful additional remedy where the complaint concerns the State's failure adequately to protect the right to life. In cases of personal injury, there is an effective but expensive domestic remedy where the injury is attributable to the State. There is also an uncertain, but equally expensive, remedy where the alleged violation by the State concerns its failure to prevent the injury by the enforcement of safety regulations. In addition, there is an issue under Article 6 of the Convention even where there is no question of a violation of Article 2. The State is responsible for its legal system, including the procedures whereby individuals can seek redress against other individuals. In other words, Article 6 is of potential application in *all* cases of personal injury, irrespective of who the defendant may be.

On the face of it, Article 6 merely provides that judicial proceedings must be fairly conducted.[44] The European Court of Human Rights has, however, held that Article 6 implies certain other guarantees. In the case of *Golder* v *UK*,[45] the Court held that 'Article 6 paragraph 1 secures to everyone the right to have any claim relating to his civil rights and obligations brought before a court or tribunal.'[46] In other words, the Article implies a right of access to court.

In that case, the denial of access to court arose from a positive obstacle placed in the way of the applicant in the form of the Home Secretary's prohibition on his consulting a solicitor. Another example of such an impediment would be a bar to legal action contained in a statute. The Court, however, has applied the right of access to court to cases where the State does not impose a positive impediment but where it arises rather from the financial circumstances of the applicant. In the case of *Airey* v *Ireland*,[47] the applicant could not obtain an order of judicial separation which was only available from the High Court in Dublin since, at the time, no civil legal aid was available in Ireland, and she did not have the financial means to pay for a solicitor to represent her.[48] The Court found that

> ...fulfilment of a duty under the Convention on occasion necessitates some positive action on the part of the State; in such circumstances, the State cannot simply remain passive ... The obligation to secure an effective right of access to the courts falls into this category of duty.[49]

The Court was at pains to emphasize that its judgement did not mean that Ireland was required to introduce free civil legal aid in all cases. In some cases, it might be possible for individuals to represent themselves before the High Court. That would depend on the complexity of the procedure, the issues and the evidence in a particular case or a particular type of case. Another possibility was for the State to simplify the procedure for obtaining a decree of judicial separation by, for example, making it available from the District Court. The essence of the matter is that the '...Convention is intended to guarantee not rights that are theoretical or illusory but rights that are practical and effective ....'[50] Therefore:

> "... Article 6 paragraph 1 may sometimes compel the State to provide the assistance of a lawyer when such assistance proves indispensable for an effective access to court either because legal representation is rendered compulsory ... or by reason of the complexity of the procedure or of the case."[51]

It is clear from the reasoning of the Court that the effectiveness of the access to court is a matter of substance and not of form. The fact that legal aid is available in personal injury litigation in Britain will not determine the issue. It will also be relevant to consider the level of financial resources at which the applicant is required to contribute to the cost and the proportion of the cost he or she is expected to bear. The formula used by the Court is access to court; this would not necessarily imply access to appeal procedures. Nevertheless, the reasoning in the *Airey* case suggests that the applicant should not be denied effective access to a *remedy* and this may involve appeal proceedings. This is reinforced by the obligation to exhaust domestic remedies, including appeal procedures, before submitting a case to the Commission. This has serious implications when one considers the contribution expected of legally-aided applicants, and, even more, the position of non-legally-aided applicants.

The Court examines each case individually. It might not be willing to say that in *all* cases of personal injury litigation the assistance of a solicitor and sometimes a barrister was required. Nevertheless, in a case of any complexity, or where the defendant was legally represented, there would be a strong argument that such assistance was required.

The cost of obtaining compensation for personal injury is examined elsewhere in this book.[52] It appears likely that, in some cases, applicants are denied effective access to court for a determination of their civil rights, in breach of Article 6(1) of the Convention, as a result of the financial costs involved. It would be unrealistic to expect the government to sign a blank cheque. As the Court in the *Airey* case emphasized, measures other than an extension of legal aid may be adopted. In addition to the possibility of a form of insurance scheme which would obviate the need to go to court, the sort of measures which need to be considered are the bringing of class actions and allowing non-legally-aided claimants to 'ride on the back' of legally-aided ones. This avenue of effective access to a remedy was denied to the Opren litigants by the courts.[53] Financial assistance could also be provided for the negotiations which might enable an out-of-court settlement to be reached. The 'Piper Alpha' compensation negotiations were lengthy and must, therefore, have been expensive. Had the case gone to court, however, the costs would have been much higher. Strictly speaking, such assistance would not come within Article 6 since that concerns access to *court*. It would, however, come within the formula of access to a *remedy* and would be cheaper for the taxpayer than obliging applicants to go to court, where they would have to be effectively legally-aided.

It is not being suggested that there are easy solutions to the problem. It is being argued, however, that in many cases the current financial limits on civil legal aid, and the level of contribution required, represent a substantial financial barrier and therefore a denial of effective access to court.

Article 6 imposes a more specific and more onerous obligation on States than does Article 13, which guarantees the right to an effective remedy before a national authority. Wherever the matter in dispute is civil in character, the applicant would be better advised to invoke Article 6. It was seen above, in the context of Article 2, that it might be necessary to challenge the failure to make any safety regulations or the non-enforcement of those already made. If such proceedings were characterized as civil, the right of effective access to court would apply.[54] If the proceedings were regarded as public in character, the guarantees of Article 6 would not apply. If no judicial remedy existed at all, which is most likely to arise where the minister is under no statutory obligation to make safety regulations and has not done so, the applicant may need to invoke Article 13. It would then be argued that the essence of the complaint – of a violation of Article 2 – cannot be brought before any national authority. It would have to be shown that there was an 'arguable claim' that the government was in breach of Article 2. It appears that this requirement is not as onerous as establishing a *prima facie* case, but its precise scope is far from clear.[55]

The European Convention on Human Rights is no substitute for effective remedies before national authorities. It does, nevertheless, fulfil a useful function in enabling national procedures to be called into question. This is all the more important in a State without anything approaching a constitutional court or constitutionally guaranteed rights. The Convention reaches the parts that other remedies do not reach. Its reach also extends into fields that may come as a surprise to the legal practitioner. In a recent case, the manner in which an 'Anton Piller' order was executed was held to raise an admissible issue under Article 8, which protects the right to respect for private and family life.[56] In the field of personal injury litigation, Convention issues may arise in individual cases under Article 2 and, more commonly, under Article 6. It is possible to envisage situations in which other provisions would also be applicable. The incoming tide in British law is not just bringing with it EEC law; it also contains the case-law under the European Convention on Human Rights.

Notes

1 There still, on occasion, seems to be some confusion in the press and amongst lawyers as to the relationship between the European Convention on Human Rights and the institutions of the EEC. The former has absolutely nothing to do with the latter. The ECHR is one of the Conventions produced by the Council of Europe. It

sets up enforcement machinery (see the section on *Procedure*) which is, at present, tied in to the structure of the Council of Europe. The European Court of Justice (that is, the EEC's court) has considered cases with a human rights dimension but it does so in the context of the Treaty of Rome and other EEC law. It has sometimes made express reference to provisions in the ECHR to identify fundamental constitutional norms in member States. As far as the European Commission and Court of Human Rights are concerned, their only task is to establish whether a Convention right has been violated in the particular case before them. This paper will not deal with EEC law or with any other international treaty obligation. Its only concern is with the use that may be made by individuals of the European Convention on Human Rights.

2 A distinction is drawn in international human rights texts between the protection and the promotion of human rights. The former is seen as requiring immediate action by the State, commonly of a negative character. The protection of rights can require positive action on the part of the State. The promotion of human rights, on the other hand, involves arriving progressively at certain targets. Generally speaking, civil and political rights are protected and economic, social and cultural rights promoted but there are exceptions in both fields.

3 As opposed to economic, social and cultural rights which are dealt with primarily in the European Social Charter.

4 For example, the classification of an offence as disciplinary under municipal law in relation to soldiers, prisoners, police officers and so on, is not conclusive as to its status for the purposes of Article 6 ECHR which deals with civil and criminal proceedings. In some cases, such proceedings have been held to be criminal for the purposes of Article 6; *Engel & Others* v *the Netherlands*, Eur. Ct. of H.R., Series A, Vol. 22. Similarly proceedings regarded as matters of public law rather than as civil proceedings within the domestic sphere may be held to be civil for the purposes of Article 6; *Konig* v *Federal Republic of Germany*, Eur. Ct. of H.R., Series A, Vol. 27; *Feldbrugge* v *the Netherlands*, Eur. Ct. of H.R., Series A, Vol. 99 and *Deumeland* v *FRG*, Eur. Ct. of H.R., Series A, Vol. 100.

5 '(1) In the determination of his civil rights and obligations or of any criminal charge against him, everyone is entitled to a fair and public hearing within a reasonable time by an independent and impartial tribunal established by law. Judgment shall be pronounced publicly but the press and public may be excluded from all or part of the trial in the interests of morals, public order, or national security in a democratic society, where the interests of juveniles or the protection of the private life of the parties so require, or to the extent strictly necessary in the opinion of the court in special circumstances where publicity would prejudice the interests of justice....'

6 *Ashingdane* v *United Kingdom*, Eur. Ct. of H.R., Series A, Vol. 93.

7 '(1) Everyone's right to life shall be protected by law. No one shall be deprived of his life intentionally save in the execution of a sentence of a court following his conviction of a crime for which this penalty is provided by law.

(2) Deprivation of life shall not be regarded as inflicted in contravention of this Article when it results from the use of force which is no more than absolutely necessary:

(a) in defence of any person from unlawful violence;

(b) in order to effect a lawful arrest or to prevent the escape of a person lawfully detained;

(c) in action lawfully taken for the purpose of quelling a riot or insurrection.'

8 *Association X* v *UK* (7154/75), 14 D & R, 31.

9 For example, Interights, Justice.

10 Under Rule 32(2) of the Rules of Procedure of the European Commission of Human Rights (1990), the applicant can be represented by 'a lawyer or any other person, resident in a Convention country, unless the Commission at any stage decides otherwise'; Under Rule 30 of the Revised Rules of Court (1982), the applicant can be represented before the court by 'an advocate authorised to practise in any of the Contracting States ... or by any other person approved by the President.'

11 This account does not deal with the inter-state complaints procedure. It also assumes that the State complained against has made a declaration under Article 25 recognising the competence of the Commission to receive and investigate petitions from individuals, groups and non-governmental organisations and that it has made a declaration under Article 46 recognising the jurisdiction of the European Court of Human Rights.

12 For further discussion, see relevant section in this chapter.

13 For example, *Huber* v *Austria*, 18 Ybk. 324.

14 Memorandum and oral intervention by Lord Wedderburn on behalf of the TUC in *Young, James & Webster* v *UK*, Eur. Ct. of H.R., Series A. Vol. 44 (the 'closed shop' case); submission of the British Government in *Winterwerp* v *the Netherlands*, Eur. Ct. of H.R., Series A, Vol. 33. This practice can be authorised under Rule 37 of the Revised Rules of Court (1982).

15 The Contempt of Court Act 1981 was made necessary by the *Sunday Times* case. *Harman* v *UK* (10038/82), 38 D & R 53, suggests that problems in this field may not all have been resolved. The case was the subject of a friendly settlement.

16 Statistics on applications to the Commission are to be found in Stocktaking on the European Convention on Human Rights and its annual supplements, produced by the Commission and published by the Council of Europe.

17 Partial decision on admissibility in 9310/81 of 15 March 1984 in which the application of the Federation of Heathrow Anti-Noise Groups (FHANG) regarding aircraft noise was declared inadmissible but that of the three individual applicants, Baggs, Rayner and Powell, was to be further investigated.

18 1611/62, Yearbook 8, 158; *X and Y* v *Switzerland* (7289/75 & 7349/76), 9 D & R 57.

19 *Cyprus* v *Turkey* (8007/77), 13 D & R 85 at 148–50.

20 Where X is killed in alleged violation of the State's obligations under Article 2, the surviving spouse can bring an action under Article 2 in right of the deceased and under Article 8 in his/her own right, alleging interference in the right to family life. *Amekrane* v *UK* (5961/72), Coll. of Dec. 44,101; Yearbook 16, 356.

21 *X* v *UK* (8416/79), 19 D & R 244; note para 7 at p 249 in which the Commission states that, whilst none of the uses of the term 'everyone' in the articles of the Convention '... indicates clearly that it has any possible prenatal application', nevertheless '... such application in a rare case – eg under Article 6, paragraph 1 – cannot be entirely excluded.' The provision referred to relates to the determination of civil rights and obligations and might therefore include a right of action for the unborn child in relation to prenatal injuries.

22 See discussion later in this chapter.

23 Eur. Ct. of H.R., Series A, Vol. 45.

24 Yearbook 21, 638.

25 Article 17 provides 'Nothing in this Convention may be interpreted as implying for any State, group or person any right to engage in any activity or perform any act aimed at the destruction of any of the rights and freedoms set forth herein or at their limitation to a greater extent than is provided for in the Convention.'

26 The effect of the Convention on third parties (*Drittwirkung*) is a matter of some con-

troversy; see Drzemczewski A. (1983), *European Human Rights Convention in Domestic Law*, Oxford: Clarendon Press, 199–204; 218–28.

27 *Supra cit.*, Note 14.

28 Application 9310/81; the *Baggs* case was declared partially admissible on 17 October 1985 and has since been the subject of a friendly settlement; the *Powell* case was declared partially admissible on the same day and the *Rayner* case likewise on 16 July 1986. The Commission Report was adopted on 19 January 1989; the judgement of the Court is to be found at Eur. Ct. of H.R., Series A, Vol. 172. See also *Arrondelle* v *UK* , 19 D & R 186.

29 Article 26 ECHR.

30 Drzemczewski, *op. cit.*, Part II.

31 Eur. Ct. of H.R., Series A, Vol. 24. See also *Abdulaziz, Cabales & Balkandali* v *UK*, Eur. Ct. of H.R. Series A, Vol. 94.

32 Eur. Ct. of H.R., Series A, Vol. 30.

33 *Donnelly et al.* v *UK* (5577–5583/72), 4 D & R 4.

34 214/56, 2 Ybk. 254; 332/57, 2 Ybk. 336; 524/59, 3 Ybk. 338; 596/59, 3 Ybk. 368. On the danger of an assessment of the merits taking place at the admissibility stage, see Jacobs F.G. (1975), *The European Convention on Human Rights*, Oxford: Clarendon Press, 243–6.

35 See *Boyle & Rice* v *UK*, Eur. Ct. of H.R., Series A, Vol. 131. Hampson, F.J. (1990), 'The concept of an "arguable claim" under Article 13 of the European Convention on Human Rights', *ICLQ*, **39**, 891.

36 See Fawcett, J.E.S. (1987), *The Application of the European Convention on Human Rights* (2nd Edn), Oxford: Clarendon Press, 37. For the text of Article 2, see *Supra* Note 7.

37 *Association* X v *UK* (7154/75), 14 D & R 31.

38 *Ibid.*, at p 32.

39 See the wording of the analogous provision in the International Covenant on Civil and Political Rights, which the UK has ratified and Article 6(1) of which provides 'Every human being has the inherent right to life. This right shall be protected by law. No one shall be arbitrarily deprived of his life.'

40 *Association* X v *UK.*, *supra cit.*, at p 34.

41 Fawcett, *op. cit.*, p 37.

42 *Association* X v *UK*, *supra cit.*, at p 32.

43 *Boyle & Rice* v *UK*, Eur. Ct. of H.R., Series A, Vol. 131.

44 For the text of Article 6(1) see *supra* note 5. On access to the law generally, Ashman, P. (1988), 'Access to Justice', in Sieghart, P. (ed.), *Human Rights in the United Kingdom*, London: Pinter; Merricks, W. (1984), 'Access to Law', in Wallington, P. (ed.), *Civil Liberties 1984*, Oxford: Martin Robertson.

45 Eur. Ct. of H.R., Series A, Vol. 18.

46 *Ibid.*, para. 36. Note: Article 6 does not apply to proceedings characterized by the Commission and Court as a matter of public law; see cases cited at note 4 *supra*.

47 Eur. Ct. of H.R., Series A, Vol. 32.

48 In 1978, the cost would have been in the range of £500 to £1 200, depending on whether the action was contested; *ibid.*, para 11.

49 *Ibid.*, para 25.

50 *Ibid.*, para 24.

51 *Ibid.*, para 26.

52 See Ch. 2 in this book.

53 See Ch. 2 in this book.

54 See cases cited at note 4, *supra*.
55 See *Boyle & Rice* v *UK*., *supra cit.*
56 *A.R.M. Chappell* v *UK* (10461/83), 42 D & R 137; in its Report, adopted on 14 October 1987, the Commission concluded by six votes to five that there had been no violation of Article 8 of the Convention. The court held unanimously that there had been no breach of Article 8; Eur. Ct. of H.R., Series A, Vol. 152.

6 No-Fault Liability on French Roads

Ruth Redmond-Cooper

A state desirous of implementing a new system to compensate for personal injury has, first of all, a number of basic choices to make. The scheme adopted may be all-embracing, as in New Zealand; there the social contract between the individual and the state requires that the individual forego his traditional right to bring an action in tort, in exchange for guaranteed compensation from the state regardless of whether a third party was involved in the accident – let alone proved to have been 'at fault'. Alternatively, the state may choose to proceed more cautiously and provide cover for a particular category of accident victim, for example those injured in medical misadventures or in road accidents. Compensation may further be payable to a category of victims based on: the nature of the injury suffered (for example, to compensate all blind people, whether blinded by accident or by disease as under standard social security provisions); or the place where the injury occurred (a scheme exists in Israel which provides compensation to any person injured on the roads, regardless of whether or not a motorised vehicle was involved in the accident); or the precise source of the damage (for example, the UK Vaccine Damage Payments Act 1979).

The systems currently in operation throughout the world may be said to fall roughly into two broad categories: either no-fault liability schemes or no-fault compensation schemes. Under the former, a notional defendant or perpetrator of the damage must be found whose presence at the scene of the accident may serve merely as a means of channelling funds from the insurance company to the injured person; under the latter, compensation is available from a central fund with no need to identify a notional innocent perpetrator. The New Zealand scheme which has been dealt with in some detail in chapter 4 in this book, serves as an example of a no-fault compensation scheme and has, on the whole and notwithstanding certain problems of operation and interpretation, been well received by the people whom it serves. The same cannot, however, always be said for no-fault liability schemes, which will often entail a refusal by the insurance company to acknowledge liability and a consequent legal action against the notional defendant. In such a case there is often a tendency on the part of the public, and sometimes even of the judge, to consider that imposition of liability implies fault.

It is proposed in this essay to examine the way in which no-fault liability in respect of road accidents has operated in France, both at common law, up to July 1985, and under the Act of 5 July 1985. As emphasized by the Royal Commission on Civil Liability and Compensation for Personal Injury[1] (Pearson Commission), the question of compensation for road accidents is worthy of special attention for a number of reasons. First, by reason of the number of victims (the annual death toll on the roads in the United Kingdom is in the region of 5 000, with a further 65 000 being seriously injured); road accidents also account for some 40 per cent of all tort claims. Second, by introducing compulsory third party insurance, the legislature has already recognised the inherently dangerous nature of road transport,[2] and an extension into some form of no-fault liability might not be seen as inappropriate. Third, in many respects, it is in the area of road accidents that the inadequacies of the fault system are most clearly perceived: only a very small percentage of victims succeed in recovering damages; administration and legal fees amount to almost the same sum as that finally awarded as damages; the suddenness of a road accident and the subsequent delay before the action comes to trial both heighten the difficulties of proof of fault. Since the roads are used by almost all members of society, we all, whether as pedestrian, cyclist or vehicle driver, run the risk of accident each time we venture out; insurance is paid in respect of all vehicles, and it is therefore pertinent to ask whether the money which is presently to a very great extent used to finance the litigation arising from road accidents could not be used in order to compensate all victims without requiring proof of fault. The Pearson Commission, after considering the various foreign no-fault road accident compensation schemes in existence at that time, proposed the introduction of a no-fault scheme financed by a levy on petrol and administered through the social security system. In France, the system finally adopted in July 1985 provides for compensation to be payable to all non-drivers injured in road accidents, irrespective of fault on the part of the driver of the vehicle involved and, in the main, regardless of contributory negligence on the part of the victim. Payments are made by the insurance company covering the vehicle involved, and, in cases of disputed liability, legal action remains possible.

However, no-fault liability has existed, in one form or another, for many years in France, first through judicial inventiveness and subsequently by virtue of the Act of 5 July 1985.

The French Common Law relating to Road Accidents

The French judiciary was quick to respond to the specific problems caused by accidents involving motorised vehicles. The general rules governing the imposition of tortious liability are to be found in Articles 1382 *et seq* of the French Civil Code. Articles 1382 and 1383 relate to a person's liability for his own negligent actions, and clearly require proof of fault. Article 1384, however, provides:

> A person is liable not only for damage which he causes by his own action, but also for that which is caused by the action of persons for whom he is liable, or for things which he has in his custody.

The wording of this provision might, on a relatively flexible interpretation, remind the common lawyer of the rule in *Rylands* v *Fletcher*[3] where Lord Cairns LC, citing Blackburn J in the Court of Exchequer Chamber, stated:

> ... the person who, for his own purposes, brings on his land and collects and keeps there anything likely to do mischief if it escapes, must keep it in at his peril; and if he does not do so, is *prima facie* answerable for all the damage which is the natural consequence of its escape.[4]

It is true that the *ratio* of *Rylands* v *Fletcher* was limited to the accumulation of dangerous things on the defendant's land. But the case surely provide the English judiciary with fertile ground in which to sow the seeds of a system of no-fault liability, by extending the concept to vehicles which are likely to do mischief if they escape from the control of their owner. In the USA the rule formed the basis of liability without fault for ultra hazardous activities; however, in the UK the courts have taken an unduly restrictive approach to the application of the rule, with the result that it has not been permitted to develop, but has been repeatedly interpreted as applying only in the context of adjoining or neighbouring landowners.[5]

In 1909 a valiant attempt was made to extend *Rylands* v *Fletcher* to the sphere of road accidents in the case of *Wing* v *London General Omnibus Co.*[6] The plaintiff was injured when the motor omnibus in which she was a passenger skidded and hit a lamp-post; she claimed damages on the basis of the defendants' negligence in placing upon the highway a dangerous machine which was liable to become uncontrollable in certain slippery or other conditions of the roadway (as was the case at the time of the accident). Fletcher Moulton LJ, after stating that the best known applications of the rule in *Rylands* v *Fletcher* concern activities of a person on land belonging to him, went on to state that:

> 'I have no doubt that analogous causes of action exist when a member of the public makes undue and improper use of the right which he enjoys in common with all others of using the public highways for traffic. If a man places on the streets vehicles so wholly unmanageable as necessarily to be a continuing danger to other vehicles, either at all times or under special conditions of weather, I have no doubt that he does it at his peril, and that he is responsible for injuries arising therefrom, even though there has been no negligence in the management of his vehicle.'[7]

However, no evidence was brought to show that such vehicles are in fact generally unmanageable or dangerous and thus the defendants were not liable. No further attempts to extend the rule to road accidents appear to have been made.

In France it was initially considered that article 1384 served merely as an introduction to the more specific forms of no-fault liability laid down in the provisions which follow it in the Civil Code: Article 1385 applies in the case of damage caused by animals and Article 1386 provides for no-fault liability on the part of the owner in the case of damage caused by defective buildings. However, it was not long before the courts were prepared to view Article 1384 as an autonomous provision capable of applying to any object which is capable of causing damage, with no distinction being made according to whether or not the object may be said to be inherently dangerous.[8] A person would be liable in respect of damage caused by an object in his custody – irrespective of fault – even where the damage resulted from an inherent, latent defect in the object. Once this principle had been accepted in respect of defective objects, the question arose as to the extension of the principle to those cases where damage resulted, not from an inherent defect in the object itself, but from the way in which it was handled. The single most notable object which would be covered by such an extension was the motor vehicle, and legal opinion and the courts themselves were sharply divided on the issue. The proponents of the fault principle maintained that Article 1384 should be strictly limited to those cases where the damage resulted from an inherent defect in the object, (for example, in the case of a motor vehicle, an unexplained failure of the brakes), and that where damage was caused by the manner in which the object was handled (for example a failure to stop in time to avoid hitting a pedestrian) the fault-based articles

1382 or 1383 should be used, with the result that the driver would be liable only if he had committed a fault.

The issue finally came before the Chambres Réunies of the Cour de Cassation in the *Jand'heur*[9] case in 1930. Then, after nearly five years of appeals, it was held that accidents involving motor vehicles should be governed by Article 1384, and therefore proof of absence of fault on the part of the driver is irrelevant. The final decision of the Cour was: first, that the presumption of liability contained in Article 1384 could be displaced only by a finding of 'act of God, *force majeure* or an external cause for which he is not responsible' ('*cas fortuit, force majeure ou d'une cause étrangère qui ne lui soit pas imputable*'); and secondly, that liability under 1384 is founded solely on the question of custody ('*garde*') of the object and therefore any attempt to distinguish on the basis of the origin of the damage (the object itself or the custodian's handling of it) is irrelevant.

Contributory Negligence and No-Fault Liability

Under the *Jand'heur* decision, the custodian of a vehicle which had caused damage could escape liability only where he could establish the existence of some external, unforeseeable and unavoidable event (*cas fortuit* or *force majeure*).[10] However, it was not long before proof of the contributory negligence of the victim was admitted as a basis for reducing the liability of the guardian.[11] By the 1960s, 'fault' on the part of those injured in road accidents was an increasingly common cause for the reduction of damages, whilst 'fault' on the part of the driver of the vehicle had ceased to be of any relevance.[12] However, a sense of the injustice and inconsistency of this approach led to its gradual abandonment, and in several cases the custodian of the vehicle was held to be responsible for the entire damage even where contributory negligence was established.[13]

The turning point with regard to contributory negligence came just over half a century after the decision in the *Jand'heur* case, when the Cour de Cassation once again emitted a strong pronouncement in favour of the victims of road accidents. The effect of the *Desmares* decision[14] was to exclude in any Article 1384 action the possibility of the plaintiff's damages being reduced on the basis of contributory negligence. The plaintiffs in this case were two pedestrians who were knocked over by the defendant's car when they were attempting to cross a busy four-lane road in the rush hour. Owing to the fact that they were either carried or thrown some small distance by the car, it was not possible to establish whether or not they had been attempting to cross the road at the pedestrian crossing. The plaintiffs brought an action under Article 1384, but the court of first instance accepted the defendant's contention that the accident had been caused by the plaintiffs' imprudence in crossing the road at the place and time they did, behaviour which constituted a breach of the Highway Code.[15] This finding was rejected by the Reims Court of Appeal, which awarded the plaintiffs full damages, without, however, fully explaining its reasoning. The second civil chamber of the Cour de Cassation confirmed this decision, stating that:

> Only an event amounting to *force majeure* exonerates the custodian of the object which has caused the damage...the fault attributed to the victims did not possess for Desmares [the defendant] the character of an unforeseeable and unavoidable event.[16]

This decision of the second chamber of the Cour de Cassation, while restoring a certain logic to the interpretation of the Article 1384 by placing the behaviour of the victim on the same basis as any other factor which is external to the defendant, was unpopular with many of the lower courts. Some of these refused to follow it (it should be noted that the *Desmares* decision, unlike the *Jand'heur* decision, emanated from a single chamber of the Cour de Cassation and therefore lacked much of the persuasive authority of the latter).[17] However, while some courts continued to apply the traditional rules of contributory negligence to injured pedestrians, others were prepared to widen the basis of the *Desmares* decision by extending it to cover contributorily negligent drivers of vehicles.[18] The situation was further complicated by the fact that the new formula of non-apportionment of damages applied only to actions brought under Article 1384: in a traditional negligence action under Article 1382 (in which fault on the part of the defendant must be proved) apportionment of damages on the basis of the plaintiff's contributory negligence is still permissible. In a French criminal action where the defendant has, as a result of his criminal act (for example, dangerous driving), caused injury or loss, the victim may be joined to the criminal proceedings as a *partie civile* and will be entitled to damages in accordance with the civil law. However, in these circumstances the defendant's liability will always be assessed under Article 1382 on the basis of fault, rather than on the basis of mere custody. The question of the plaintiff's contributory negligence or fault will therefore continue to be relevant in such cases.

The notion of 'fault' under 1382 has traditionally been interpreted in a very wide manner in order to help the victims, with insurance providing the implicit justification. The standard of care has therefore been totally objective and rather high. However, in cases of alleged contributory negligence, this wide interpretation of fault rebounds on the victim. Even where it is clear that the plaintiff whose contributory negligence is in question was too young to realise the danger, the court may not take this into account when assessing the total amount of damages to be paid by the defendant driver and his insurance company.[19] In *Derguini* v *Tidu*[20] the defendant was convicted of the manslaughter of a five year old girl who had started to cross the road on a pedestrian crossing, but upon becoming aware of the approach of the defendant's car had panicked and tried to run back to the pavement. It was agreed that the girl's sudden action had made it impossible for the defendant to avoid hitting her and the damages claimed by the parents were accordingly reduced by 50 per cent. However, it is important to stress that the girl was killed on a pedestrian crossing at a place where motorists were warned by road signs that there were likely to be children in the vicinity.

A huge and inequitable difference in treatment thus existed according to whether the victim of the road accident brought his action under Article 1384 against the driver as custodian of the vehicle which injured him, or under Article 1382 against the driver in respect of his personal negligence as an adjunct to criminal proceedings.[21] In *Desmares* the victims were adults, presumably aware of the dangers of crossing a busy road, and it was never positively established that they were using the pedestrian crossing; yet damages were awarded in full. In *Derguini* the victim was probably too young to appreciate fully the dangers of road traffic, but she was at least crossing in the correct place, yet damages were reduced by 50 per cent (it is possible of course, that, had the child survived the accident and sued in respect of her own injuries, the court may have been more lenient in assessing the extent of her contributory negligence).

This then at the end of 1984 was the situation confronting plaintiffs seeking damages under French law in respect of personal injuries sustained in road accidents.

In the meantime, the French (socialist) Government had been pushing through Parliament a bill designed to rationalise this confused and illogical situation, by introducing a system of compensation which would no longer be entirely fault-based. The impetus for such reform was not new: in 1965 the Ministry of Justice had examined the 'Tunc Project' which had proposed automatic compensation for road accident victims, with no account being taken of *force majeure* or of contributory negligence. This project was however rejected.[22] The idea was then taken up once more by the socialist government in the early 1980s and, after much debate and opposition from the legal profession, was passed unanimously by Parliament on 5th July 1985.

An Act Designed to Improve the Situation of the Victims of Road Traffic Accidents

The Act's optimistic title described its aim: 'An Act designed to improve the situation of the victims of road traffic accidents and to accelerate compensation procedures'. It was expected by Parliament, and indeed feared by many members of the French Bar Association, that the introduction of such a system would result in the majority of road traffic accident cases being decided, not by the courts, but by the insurance companies. However, a combination of infelicitous drafting, an inability to agree on a uniform system applicable to all victims of road accidents, and a certain hostility on the part of the legal profession, has resulted in a far higher initial level of litigation than had originally been anticipated. A further factor explaining the huge number of cases coming before the courts on the new Act is that Articles 1–6 (relating to the principle of compensation) came into force immediately upon promulgation of the Act and applied not only to accidents which had occurred in the three years prior to July 1985, but also to those cases where proceedings had already begun under the 1382/1384 system, including those pending before the Cour de Cassation.[23] In many instances, cases pending before the Cour de Cassation had deliberately been held in abeyance, and this therefore explains the very large number of cases on which the French supreme court had to pronounce within the first year of the enactment of the new legislation.

The Main Provisions of the Act

By virtue of its Article 1, the Act applies to the victims of road accidents involving 'terrestrial motorized vehicles' (including trailers), but not railways or trams running on their own tracks. The driver or custodian of such a vehicle may no longer raise the defence of *force majeure* or act of a third party as against any victim. In respect of a claim for personal injury, if the victim is anyone other than a driver of a terrestrial motorised vehicle, contributory negligence will be irrelevant unless it was such as to amount to an inexcusable fault which was the sole cause of the accident (although in the case of a 'super-privileged victim' as defined below, even an inexcusable fault will not result in an exclusion or reduction of damages). Any degree of fault on the part of the driver of a vehicle involved in an accident will reduce his claim for damages accordingly. Evidence of contributory negligence will continue to be relevant in respect of claims for property damage from all classes of victim.

Major problems of interpretation have arisen in respect of these provisions, and the solutions favoured by the case-law will be examined below.

The concept of a traffic accident It is clear from the case-law that the notion of a traffic accident (‘*accident de la circulation*’) should not be confined to accidents on the public highway, but may include accidents in a field,[24] in a parking area,[25] on the ski slopes[26] or on the slip road leading to a shop's car park.[27] The interpretation given to the concept of a traffic accident is thus wide and will include most places where motorised vehicles are found circulating normally, including, it would seem, private property (such as a shop's car park, and presumably private roads at factories, farm land, university campuses or stately homes). In respect of accidents occurring on private property, there has been no discussion as yet on the applicability of the Act to trespassers. It would seem reasonable to assume that where the presence of a trespasser is foreseeable, the driver of the vehicle which injures him may be liable under the Act. However, where this was not foreseeable, it may be possible to argue that there is no liability since the plaintiff has committed an ‘inexcusable fault, sole cause of the accident’ (Article 3(1), see below).

‘Terrestrial motorised vehicle’ The new rules relating to liability for traffic accidents apply only to ‘terrestrial motorised vehicles’ and their trailers. They do not apply to railways and tramways running on their own tracks. Just as the notion of ‘traffic accident’ has been interpreted generously by the courts, so, on the whole, has the concept of a ‘terrestrial motorised vehicle’. It clearly includes cars, lorries, motorcycles, buses and other ‘normal’ motorised traffic, but has also been held to extend to a tractor in a field,[28] a motorised road sweeper,[29] and a ‘pistemobile’ (‘*engin de damage*’).[30] However, other decisions of some of the lower courts have been far more restrictive in their interpretation of the meaning to be given to the term: a ski drag lift,[31] a mechanical excavator[32] and an electrical compressor supplying power for road works[33] have all been held not to be included in the definition, and thus persons injured in collisions with such vehicles must rely on Articles 1382/1384 of the Civil Code in order to obtain compensation.

As stated above, railways and tramways running on their own tracks (‘*circulant sur des voies qui leur sont propres*’) are excluded from the operation of the Act. The extent of the protection thereby given to the operators of railways and tramways is not altogether clear from the wording of the Act: one possible reading would have been to grant the exclusion only when the train or tram involved in an accident was travelling on its own tracks away from normal traffic or pedestrians. Thus a person injured while trespassing on *Société National de Chemins de Fer* (SNCF) tracks would not be entitled to rely on the Act, while those injured in an accident on a level crossing should be able to claim protection under the Act on the basis that the train is not at that point running on its own (that is, exclusive) tracks (*'des voies qui leur sont propres'*). Unfortunately the Cour de Cassation has decided in favour of wide protection of the SNCF by holding that the occupants of a car which collided with a train on a level crossing must found their action on the ordinary Civil Code rules of liability, while the SNCF is entitled to rely on the Act in order to claim compensation for physical damage caused in the accident.[34] Such a distinction is to be regretted.

Trailers for motorised vehicles expressly fall within the terms of the Act, and the Cour de Cassation has declared the Act applicable to a trailer pulled by a tractor,[35] a rotovator pulled by a tractor,[36] and a caravan pulled by a car.[37] It is thus clear that the Act will apply not only to a trailer which is actually in the process of being towed, but also to a trailer which is parked unattached to a vehicle at the time of the accident.[38] Problems of application have arisen in relation to accidents involving objects such as cement mixers, which, whilst they are usually towed to the place where they are to be used, have an identity separate from the vehicle which tows them. The Act does not define the term 'trailer' (*'remorque'*), and early decisions of the lower courts had held that in an accident involving a collision with a stationary, unattached cement mixer, the victim was entitled to the protection of the Act.[39] However, a recent decision of the Cour de Cassation[40] has placed a more restrictive interpretation on the term, holding that where an object is neither specifically designed as a trailer to a vehicle nor in fact being towed at the time of the accident, it should not be regarded as falling within the Act.

When is a vehicle 'involved' in an accident? In order for the Act to apply, Article 1 requires that the motorised vehicle be 'involved' (*'impliqué'*) in the accident.[41] Depending on the circumstances of the case, a vehicle may be said to be involved in an accident whether it is moving or stationary, whether it comes into contact with the victim or not. In each case it will be up to the plaintiff to establish that the defendant's vehicle was effectively 'involved' in the accident.[42] However, it should be emphasized that the victim need only establish involvement in the *accident*; it is not necessary to go further and show that the vehicle was involved in the *damage* which has occurred.[43]

Before 1985, under Article 1384, the plaintiff could proceed against the custodian of a vehicle only where he could show that the vehicle had played an 'active role' in causing the damage. By referring to involvement rather than causality, the Act would appear to have a wider application than Article 1384, and thus to eliminate the defence of 'passivity'. This was clearly the intention of the framers of the Act: Robert Badinter, the Minister of Justice responsible for pushing the Act through Parliament, stated that the term 'involved' is 'voluntarily very wide'[44] and that the Act should be applicable:

> ...even where the vehicle is correctly parked, even where it arrives on the scene after another accident; but it is necessary in such cases that it should have played some role in the damage. It should not therefore be necessary to discuss the question of causal effect, the active or passive role of the vehicle in order to determine the sphere of application of the text.[45]

The Government's intention was to eliminate completely any question of causality between the vehicle and the damage, fault on the part of the custodian of the vehicle have ceased to be of any relevance following the *Jand'heur* decision in 1930. However, in order to achieve some logical basis for requiring the defendant's insurance company to compensate the plaintiff, the defendant's vehicle should have been 'involved', even if purely fortuitously. In many ways, the problems of interpretation to which this term has given rise seem to embody the very essence of the problem of the way in which the Act should be regarded in terms of legal theory.

Although the Act seeks to eliminate the requirement of fault on the part of the defendant in many instances, there have been some compromises. These were necessary in order to satisfy both financial concerns and those critics who believed that it would be morally wrong to compensate all victims simply on the basis of the injury suffered, with no account being taken of contributory negligence. As will be seen below, contributory negligence, in one form or another, continues to play a role under the new system. It is perhaps in an attempt to introduce a certain symmetry into the operation of the Act, that the courts have often seen in the requirement for 'involvement' something more than the mere fortuitous presence of a vehicle at the scene of an accident.

It is now clear that, following a strong lead from the Cour de Cassation, the courts have accepted that the concept of involvement ('*implication*') does not require that the vehicle should have played an active role in the creation of the damage. Some early judgements of the lower courts appeared to cling to the old requirement of causality, declaring that, since a vehicle had played only a passive role in the production of the damage, and no fault could be attributed to the driver, there could be no question of the vehicle being 'involved'.[46] The passive role of the vehicle has now been formally rejected as a basis for denying the victim compensation.[47] However, there still appears to be a certain tendency to associate the notion of involvement with some degree of shame for the motorist concerned. Whilst the passive role of the vehicle can no longer be expressly relied on, the courts have sought, particularly in cases concerning stationary vehicles, other means of declaring that the vehicle was not involved. Even at the level of the Cour de Cassation there still exists a clear desire not to attach any degree of censure to a motorist who is completely blameless, with the result that the victim is deprived of the right to compensation from the motorist's insurance company. This is most evident in the area of accidents 'involving' parked vehicles.

In cases where a vehicle has been parked at a junction in such a way as to obstruct another motorist's view[48] or to block a pedestrian crossing,[49] the vehicle in question, although not itself physically involved in the collision, has been held to be 'involved' for the purposes of the Act. However, where the vehicle in question was parked correctly and in such a manner that it is not disturbing the flow of traffic, the Cour de Cassation has declared consistently that the vehicle is not involved when another vehicle collides with it. Thus, where a moped rider was killed when he collided with the back of a stationary lorry, it was held that the lorry was not involved in the accident since it was correctly parked in a well lit area where visibility was good.[50] Similarly, when a fire engine skidded on an icy road and collided with a parked car, the car was held not to have been involved in the accident since it was not possible to determine exactly where the car had been parked and thus whether it had played a role in the realisation of the damage.[51]

In such cases, where an accident is caused by the negligence of another driver (as in the *Boisgérault* case[52]) or by bad weather conditions (as in *Champagne*[53]), it is tempting to say that a correctly parked car which has been hit in the accident is merely fortuitously concerned and is therefore not involved within the meaning of the Act. In these cases the result reached was probably correct since in the first case the plaintiff was a driver of another motor vehicle and in the second the plaintiff was claiming for property damage; in each of these situations the court is entitled to consider contributory negligence.[54] However, by holding that an innocently parked vehicle is not involved in an accident in which it has been hit, the Cour de Cassation is removing such cases altogether from the ambit of the Act, which may have important consequences where the plaintiff is different and the damage suffered is to the person rather than to property. Thus where the person involved in a collision with a parked vehicle was a racing cyclist rather than a motorcyclist, the Paris Court of Appeal still held that the vehicle was not 'involved' and therefore the plaintiff was not entitled to compensation.[55] The Court of Appeal applied a stricter test than the Cour de Cassation to determine whether the vehicle was involved: was the vehicle in question parked in such a position as to hinder the plaintiff's progress with the result that he could not avoid hitting it?[56] By holding that the vehicle was not involved in the accident the Court of Appeal was able not only to deny any award of damages to the injured cyclist, but also to order him to pay the insurance company for the damage sustained by the defendant's car, and in addition, the costs of the action. As in the Cour de Cassation cases, the Court relied on the absence of fault on the part of the custodian of the vehicle, but went further, since in this case parking had in fact been banned in the area in question for the duration of the race. The defendant had not been informed of this ban, and the Court clearly felt that it would be unfair to declare his vehicle to be involved in the accident. The unfortunate cyclist was therefore personally responsible for the entire loss resulting from the accident. Such a result is clearly against at least the spirit of the Act, which was intended to provide compensation for victims in exactly such circumstances as these. Had the Court held that the vehicle was involved in the accident, it would then have been difficult to avoid granting full damages to the plaintiff since he was cycling in a road where there should have been no parked vehicles and cannot reasonably be said to have committed an inexcusable fault.

A finding that an 'innocent' car was not involved in an accident may also adversely affect passengers, who, like cyclists and pedestrians, are accorded a privileged status under the Act, and are entitled to full compensation unless they have committed an inexcusable fault which was the sole cause of the accident (Article 3). In the case of an accident between two vehicles, the driver of one of which was clearly to blame, the courts prefer to find that only the 'guilty' vehicle was involved (whether the other was stationary or moving). In many cases an injured passenger in the 'guilty' vehicle will be able to claim against the driver's insurance, but where he is not insured the passenger will be left without compensation. In the case of cars, such a problem will probably not be frequent.[57] However, the problem of young moped riders carrying illegal passengers is common enough in France, and there may well be no cover for such victims. Thus, where a car failed to give right of way to a moped, thereby injuring both the driver and the illegal passenger, it was held that the car was not involved in the accident, since the driver of the moped alone had committed the faults leading up to the accident by riding at night without lights, without a crash helmet and carrying a passenger. These faults on the part of the driver of the moped rendered the accident unforeseeable for the driver of the car and consequently the car was held not to be involved.[58]

Much of this may perhaps be perceived as an emotional response to awarding damages to a person who is clearly seen as being at fault, against a person who is seen to be blameless. In many ways this is the central argument against the administration of a no-fault system through the private insurance industry; if the 'involvement' of a vehicle is a prerequisite to compensation, there will always be a subconscious linking of 'involvement' and 'fault'. In its more recent decisions the Cour de Cassation has, however, tended to stress that a vehicle may be 'involved' in an accident even where it is merely the setting for the accident and has played no causal role whatever in either the occurrence of the accident or the damage. Thus a person who is injured in a fall inside a stationary bus will be entitled to the protection of the Act, notwithstanding that the fall was caused by jostling from another passenger and was in no way related to the functioning of the vehicle.[59]

Force Majeure no longer a defence for the driver Article 2 provides that *force majeure* and acts of a third party can no longer be relied on in any circumstances in order to exonerate the custodian of a vehicle which has been involved in an accident. The provision has given rise to little dispute.[60] *Force majeure* has been interpreted as any event external to the victim[61] such as a dog wandering on the motorway,[62] or black ice.[63]

Compensation for non-drivers Compensation for physical injury sustained by persons other than drivers of motor vehicles is covered by Article 3. Article 3(1) provides that persons other than 'drivers' of motorised vehicles are entitled to full compensation for personal injury, irrespective of any fault which they may have committed, unless that fault may be classified as 'inexcusable' and the 'sole cause of the accident'.[64] Perhaps it would have been difficult, *vis à vis* public opinion, to omit such an exception to an otherwise blanket coverage for non-drivers. However it is clear that its inclusion – as with the concept of involvement – has opened the door to extensive litigation whereas it was hoped that insurance companies would settle quickly with victims out of court.

Inexcusable fault The concept of 'inexcusable fault' comes from the field of labour law: under the Act of 9 April 1898 on Accidents at Work, a worker injured at work is entitled to a greater sum in compensation than he would be if no such fault had been committed.[65] The Cour de Cassation, sitting in plenary session in 1941, determined a formula which has since been used widely in order to determine when a fault should be qualified as inexcusable. For the Cour de Cassation such a fault[66] is 'of exceptional seriousness, arising from a voluntary act or omission, from the awareness of danger which the perpetrator should have had, from the absence of any justification'.[67] This formula, widely applied in labour law cases, is now being used by certain Courts of Appeal and courts of first instance when assessing whether or not an insurance company is entitled to refuse compensation to non-drivers. It should however be noted that, whilst in the field of labour law a finding that an inexcusable fault has been committed serves to increase the compensation payable to an injured person, under the Act of 1985 such a finding will result in the injured person receiving no damages at all. It would therefore seem logical to abandon the labour law interpretation of the concept of inexcusable fault, and replace it with one which is more fitting to the aims of the Act.

The *travaux preparatoires* show that the intention of Parliament was to limit the use of the concept of inexcusable fault to those few cases where the victim has been guilty of 'asocial behaviour in the context of road traffic'.[68] The victim should therefore be deprived of damages only in those exceptional circumstances where he has acted in a way in which the *ordinary* man or woman (as opposed to the English law standard of the *reasonable* man) would never do. However, early decisions of many of the lower courts indicated a desire to maintain a more definite link between foolish behaviour on the part of the victim and the total amount of damages to which he is eventually entitled. The 1941 Cour de Cassation labour law definition of inexcusable fault has therefore been used in order to reduce damages in those cases where the pedestrian or cyclist, without justification, has behaved in such a way that he must be aware that an accident is possible. Thus, a pedestrian who crossed at a time when the pedestrian crossing light was red,[69] or away from a designated pedestrian crossing[70] could be declared to have committed an inexcusable fault, and as a result would lose all rights to damages under the Act. Such behaviour may certainly be classified as irresponsible by the standard of the mythical 'reasonable man'. Nonetheless most pedestrians are occasionally guilty of such irresponsibility, and it was not the intention of Parliament to remove the protection of the Act for faults such as these; rather it was their intention to deny compensation only where the victim had either deliberately sought to be injured (Article 3(3)), or, in the case of 'inexcusable fault' where he was guilty of totally reprehensible, asocial behaviour.

Recent decisions of the Cour de Cassation have sought to emphasize the criteria for a fault to be considered as 'inexcusable' for the purposes of Article 3(1). These indicate that the fault committed by the victim should be voluntary and of exceptional seriousness ('ordinary' foolishness is therefore ruled out), exposing its author without justification to a danger of which he should have been aware.[71] In determining the voluntary nature of the victim's actions, the court should have regard to whether or not the resultant damage was intended by the victim.[72] Many of the earlier cases which had denied a remedy to pedestrians or cyclists found to be guilty of imprudent behaviour have now been quashed by the Cour de Cassation, on the basis that the fault committed was not of such seriousness as to be considered inexcusable. Compensation should be denied only in those cases where the victim may be said to have acted with complete disregard for his own safety; as where he crosses a badly lit dual carriageway at night, climbing over the central reservation barrier without paying any heed to oncoming traffic instead of using the pedestrian crossing situated nearby.[73] Running across a busy road without looking, whilst irresponsible behaviour, should not be seen as taking the victim outside the protection of the Act.[74]

'Sole cause of the accident' Before excluding the right to damages, the court must find, not only that the fault of the victim was inexcusable, but also that it was the sole cause of the accident. Thus where a motorist was aware from a certain distance of a cyclist's dangerous manoeuvre, and could therefore have avoided hitting him, the cyclist's fault – while it may have been inexcusable – was not the sole cause of the accident and he was entitled to full compensation under the Act.[75] The foreseeability of such action by the victim and the speed at which the vehicle is travelling are both relevant to a determination of whether the victim's fault constituted the sole cause of the accident. Thus for the Cour de Cassation, it is not unforeseeable for the driver of a motor vehicle that, when he goes through a green traffic light, a pedestrian may risk crossing at the same time.[76] The determining factor in these cases must always be the extent to which the driver of the vehicle involved in the accident could have foreseen the presence or the actions of the victim. It is probably true to say that some of the earlier cases might now be decided differently upon a strict application of this foreseeability test.[77]

Contributory negligence on the part of drivers The benefit laid down in Article 3(1) does not apply to the drivers of motorised vehicles. If such a driver is injured in a motor accident, proof of his contributory negligence, not amounting to an inexcusable fault, will be admissible and his damages reduced accordingly.[78] Attempts have been made to justify this anomaly on the basis of a difference in nature between "drivers", who create the risk of accidents by the mere fact of the kinetic force of their vehicles, and pedestrians or cyclists (or indeed horse riders[79]) who are most likely to suffer serious injury in the event of a collision. In the course of debates in the National Assembly, Robert Badinter stated that the driver of a car is protected by a steel envelope which effectively protects him from the effects of his mistakes, whereas the pedestrian or cyclist often pays for a moment's inattention with his life.[80] However, the motorcyclist, who would seem to be just as vulnerable as the ordinary cyclist, is denied the protection given to cyclists and pedestrians. In fact, according to figures presented in the report of the Parliamentary *rapporteur*, Mme Gaspard[81] the vast majority of accident victims receiving no compensation for their injuries are the drivers of motor cycles. However, a system providing automatic compensation for anyone injured in a road accident would have been too expensive; in addition, such a system would have destroyed the ordinary person's illusion (and desire) that those 'responsible' for motor accidents 'pay' for their faults. Both of these were important considerations in 1985 with Parliamentary elections imminent.

The distinction between driver and non-driver may therefore be crucial in determining the damages which the victim is entitled to receive. If he is held to be a driver his own contributory negligence may be held against him; whereas in the case of a non-driver, only an inexcusable fault decreed to be the sole cause of the accident will affect his right to compensation. Although in most instances the category to which the victim belongs will be immediately clear, difficult cases have arisen.

The test used in determining whether or not a victim has the status of 'driver' seems to be his position in relation to his vehicle, rather than any degree of control which he may have over the vehicle. In many cases this has proved beneficial to the victim since, as soon as a driver is for some reason outside or off his vehicle, he acquires the status of pedestrian. Thus a victim, following an accident in which he was involved as a driver, got out of his car in order to warn of the accident and was struck by a third vehicle. He was treated as a non-driver in respect of this second accident, and his contributory negligence was not relevant to the assessment of compensation.[82] Similarly, a person hit by a car as he was about to get into his own car was held to be a pedestrian rather than a driver.[83] Where the motorised vehicle is being pushed by the victim at the time of the accident, he will be a pedestrian;[84] but if he is inside a vehicle which is being towed, he may be considered to conserve a certain degree of control over his vehicle which may cause him to be classified as a driver[85]; similarly if he is attempting to start the engine of his moped by pedalling.[86] In those cases where it is unclear from the circumstances of the accident exactly where the victim was at the moment of impact, the defendant will be required to prove that the victim was a driver rather than a pedestrian.[87]

The avowed aims of the Act were the improvement, acceleration and simplification of compensation procedures for road accident victims. However the introduction of this somewhat artificial distinction between drivers and non-drivers has served not only to destroy much of the logic of the system – there being no conceptual reason for introducing such a distinction – but also to introduce yet more delays and uncertainties into the system.

'Super-privileged victims' Article 3(2) provides that the non-motorised victim who is either aged below sixteen or over seventy years, or who is in receipt of a certificate attesting a permanent degree of handicap of 80 per cent or more, will always be compensated for personal injuries incurred in road accidents, and that their own inexcusable fault may not be held against them. The majority of road accidents in which pedestrians are injured concern persons in these categories, who by reason of age or incapacity often commit grave errors of judgement when negotiating traffic. The objective test applied in cases such as *Derguini*[88] therefore disappears, and such a person will always be entitled to full compensation unless it can be shown that the victim voluntarily sought the damage which occurred. It is not enough therefore to show that the plaintiff acted in a manner which the ordinary person would immediately condemn as dangerous; it must be shown that the victim actually intended to be injured. Where a victim, intending to cross the road, steps out without looking in front of a fast moving vehicle, this may be evidence of an inexcusable fault should he be an 'ordinary' pedestrian. A person falling into one of the categories above, however, will receive full compensation unless he tried to jump under the vehicle deliberately in order to commit suicide.

Unfortunately, the Cour de Cassation has chosen to interpret Article 3(2) in a somewhat restrictive fashion, considering that where a mentally handicapped person does not have a medical certificate testifying to 80 per cent disablement, that mental handicap cannot be taken into account for the purpose of assessing whether or not the victim has committed an inexcusable fault.[89] Such reasoning appears to confuse the separate roles of Article 3(1) (which allows the court to refuse to award damages where the victim has committed an inexcusable fault which was the sole cause of the accident) and Article 3(2) (which provides that such a refusal will not be permitted where, prior to the accident, the victim was in possession of the necessary medical certificate), Behaviour which, in the case of a person with unimpaired mental faculties, would be regarded as amounting to an inexcusable fault, may in the case of a person suffering from a mental handicap – albeit not 80 per cent – be excusable.

Conclusion

It is perhaps all too easy to take the teething problems of a radical piece of law reform, such as the Act of 5 July 1985, and subject them to criticism with the benefit of hindsight and without the constraints of either politics or economics. However, it was clear from the outset that there would be problems both of interpretation and of moral responsibility. These were inevitable since the Act was a compromise between the principle of no-fault compensation, based purely on injury suffered, and the traditional French tort system under which the victim was obliged to prove, if not fault, at least active causation between the vehicle and the injury. It is the author's opinion that a no-fault compensation system, centrally funded and administered, will operate more effectively and more fairly toward victims than a no-fault liability system which leaves in place the traditional litigation process. Certainly problems of definition will always arise, and an emotional element will always remain in relation to compensation of those victims who are seen as being in some way responsible for their own injuries. There is also the argument that the driver who is truly at fault should be made to 'pay' for the damage which he has caused. Various solutions may be suggested to counter these objections. Those who fear that 'undeserving victims' will receive compensation might be reassured by a system whereby the victim receives automatic compensation merely to cover the special needs which arise out of the accident. In order to recover full damages he must use the traditional tort system (either on the basis of showing lack of fault on his own part, or as at present, showing fault on the part of the driver). Retention of some aspects of the tort system might also satisfy those who perceive some deterrent role in the law of tort; however, it would seem that the deterrence aim would be better satisfied if the criminal system were more widely used in order to prosecute those drivers who are clearly at fault.

Notes

1 Cmnd. 7054/1978.
2 Other legislative measures aimed directly at the prevention of road accidents, rather than mere compensation, include the compulsory wearing of seat belts (Road Traffic Act 1984) and recent proposals to reduce the speed limit in residential areas to 20 mph as part of the Government campaign against child road deaths. It should also be noted that it is not only the drivers of motorised vehicles who are at risk of causing accidents: following a number of claims against cyclists, including one expected to amount to at least £500 000, calls are being made for the extension of compulsory third party insurance cover to cyclists (see *Sunday Times* 7 January 1990).
3 (1868) LR3 HL 330.
4 Pp 339–40.
5 See *Read* v *J Lyons & Co* [1947] AC 156 where Lord Porter expressly stated that any extension of the rule would be undesirable.
6 [1909] 2 KB 652.
7 *Ibid.*, at p 665.
8 Ch. Reunies 13 Feb 1930; DP 1930.I.57.
9 Ch. réun. D.1930.1.57; conclusions of Procureur General Matter D.1930.1.64.
10 See *l'Affaire Franck* Ch. Reunies 2 Dec 1941 S.1941.1.217 where the Cour de

Cassation, after a number of appeals, finally held that the owner of a stolen car loses the custody of the vehicle once it is stolen and cannot therefore be held liable under Article 1384 in respect of any accidents.

11 Req 13 April 1934, D.1934.1.41.

12 Cass. 2e Civ. 15 Jan 1960, S.1962.2.

13 Cass 2e Civ. Mar 1970.

14 Cass. 2e Civ. 21 July 1982, D.1982.J.449.

15 Article R219 Code de la Route.

16 'Seul un événement constituant un cas de force majeure exonère le gardien de la chose, instrument du dommage... la faute imputée aux victimes n'avait pas pour Desmares le caractère d'un événement imprévisible et insurmontable.'

17 See Serverin, (1985), and Rondeau-Rivier, 'Un Essai d'Evaluation du Changement du Droit: la Mesure des Incidences de l'Arrêt Desmares' D.Chr.227 at 229.

18 Gaz Pal 1982, 2, 597.

19 English law has never adopted such a harsh attitude: see *Gough* v *Thorne* [1966] 3 All E.R.613.

20 Cass. Ass. Plen. 9 May 1984, JCP.1984.II.20256.

21 Where, in a civil action, a claim was made under both 1382 and 1384, the tendency of the judges was to decide on the basis of 1384: Civ 2e 25 Jan 1984, D.1984.242.

22 See Tunc, A. (1966), 'La Sécurité Routiere, Esquisse d'une Loi sur les Accidents de la Circulation', and (1967) 'Sur un Projet de Loi en matière d'Accidents de la Circulation' *Rev. Trim. Dr. Civ.* 82.

23 Article 47 provides that Articles 1–6 should come into force immediately upon publication of the Law, and should have retroactive effect in respect of accidents which occurred in the three years preceding its publication. Logically, however, where a case had already been finally settled under the old system, the new Law does not permit a re-opening of the case in order to found a claim on the new basis of liability.

24 Cass 2e Civ 5 Mar 1986 and 25 June 1986, Bull. Cass. no. 28.

25 *Darodes de Tailly* v *Vico* Cass. 2e Civ. 25 June 1986, Bull. Cass. no 28.

26 CA Gren. 9 Feb 1987, D.87.245.

27 Cass. 2e Civ. 25 June 1986.

28 Cass. 2e Civ. 5 Mar 1986, Bull. Cass. no 28.

29 Cass. 2e Civ. 13 Nov 1985 *Khelifa*.

30 CA Gren 9 Feb 1987, 1987.D.245.

31 TGI Albertville 3 Jun 1986.

32 TGI Cahors 27 Feb 1986, 1986 Gaz. Pal. I.416.

33 CA Paris 18 Nov 1987, 1988 Gaz Pal I 23.

34 Cass. 2e Civ. 17 Mar 1986, Bull. Cass. no 40.

35 Cass. 2e Civ. 18 Mar 1986.

36 Cass. 2e Civ. 5 Mar 1986.

37 Cass. 2e Civ. 19 Nov 1986.

38 Cass. 2e Civ. 24 Nov 1986 and 17 Mar 1986.

39 See Cass 2e Civ. 5 Nov 1986.

40 Civ 2e 7 Jun 1989; 1990 D.J.116, note Legier.

41 The translation is not an easy one to make, precisely since the term *impliqué* has given rise to such severe problems of interpretation.

42 *Guyolot* v *Rameau* Cass. 2e Civ. 28 May 1986, 1987.D.160; *Gervais* v *Bius* Cass. 2e Civ. 21 Jul 1986, 1987.D.161.

43 Civ 2e 8 Nov 1989; Dalloz 1989.IR.309.

44 Parliamentary session of 10 April 1985; J.O. Deb. Senat 11 April p.193.
45 *Ibid.*
46 TGI Abbeville, 12 Dec 1986; 1986 Gaz Pal 1–3 June.
47 Cass. 2e Civ., 4 Dec 1985, *Helvetia Accidents* v *Erbel*; Cass. 2e Civ.25 Jun 1986, *Sternberger* v *Bonhours*.
48 CA Versailles 13 Dec 1986.
49 Cass. 2e Civ. 21 Jul 1986.
50 Cass. 2e Civ., 21 Jul 1986, *Boisgerault* v *Vedrenne*, 1987.JCP.20768.
51 Cass. 2e Civ. 21 Jul 1986, *Prefet de Police* v *Champagne*, 1987,JCP.20768. 'La position exacte de l'automobile de M. Champagne sur la chaussée était restée indeterminée, de sorte qu'il n'etait pas établi que son stationnement eût joué un rôle dans la réalisation de l'accident.'
52 *Supra cit.*
53 *Supra cit.*
54 Articles 4 and 5 respectively.
55 1987.D.149 *Rousseau* v *Moison*.
56 'Pour qu'un véhicule terrestre à moteur en stationnement puisse être impliqué dans la réalisation d'une collision, il est nécessaire qu'il se soit trouvé dans une position de nature à gêner la progression normale du véhicule ou de l'engin dont le conducteur n'a pu éviter de le percuter.'
57 However, see Trib. Corr. Dijon, 26 May 1986; 1987 Gaz Pal 2 Jan.
58 CA Bordeaux, 18 Mar 1986; 1987 Gaz Pal 27 Mar.
59 Civ. 2e 11 Oct 1989; Dalloz 1989.IR.272. See also Civ 2e 7 Jun 1989; 1989.D.IR.193.
60 See, for example, Civ 2e 11 Oct 1989; 1989.D.IR.272, *supra*.
61 CA Paris 8 Nov 1985; 1985.D.Flash no 43.
62 Cass. 2e Civ. 6 Nov 1985 Bull. Civ. II no 166.
63 Cass. 2e Civ. 17 Mar 1986; 1986 JCP IV 153.
64 Article 3(1) provides: 'Les victimes, hormis les conducteurs de véhicules terrestres à moteur, sont indemnisés des dommages resultant des atteintes à leur personne qu'elles ont subis, sans que puisse leur être opposée leur propre faute à l'exception de leur faute inexcusable si elle a été la cause exclusive de l'accident.'
65 Article L. 452–1 Code Sécurité Sociale. Although there is provision in Article L. 453–1 for a reduction in damages where an inexcusable fault is found to have been committed by the employee, this provision is rarely invoked.
66 1941.JCP.II.1705.
67 '...d'une gravité exceptionnelle, derivant d'un acte ou d'une omission voluntaire, de la conscience du danger que devait en avoir son auteur, de l'absence de toute cause justificative.'
68 '...un comportement asocial dans le domaine de la circulation'; Robert Badinter, J.O. deb. Ass. Nat. 17 Dec. 1984.
69 CA Aix en Provence 22 Nov 1985, *Kerrouche* v *Jordan*; CA Paris 12 Dec 1985, *Nougier* v *RATP*.
70 CA Versailles 28 Nov 1985, *Fossemale* v *Poisson*.
71 See particularly Cass. 2e Civ. 20 July 1987 (10 decisions), 3 reported in 1988 Gaz Pal 8/9 Jan.
72 Crim 7 Nov 1988; 1989.D.IR.34.
73 *Consorts Mannois* v *Anfry*, *supra*.
74 CA Paris 11 Jan 1989; Dalloz 1989.IR.59.
75 Cass. 2e Civ. 25 Jun 1986, *Debontrider* v *Rybak*.
76 Cass. 2e Civ. 14 Jan 1987.

77 See discussion in CA Versailles 3e Ch 20 Oct 1989; 1990.D.IR.14.

78 Article 4 provides: 'La faute commise par le conducteur du véhicule terrestre à moteur a pour effet de limiter ou d'exclure l'indemnisation des dommages qu'il a subis'. ('Any fault committed by the driver of a terrestrial motorised vehicle will have the effect of limiting or excluding compensation for damage which he has suffered.')

79 Cass. 3e Civ. 12 Nov 1986, *Sté des Cars Compain* v *Colas*.

80 J.O. Deb. Ass. Nat. 18 Dec 1984 p7024. 'L'automobiliste est protégé par une enveloppe d'acier et le plus souvent, fort heureusement, ses erreurs n'entraînent pour lui que des dommages minimes. Rien de tel pour le piéton et le cycliste, dont la plus légère négligence, le plus bref moment d'inattention mettent en jeu l'intégrité physique et parfois la vie même.'

81 Doc. Ass. Nat. no 2485 p9.

82 Cass. 2e Civ. 9 Jul 1986, *Petit* v *L'hoste* 1987.D.88.

83 CA Paris, *Pungier* v *Gaberand* 26 Sep 1986, 1987.D.88.

84 Cass. 2e Civ. 14 Jan 1987, *CPAM de Saone et Loire* v *Morin*; CA Paris 11 Feb 1986, *Dary* v *Saintini* 1986 Gaz Pal 28/29 May.

85 Cass. 2e Civ. 14 Jan 1987 *Brival* v *Tixier Vignancour*, 1987.JCP.II.20768.

86 Cass. 2e Civ. 28 Apr 1986, *Limouzy* v *Gimenez* 1987.D.88.

87 Cass. 2e Civ. 9 Jul 1986, *Brown* v *Gerin*, 1987.JCP.II.20747.

88 See Note 20, *supra cit*.

89 Civ 2e 1989.D.J.559, note Aubert.

7 Oil Pollution Damage Compensation under the Civil Liability Convention 1969

Benjamin Browne

Introduction

Over the last 25 years, the law on shipowners' liability for damage by oil spillage from ships has changed beyond all recognition. The main reason behind the changes is the greatly increased risk of major catastrophes due to oil spills. That incidents of this nature were bound to occur sooner or later was easy to predict. The size of tankers for the carriage of oil had been increasing with accelerating speed from the end of the Second World War up to the mid-1970s. In 1947 the largest tanker of the Norwegian fleet was about 16 000 metric tons deadweight, by 1957 this figure had reached 39 000, by 1967 it had reached 203 000 and by 1977 it had increased to 417 000 tons.

The safety requirements for the building and the rules concerning the navigation of large tankers did not keep abreast of this development, and nor did the law.

At common law, there were great difficulties in establishing that a tort had been committed. Trespass was available as a cause of action only to occupiers of land whose property had been physically invaded. Nuisance contains similar doubts and problems relating to the standing of a plaintiff, as well as being restricted by the availability of the defence of necessity and the so-called 'traffic rule'. Negligence suffered from two main defects: first, it was hard to establish failure on board a vessel to take due care; secondly, the recoverability of pure economic loss in tort was doubtful.

Probably the leading case on oil pollution liability at common law is *Esso Petroleum v Southport Corporation.*[1] This was a case where an oil tanker was stranded in a river estuary and, to prevent her breaking her back, the master jettisoned 400 tons of her oil cargo which the tide carried onto a foreshore, occasioning damage. The foreshore owners brought proceedings against the shipowners in an action based on trespass, nuisance and negligence alleging that the stranding was caused by faulty navigation. The defendants denied negligence. The House of Lords upheld the trial judge's finding that the defendant shipowners were not negligent. They further held that in the absence of negligence or proving unseaworthiness, the plaintiff foreshore owners could not succeed in tort.

In the *Amoco Cadiz* case[2], however, the plaintiffs were successful in claiming substantial damages in the District Court for the Northern District of Illinois, Eastern Division. These were awarded against not only the registered owners of the '*Amoco Cadiz*' but also their parent company, Standard Oil, principally on the basis of negligence.

Writers have speculated that international law could be used as a vehicle for making a recovery in respect of oil pollution, by virtue of the doctrines of 'hazardous activities' and 'abuse of rights', but this has not yet been done. The doctrine of hazardous activities is perhaps best formulated in the well-known case of the *Trail Smelter.*[3] It imposes on states the obligation not to permit the use of their territory in such a manner as to cause injury to the territory of another, or property or persons therein, when the case is of serious consequence and the injury is established by clear and convincing evidence. This doctrine would probably support the proposition that states are not free simply to sit back and let ships under their flags sail the seas totally unregulated. Another possible method of exerting pressure on states which do not regulate vessels registered under their flag arises from the doctrine of abuse of rights, as specifically developed in the Convention on the High Seas 1958. Article 24 of the Convention states: 'Every state shall draw up regulations to prevent pollution of the seas by the discharge of oil from ships...taking account of existing treaty provisions on the subject.'

Article 2 of the Convention provides that all states must have reasonable regard to the interests of other states in the exercise of their freedom of the high seas.

Common law and international law, therefore, provided scanty remedies for oil pollution victims in view of the increasing number of substantial oil pollution incidents which occurred in the 1960s and 1970s.

In 1967 the 'Torrey Canyon' (a Liberian flag tanker) foundered off the South-West tip of England, spilling some 111 000 tons of oil. The global limitation fund of the 'Torrey Canyon' was quite insufficient to cover the claims for oil pollution damage and victims went uncompensated. The

British Government initiated the drafting of new rules on civil liability for oil pollution through the International Maritime Organisation (IMO). In 1969, the IMO convened a Diplomatic Conference in Brussels which adopted the International Convention on Civil Liability for oil pollution damage – 'Civil Liability Convention' (CLC). This Convention lays down the principle of strict liability for shipowners and provides for a system of compulsory insurance. The 1969 Conference noted that the CLC did not provide full compensation to oil pollution victims and recognised the need for a scheme providing supplementary compensation.

A second IMO Conference in Brussels in 1971 adopted the International Convention on the Establishment of an International Fund for Compensation for Oil Pollution Damage (Fund Convention) which set up the International Oil Pollution Compensation Fund (IOPC Fund) to administer the system of compensation created by the Fund Convention. The CLC entered into force in 1975 and the Fund Convention came into force in October 1978.

As at 9 September 1992 the CLC had 74 contracting states and the Fund Convention had 49 contracting states with more expected to join in the near future.

The CLC was enacted in the UK by the Merchant Shipping (Oil Pollution) Act 1971. Subsequently two Protocols have extended and amended the CLC in its original form. The second Protocol of 1984 ('the 1984 Protocol') has not yet come into force, due principally to the reluctance of a major contributor to increase its contribution to the IOPC Fund. A convention is being held in London in November 1992 at which it is hoped a solution can be found to this; it is likely that a 1992 Protocol will result very much along the lines of the 1984 Protocol. In addition the Prevention of Oil Pollution Act 1971 and the Merchant Shipping (Prevention of Oil Pollution) Regulations 1983 create criminal liability for oil pollution and lay down certain anti-pollution requirements which must be observed by UK registered oil tankers.

In addition to this legislation, most tanker owners, bareboat charterers and major oil companies have entered into one or both of two agreements:

(1) Tanker Owners' Voluntary Agreement Concerning Liability for Oil Pollution (TOVALOP) which came into effect in October 1969, and its supplement which came into effect on 20 February 1987.
(2) Contract Regarding a Supplement to Tanker Liability for Oil Pollution (CRISTAL).

TOVALOP provides further provision for compensation for loss suffered from oil pollution, or threat of it, caused by tankers owned or bareboat chartered by TOVALOP members (which now constitute 97 per cent of the world tanker tonnage).

TOVALOP supplements the CLC by providing compensation (limited to a maximum US$16.8 million) for pollution occurring in non-CLC waters; for measures taken in the face of a threat of oil pollution by offering protection to the bareboat charterer (who is deemed to be the shipowner); and by covering pollution from a tanker in ballast. TOVALOP also requires that all members are insured against liability for oil pollution to an extent which enables them to fulfil their obligations under TOVALOP. The TOVALOP supplement applies only when the cargo concerned is owned by a CRISTAL member and introduces *inter alia* significantly higher limits of liability (a maximum of US$70 million for tankers of 140 000 gross tons or more) for owners than are provided by the original Standing Agreement.

CRISTAL provides for the payment of compensation in respect of oil pollution damage supplemental to that paid by tanker owners or bareboat charterers, up to the monetary limits provided for in the TOVALOP Supplement. Unless the tanker owner first pays compensation up to the TOVALOP Supplement limit, no payment will be made under CRISTAL. As with TOVALOP the limit of liability depends on the ship's gross tonnage, but for vessels of 140 000 tons or more CRISTAL will pay the layer between US$70 million and US$135 million.

Both TOVALOP and CRISTAL are due to expire on 20 February 1994. Their short term future thereafter is reasonably assured but in the longer term many foresee their eventual disappearance.

Civil Liability Convention's Scope of Application – CLC Article II

Article II of the CLC states:

> This convention shall apply exclusively to pollution damage caused on the territory including the territorial sea of a Contracting State and to preventive measures taken to prevent and minimise such damage.

A number of points arise from this definition:

(a) Oil pollution damage – by Article I (5) 'oil' means 'persistent oil' such as crude oil, fuel oil, heavy diesel oil, lubricating oil, whale oil and other persistent oils. It does not apply to distillate oils (for example gas oil or automotive diesel oil), kerosene, white spirit, gasolene, and so on.

(b) The pollution must result from escapes or discharges from laden tankers. The CLC would not therefore cover a spill from a ruptured loading pipeline to a tanker at an offshore terminal, for example.

(c) The pollution must be suffered in 'the territory including the territorial sea of a Contracting State'. In the 'Haven' incident in April 1991 pollution occurred in the territory of three adjacent CLC states (Italy, France and Monaco) but all claims are being made against the only fund established by 'Haven''s owners in Italy.

(d) The CLC also applies to 'preventive measures' as defined in Article 1(7) which means 'any reasonable measures taken by any person after an incident has occurred to prevent or minimise pollution damage'. This definition would appear to exclude the costs of so-called 'pre-spill measures'.

Strict Liability

Article III of the CLC states:

> ...the owner of a ship at the time of an incident, or where the incident consists of a series of occurrences at the time of the first such occurrence, shall be liable for any pollution damage caused by oil which has escaped or been discharged from the ship as a result of the incident.

Thus, the tanker owner is under a strict liability for oil pollution damage caused by an escape or discharge of oil from his ship. The word 'ship' is defined as 'any sea-going vessel and any sea-borne craft of any type whatsoever actually carrying oil in bulk as cargo' (CLC Article I(1)), so that this strict liability does not apply, for example, in respect of damage caused by bunkers escaping from a tanker whilst sailing in ballast.

By Article III(2) and (3), the CLC provides certain specific exceptions to this strict liability. In order to avail himself of the benefit of the exceptions, the owner must prove that the damage:

(a) resulted from an act of war, hostilities, civil war, insurrection or a natural phenomenon of an exceptional, inevitable and irresistible character, or

(b) was wholly caused by an act or omission done with intent to cause damage by a third party, or

(c) was wholly caused by the negligence or other wrongful act of any Government or other authority responsible for the maintenance of lights or other navigational aids in the exercise of that function.

Also, if the owner can show that the damage resulted wholly or partially from the victims' negligent, reckless or intentional act, the owner may be exonerated wholly or partially from his liability to that victim.

Claims for compensation may only be made against a tanker owner by virtue of Article III(4) of the CLC. The owners' servants or agents (such as master, crew and ships' managers) are therefore exempt from actions in respect of oil pollution damage. Pollution victims may, however, bring claims against persons other than the owner, his servants or agents. This was done in the *Tanio.* [4] In this case a Malagasy tanker, 'Tanio' (18 048 gross registered tons), carrying 24 000 tons of fuel oil, broke amidships in heavy weather conditions off the coast of Brittany, France. About 13 500 tons of cargo spilt from the wreck, polluting more than 200 kms of the Brittany and Channel Islands coasts. The stern section, with about 5 700 tons of cargo aboard, remained afloat and was towed to Le Havre. The bow section, with about 5 000 tons of cargo on board, sank to a depth of 90 metres. The oil contained in the sunken bow section had to be pumped out in order to prevent further pollution from the wreck.

The incident occurred in March 1980 and it soon became clear that the claims would far exceed the shipowners' limit of liability under the CLC of about £1.2 million. In the end, the IOPC Fund received and accepted claims of about £34 million, much of which was paid by the IOPC Fund.

In 1983, the IOPC Fund took legal action in the Court of Brest, France, by virtue of its subrogated rights against:

(i) the shipyard that repaired the 'Tanio' in 1979;
(ii) the registered owner of the 'Tanio' at the time of the incident;
(iii) the charterer of the 'Tanio' at the time of the incident;
(iv) the chartering managers of the 'Tanio';
(v) the technical managers responsible for the repairs carried out to the 'Tanio' in 1979;
(vi) Bureau Veritas, the classification society that monitored the repairs to the 'Tanio' in 1979;
(vii) The P&I Club, the United Kingdom Mutual Steamship Assurance Association (Bermuda) Ltd, in its capacity as insurers of the civil liability of certain defendants.

The French Government, which had not received full compensation from the IOPC Fund, also took action against these parties. Eventually, the IOPC Fund and the French Government accepted US$50 million from the UK Club and 'Tanio's registered owners in full and final settlement of their claim. This settlement, however, did not cover the claims of French local authorities and private claimants who had also instituted legal proceedings against the defendants referred to above.

The system whereby claims for oil pollution damage may not be made against the tanker owner's servants or agents does not of course function where claimants in contracting states sue defendants in non-contracting states, as was done in the *Amoco Cadiz*[5] where the claimants brought proceedings in Illinois.

However, in the vast majority of incidents there will be no real temptation for claimants to sue shipowners or their servants or agents in non-contracting states. Up to certain limits, claims in excess of the shipowners' limit of liability will be paid for by the IOPC Fund and, in certain circumstances, claims in excess of IOPC Fund limits will be borne by the voluntary schemes, up to their limits of liability. Thus, it will generally only be in quite exceptionally large incidents that claimants will be tempted to sue shipowners in non-contracting states.

Under the 1984 Protocol, Article III(4) would be amended expressly to bar claims not only against servants or agents of the owner (including crew members) but also against pilots, charterers, managers and operators of the ship, salvors and those taking preventive anti-pollution measures and their servants or agents.

Limitation of Liability – CLC Article V and 1976 Protocol Article II

By virtue of these Articles, tanker owners may limit their liability, in respect of any one incident, to 133 Special Drawing Rights (SDRs) – about US$ 197.54 as at 4 September 1992 – per ton of the ship's limitation tonnage, or 14 million SDRs (about US$20.8 million as at 4 September 1992), whichever is the lesser. For this purpose, the ship's tonnage is its net tonnage plus engine room space. If the 1984 Protocol comes into force those limits will rise to 3 million SDRs for ships not exceeding 5 000 gross tons and 420 SDRs per ton for every ton in excess thereof up to 59.7 million SDRs. Furthermore, a ship's limitation tonnage under the 1984 Protocol would be its gross tonnage calculated in accordance with the International Convention on Tonnage Measurement of Ships 1969. Since most ships have not been measured in accordance with this Convention, it will often become necessary to re-measure the vessel for the purposes of constituting a valid limitation fund. Generally speaking this will result in larger limitation tonnages and consequently larger limitation funds if the 1984 Protocol comes into force.

An owner may not limit his liability if the incident occurred 'as a result of the actual fault or privity of the owner'. These words are drawn directly from the 1924 and 1957 Conventions on Limitation of Liability for Maritime Claims. Until 1 December 1986, English law on shipowners' limitation applied this test when considering whether shipowners could limit their liability under Section 503 of the Merchant Shipping Act 1894 (as amended). There is therefore a good deal of judicial authority on the meaning of the words.

The first point that should be noted is that fault or privity must attach not to any person in the employment of the shipowning company, but only the senior employee(s) who is the '*alter ego*' of the company. The '*alter ego*' is the person on the Board of Directors or in the senior management of the company who is the controlling mind of the company.

But what do the words 'actual fault or privity' mean?

Recent authorities usually quote with approval the words of Buckley L.J. in *Asiatic Petroleum Co.* v *Lennards Carrying Co. Ltd.*:[6]

> ...the words "actual fault or privity" in my judgment infer something personal to the owner, something blameworthy in him as distinguished from constructive fault or privity such as the fault or privity of his servants or agents. But the words "actual fault" are not confined to affirmative or positive acts by way of fault. If the owner be guilty of an act or omission to do something which he ought to have done, he is no less guilty of an actual fault than if the act had been one of commission. To avail himself of the statutory defence, he must shew that he himself is not blameworthy for having either done or omitted to do something or been privy to something. It is not necessary to shew knowledge. If he has means of knowledge which he ought to have used and does not avail himself of them, his omission so to do may be a fault, and, if so, it is an actual fault and he cannot claim the protection of the section....[7]

In practice, the British courts have applied these words strictly and have been quick to hold that shipowners, particularly through defective systems of management and superintendence, are personally at fault in relation to matters giving rise to claims.

In the case of the *Lady Gwendolen*,[8] a collision was caused by a vessel owned by Arthur Guinness & Co, proceeding at too high a speed through fog. Captain Meredith, the Master, had frequently travelled at too high a speed in fog, relying upon the ship's radar to protect him. Unfortunately, however, he did not know properly how to operate the radar equipment. The managers of the vessel should have known that Captain Meredith had had inadequate instruction in the use of the radar, and could have seen from the log books that he had been travelling too fast in fog on previous voyages. However, they did nothing. The Court of Appeal held that the collision had occurred with actual fault on the part of the owners in the management of the navigation of the vessel.

In the case of the *Marion*,[9] the Master used an out-of-date chart to anchor his vessel off Teesport. He dropped his anchor onto an underwater pipeline not marked on his old chart, causing serious damage. Even though the vessel had on board an up-to-date chart showing the pipeline, which the Master failed to use, the owners were held not entitled to limit their liability because of management deficiencies in their system of supervision of the vessel and the maintenance of charts on board. Those deficiencies were held to be sufficient to make it impossible for the owners to show that the accident had occurred 'without their actual fault or privity' and they therefore forfeited their right to limit their liability.

The last case to which attention should be drawn in this connection is the *Garden City*,[10] which was similar in its facts to the *Lady Gwendolen*. In the *Garden City*, the vessel in question, the 'Zaglebie Dabrowski' was owned by Polsteam, the Polish state-shipowning organisation. It was held that there was a failure to check on the navigational habits of the Master of the vessel, and that the Chief Navigator of Polsteam (a post somewhat similar to a Marine Superintendent in English practice) was at fault. However, Staughton J. held that his fault was not the fault of Polsteam. The duties he carried out negligently had been delegated to him. The only relevant issue was whether the system of management adopted by the Manager of Technical & Investment Affairs, including the delegation, was faulty. Staughton J. held that it was not and there was therefore no actual fault on the part of Polsteam itself. The decision in the *Garden City* would appear to support the view that where authority has been delegated by the '*alter ego*', there can only be actual fault on the part of the shipowner if the system of delegation was itself a faulty one; the negligence of the delegate would not, of itself, amount to actual fault of the delegator.

The test of actual fault or privity may be replaced, if the 1984 Protocol comes into force, by a test that would make it much easier for shipowners to limit their liability. The new test would only deprive the shipowner of his right to limit if it is proved that the pollution damage resulted from the owners' personal act or omission, committed with the intent to cause such damage, or recklessly and with knowledge that such damage would probably result.[11]

Once the limitation fund has been constituted and a decree of limitation granted, the fund is distributed amongst claimants in proportion to the amounts of their claims. The limitation fund, which is set up under the CLC, is additional to other limitation funds for damage or personal injury claims not covered by oil pollution.[12] However, once the CLC Limitation Fund has been constituted and the owner has been found entitled to limit his liability, none of the owners' assets can be seized, arrested or detained in relation to claims for oil pollution damage and all assets under seizure, arrest or detention in relation to such claims must be released.[13]

The limitation provisions in the CLC require considerable thought on the part of each contracting country, to ensure that existing limitation provisions applying to shipowners and others dovetail with the pollution limitation rules. An example of this is the position of a charterer who may be liable under the *lex fori* for pollution damage, for instance in negligence. It will be remembered that the CLC provides that:

> No claim for compensation for oil pollution damage shall be made against the owner otherwise than in accordance with this Convention. No claim for pollution damage under this Convention or otherwise may be made against the servants or agents of the owner.[14]

This does not exclude actions against the charterer, however. In the 14 CLC countries which also operate the 1957 Shipowners' Limitation Convention, the charterer would be entitled to the benefit of the 1957 Convention; but as both he and the owner would have separate limitation funds, the effect would be that greater compensation would be available from them combined in respect of oil pollution than it was thought proper to impose under the CLC alone. This anomaly was corrected in the United Kingdom by Section 7 of the Merchant Shipping (Oil Pollution) Act 1971. Since 1 December 1986, the UK and many other countries have no longer applied the 1957 Limitation Convention but the 1976 Convention, Article 3(b) of which provides that the 1976 Convention does not apply to claims for oil pollution damage within the meaning of the CLC.

This wording does not make it clear whether the exclusion in the 1976 Limitation Convention applies merely to claims against the registered shipowner for oil pollution damage, or to *all* claims for pollution damage as defined in the CLC. If the latter interpretation is preferred, then it would seem that the charterer is in an even worse position than he would be in a 1957 Convention Country, because he would be unable to limit his liability under either the 1976 Convention or the CLC. It is, therefore, arguable that a charterer in such circumstances might be liable without limit for oil pollution claims, whereas the registered owners could limit under the CLC. Similarly, let us consider the hypothetical case of a ship which through its own fault collides with a tanker, causing oil to be spilt from the latter resulting in oil pollution. On a wide construction of the exclusion, the owners would not be entitled to limit their liability in an action brought directly against them for pollution damage by a third party. Clearly, a narrow construction of the exclusion is preferable, to limit it only to claims against the registered owner for oil pollution damage for which liability under the CLC may arise. Although the 1984 Protocol Article 4 would exempt the charterer (and certain others) from liability for compensation for oil pollution damage, it would not allow the colliding ship's owner to limit his liability for such compensation. It therefore only partially solves the problem.

There are other examples of difficulties which arise out of the 'intermeshing' of limitation provisions of the CLC and other limitation conventions.

Compulsory Insurance – CLC Article VII

By CLC Article VII, owners of tankers carrying more than 2 000 tons of persistent oil as cargo are obliged to maintain insurance to cover their oil pollution damage liability under CLC. Tankers must carry on board a certificate, issued by the state of the ship's port of registry, attesting the insurance coverage of the ship. Furthermore, contracting states are obliged to ensure that ships entering or leaving their ports or terminals, and actually carrying more than 2 000 tons of oil in bulk as cargo, are in possession of that certificate and are therefore insured. In practice, a tanker owner's liability under the CLC is usually underwritten by his P&I Club.

Under the CLC, the position of an insurer is complicated by two factors:-

(a) Direct action – CLC Article VII(8) provides that oil pollution compensation claims may be brought directly against the insurer up to the owner's limit of liability, irrespective of the owner's actual fault or privity. This is one of the very rare examples of direct action against insurers now in force in English law.

(b) Insurers may constitute a limitation fund even in the event of the owner's actual fault or privity.[15] In the event that the owner is unable to limit, because the incident occurred with his actual fault or privity, the fact that the insurer has constituted a limitation fund does not prevent a claimant suing the owner – in separate proceedings – for any amounts in excess of the limitation fund.

Jurisdiction – CLC Article IX

Actions for compensation may only be brought in the Courts of the Contracting State which has suffered pollution damage in its territory, including its territorial waters. Thus, once the first action has been brought in a Contracting State, that State has exclusive jurisdiction over all the claims for compensation for oil pollution damage arising out of the incident, and over the distribution of the limitation fund. Obviously, claims unrelated to oil pollution, although arising out of the same incident, may be brought in another jurisdiction provided that the rules relating to Conflict of Laws in that other jurisdiction permit. In English law jurisdiction is dealt with in relation to defendants domiciled in the European Community (except Portugal) by the Civil Jurisdiction and Judgments Act 1982. For defendants domiciled outside the European Community, the criteria laid down by the House of Lords in *Spiliada Maritime Corporation* v *Cansulex Ltd* are applied.[16] Since the *Spiliada* it is established that an English Court will grant a stay of proceedings where it is satisfied that there is another forum which is *the* appropriate forum for the trial of the action, that is, one 'in which the case may be tried more suitably for the interests of all the parties and the ends of justice'. This test was applied recently by the Gibraltar Court of Appeal in *Aldington Shipping Ltd* v *Bradstock Shipping Corp. & Anor* (the *Waylink* and *Brady Maria* case).[17] This arose out of a collision in January 1986 in the River Elbe, West Germany. The 'Brady Maria' was a tanker and as a result of the collision, some of her oil was spilt causing pollution. Shortly after the collision, owners of the 'Waylink' instituted proceedings against owners of the 'Brady Maria' for damages in the Regional Court of Hamburg and also constituted a limitation fund in West Germany in the sum of DM 440 185. The claims against the fund brought by the 'Brady Maria''s owners, the West German Government and the IOPC Fund greatly exceeded DM 440 185. Therefore the owners of the 'Brady Maria' instituted proceedings in Gibraltar against the 'Waylink''s owners hoping thereby to increase their recovery. The Gibraltar Court of Appeal held that the action should be stayed, applying the test in the *Spiliada* that on the facts and the evidence West Germany was the place with which the action had the most real and substantial connection, and that there was a balance of convenience in favour of West Germany which made it the natural and appropriate forum for these proceedings.

Perhaps it is worth noting that ships owned by states may raise Sovereign Immunity as a defence to proceedings under the CLC. However, their ability to raise this defence in most West European jurisdictions will be limited by the European Convention on State Immunity (enacted in the UK by the State Immunity Act 1978) which provides *inter alia* that no state ship will enjoy immunity if, at the time when the cause of action arose, it was being used for commercial purposes.

IOPC Fund

The IOPC Fund was created by the Fund Convention and is financed by persons in Contracting States receiving 'contributing oil' exceeding 150 000 tonnes *per annum*. By Article II of the Fund Convention, the Fund's main functions are to:

(a) provide supplementary compensation for oil pollution damage for those who cannot obtain full compensation under CLC.
(b) to indemnify tanker owners flying the flag of a Fund Convention country, or their insurers, up to 33 SDRs (about US$49 as at 4 September 1992) per ton, or 5 667 000 SDRs (about US$8.4 million) – whichever is the less – of their liabilities under CLC. This will normally cover about 25 per cent of the limitation fund. The Fund is relieved of this obligation if the damage was caused by the wilful misconduct of the tanker owner or, if due to the actual fault or privity of the tanker owner, the polluting ship did not comply with certain conventions and the incident was caused wholly or partially by such non-compliance.

Assessment and Quantification of Oil Pollution Claims

Most oil pollution claims against ships are settled by P&I Clubs confidentially. However, IOPC Fund settlements are made public in the IOPC Fund Annual Reports and are, broadly speaking, based on the English legal principles of foreseeability and remoteness. Generally, the IOPC Fund will only pay compensation if a claimant who has a legal right to claim under national law has suffered quantifiable economic loss.

When considering a claim, particular regard should be had to the definitions in Article I of the CLC. The principal relevant definitions are:

> '**pollution damage**' means loss or damage caused outside the ship carrying oil by contamination resulting from the escape or discharge of oil from the ship, wherever such escape or discharge may occur, and includes the costs of preventive measures and further loss or damage caused by preventive measures.
> '**preventive measures**' means any reasonable measures taken by any person after an incident has occurred to prevent or minimise pollution damage.
> '**incident**' means any occurrence or series of occurrences having the same origin, which causes pollution damage.

Oil pollution can give rise to a number of different kinds of claim some of which are discussed below:-

Damage to property Most jurisdictions recognise the principle of *restitutio in integrum* or compensation for the reduction in value or for necessary costs of repair. The same can be said of consequential losses suffered by owners or users of property that has been contaminated or damaged.

Thus for example the owner of a fishing boat damaged by oil pollution may be prevented from using his boat for some time while the boat is being cleaned, thereby suffering loss of income. The fisherman whose fishing gear has been damaged by pollution may lose earnings during the time he is prevented from fishing, pending the cleaning of the nets or the purchase of new equipment. Generally speaking, most systems of law will compensate the fisherman for his loss of earnings.

Similarly, most systems will recognise that money spent on measures to prevent or minimise the effect of oil pollution should be recoverable. However, the definition of 'preventive measures' would appear not to apply to what have been called 'pure threat removal measures', that is, measures which are so successful that there is no actual spill of oil from the tanker at all. Additionally, the IOPC Fund takes the position that if a spill occurs, only damage caused or costs of measures taken after the spill are compensable; costs of so-called pre-spill measures are thus not compensated. However, if a tanker is damaged and oil is spilt, the costs of measures to prevent more oil from escaping into the sea are regarded as being, in principle, compensable.

Clearly, the Fund will pay for the reasonable costs of clean-up operations including the salaries of personnel specially used for the operations. The IOPC Fund has also, in the past, agreed to pay not only the costs of overtime allowances and so on, but also the normal salaries of persons involved in clean up operations who are permanently employed by public authorities. It could be argued that the public authorities would have had to pay the normal salaries even if no incident had occurred, so this stance is by no means self-evident. However, the IOPC Fund's position in this regard has been upheld in the Swedish case of the 'Tsesis'[18] and the Australian case of the 'Stolt Chief'.[19]

Salvage operations Broadly speaking, the IOPC Fund will only regard the cost of salvage operations as pollution damage if the primary purpose was to prevent or minimise pollution damage. Usually this is not the case: in most cases the prime objective of salvage operations is to protect the ship or cargo concerned.

This often narrow distinction can give rise to disagreement. An example of such a dispute arose out of the collision between the Greek tanker 'Patmos' (51 627 gross registered tons) carrying 83 689 tons of crude oil and the Spanish tanker 'Castillo De Montearagon' (92 289 gross registered tons) which was in ballast. The collision took place off the coast of Calabria in the Straits of Messina, Italy. Fire broke out on the main deck of the 'Patmos' and spread to the accommodation and wheelhouse. Three crew members died and the ship had to be abandoned. The ship suffered hull damage. Driven by strong winds and currents, the 'Patmos' drifted onto a beach by a village on the Sicilian coast. The ship was refloated and tugs held the vessel in the Straits of Messina. The tugs also fought the fire which took two days to extinguish. The casualty was then towed to the port of Messina and moored at the SMEB shipyard where the oil was discharged. Altogether about 700 tons of oil escaped from the 'Patmos'. Most of it dispersed naturally, but a few tons came ashore on the Sicilian coast. The Italian authorities undertook extensive measures in order to contain the spilt oil and prevent it from polluting the Sicilian and Calabrian coasts.

The incident gave rise to 43 claims against the limitation fund, totalling £35 million. Of these, 12 claims totalling £18.3 million related to salvage operations and related measures, and as such the IOPC Fund resisted them. As a result of the IOPC Fund's stand, two of the claims were withdrawn, but the others became the subject of proceedings in the Court of Messina in 1986. In its judgement the Court made a general statement to the effect that salvage operations could not be considered as preventive measures since the primary purpose of such operations was that of rescuing ship and cargo; this applied even if the operations had the further effect of preventing pollution. On the basis of this principle, the claims were either rejected in full or substantially reduced by the Court.

Pure economic loss Claims for pure economic loss are regarded by the IOPC Fund as being only recoverable by claimants who depend directly on earnings from sea related or coastal activities. For example, loss of earnings suffered by fishermen, hoteliers and restauranteurs at seaside resorts would be recoverable, but losses suffered indirectly would not be recoverable: thus loss of tax revenues by municipal authorities would not be recoverable. This is probably consistent with the position in English law as regards those who own the hotels, restaurants and fishing boats and so on: *Junior Books Ltd.* v *The Veitchi Co. Ltd.*[20] However, in English law it is probably not correct to compensate a person who only has a contractual right to have the use or services of the chattel damaged for the purposes of making profits or gains without possession or property in the chattel: *Candlewood Corporation* v *Mitsui Limited.*[21]

Damage to the environment The IOPC Fund does not accept claims by governments for damage to the environment as they are unquantifiable. In the case of the 'Patmos' the Italian government lodged a claim in respect of damage to the marine environment which the Court of Messina rejected. The Court declared that the state had not suffered any loss of profit or incurred any costs as a result of the alleged damage to the territorial waters or the flora and fauna and had therefore not suffered any economic loss. The Court of Messina's judgement was appealed by the Italian Government and the Court of Appeal delivered judgement on 30 March 1989. In their judgement the Court of Appeal ruled that the Owners of the 'Patmos', the UK P&I Club, and the IOPC Fund were liable for the damage claimed; by an order of the same date the Court appointed three experts to ascertain the existence of oil pollution damage to marine resources caused by the incident, and to quantify it. The Court experts found that some fishermen were prevented from fishing for 15 days and that this damage could be quantified at not less than L.It. 1 000 million. However, they stated there was a lack of data on the impact on other economic activities and that a precise assessment of the damage to such activities was impossible. The experts thought the Court should carry out the evaluation. The Court of Appeal has now sought further guidance from the experts and their judgement is now not expected before the middle of 1992. This issue has assumed a new importance in the light of the fact that, of claims of US$1.4 billion so far made for oil pollution damage compensation arising out of the 'Haven' incident off Genoa in April 1991, US$400 million relate to environmental damage.

Oil Pollution which is not Covered by the CLC

It will already be evident that there are a number of types of oil pollution damage not covered by the CLC. While some non-CLC oil pollution damage may be recovered from the tanker owner, or in certain circumstances under TOVALOP, CRISTAL or the owners' insurers, innocent victims of pollution can still go without any form of compensation at all. Much depends on local law.

There are a large number of incidents each year which fall outside the CLC, not only because the pollution occurs outside Convention countries, but also because it falls into one of the categories shown in Table 7.1. For example, on 10 August 1987, the Panamanian registered tanker 'Texaco Caribbean' (270 015 deadweight tons) fully laden with a cargo of Iranian crude oil was struck by a mine off Fujariah in the United Arab Emirates (UAE), spilling 7 500 tons of oil. Fortunately the oil dispersed naturally after a few days, but here was a situation with the potential for causing

Table 7.1 Types of Pollution Damage not Covered by the CLC

Type of Pollution Damage	*Potential Loss Bearer (Apart from Shipowner)*
War, etc. Intent of third party Government negligence in maintenance of lights or other navigational aids	CLC Article III(2) & (3). No compensation – but owners' liability may be covered by P&I insurance or war risks insurance
Non-persistent oil	No compensation but may be covered by owners' P&I insurers
Pollution not by tankers	No compensation but may be covered by owners' P&I insurers
Pure threat removal measures	TOVALOP/CRISTAL and may be covered by owners' P&I insurers
Tankers on ballast voyages	TOVALOP/CRISTAL and may be covered by owners' P&I insurers
Offshore drilling rigs and other operations	No compensation under CLC, TOVALOP or CRISTAL, but the licensee and the operator or contractor (depending on the terms of the drilling contract) will usually be liable. Their liability for pollution damage will normally be insured under the P&I cover[22]
Pollution losses caused by owners' actual fault or privity	May be covered by TOVALOP CRISTAL and/or P&I insurers in certain circumstances

severe damage to the UAE coastline. That damage would have been due to war, which is specifically excluded from the Convention. Oil pollution caused other than by laden tankers is not covered by the CLC, but out of thirty pollution incidents reported to the International Tanker Owners' Pollution Federation Limited (who run TOVALOP) in 1987, nine incidents originated from dry cargo vessels and were therefore not covered by either the CLC or the voluntary schemes. Perhaps more would have been heard about these gaps in cover if it were not for the voluntary schemes, and for the fact that the number of spills was at a markedly lower lever in the 1980s than the levels reached in the 1970s.

Rights of Recourse

Of the Shipowner

Article III(5) of the Civil Liability Convention states 'Nothing in this Convention shall prejudice any right of recourse of the owner against third parties.'

Thus, the owners of a ship damaged in a collision can sue the owners of the colliding ship at fault for an indemnity in respect of payments made to oil pollution damage claimants who suffer loss as a result of the collision, as was demonstrated in the *Waylink* and *Patmos* cases. Similarly, a shipowner who is liable to pay oil pollution claims caused by the negligent design or construction of his vessel may recover an indemnity (full or partial depending on the circumstances) from the negligent shipbuilders (as for example in the *Amoco Cadiz* case).

Of the IOPC Fund

We have already seen, in relation to the *Tanio*, that the IOPC Fund has rights of recourse against both the shipowner or his guarantor and persons other than the shipowner and his guarantor. These rights are conferred by Article 9 of the Fund Convention and were used to considerable effect in the 'Tanio' affair. In practice, the IOPC Fund's rights of recourse are one of the most important factors in most sizeable pollution incidents, and for those advising shipowners and P&I Clubs, they are ignored at one's peril.

Conclusion

It has been necessary to gloss over or omit many important aspects of the way in which the CLC functions. The compensation regime established by the CLC provides only a partial answer to the problem of compensating victims of oil pollution. Although some of the omissions are dealt with by voluntary schemes, and perhaps in the future by the 1984 Protocol (or something like it) there are still circumstances where innocent victims receive no compensation for pollution damage. This is easily the most significant failing of the present system. Perhaps the problem owes its origin to the fact that when the CLC was drafted, people were concerned primarily with arriving at a compensation framework which would gain maximum endorsement worldwide. In the light of the difficulties which faced oil pollution damage claimants in 1969, the CLC was a considerable advance. However, attitudes to concepts like strict liability have now modified and time is ripe for further advances. We need now to consider whether the CLC should be extended to cover at least some of the excluded areas of oil pollution liability outlined in Table 7.1. Recent disasters like the 'Exxon Valdez' have led the USA to introduce a radical new piece of legislation, the Oil Pollution Act 1990. In conjunction with State legislation this will result in a regime which in practice can often mean that not only strict but also unlimited liability will fall upon Shipowners, and certain others, for all commonly encountered kinds of marine oil pollution from ships. Since the 'Haven' incident in Italy in April 1991 there has been talk of the introduction of similar legislation in Europe.

There are still anomalies; for example, the CLC can be circumvented by litigants who choose to pursue owners in non-Convention countries, as was done in the '*Amoco Cadiz*' case. It is hoped that this difficulty will diminish in importance as more littoral states accede to the CLC, and as the IOPC Fund's limits increase. The problems posed by the interaction of Conventions, particularly on the subject of limitation of shipowners' liability, can generally be resolved by local legislation; but careful thought has to be given to this aspect by contracting countries. It is now approaching 25 years since work was started on drafting the CLC and the legislation, case-law and practice surrounding it is still in the process of evolution. However, now that the system is functional and has been shown to be viable, year by year more countries accede to it.

Strict liability under the CLC has not resulted in a significant reduction in expensive international litigation, due partly to the rights of recourse enjoyed by the IOPC Fund. It has however resulted in the more rapid and fuller payment of pollution damage claims in respect of incidents to which the Convention does apply. Altogether the CLC, and the voluntary schemes TOVALOP and CRISTAL, have, for all their omissions, dramatically improved the position of the majority of oil pollution claimants over the last 25 years.

Notes

1 [1965] AC 218.
2 [1984] 2 Lloyd's Report 304.
3 [1935] U.N.R.I.A.A. iii. p 1905.
4 *IOPC Fund Annual Report* 1987, pp 10–16.
5 *Supra cit.*
6 [1914] 1 KB 419.
7 *Ibid.*, at p 432.
8 [1965] 1 Lloyd's Report 335.
9 [1984] AC 563.
10 [1982] 2 Lloyd's Report 382.
11 1984 Protocol, Article 6(2).
12 Limitation of Liability Convention (1976), Article 3(6).
13 CLC Article VI.
14 CLC Article III(4), *supra cit.*
15 CLC Article V(8).
16 [1986] 3 WLR 972.
17 [1988] 1 Lloyd's Report 475.
18 The Sven Court of Appeal, Sweden. The case was taken to the Swedish Supreme Court on another issue but is discussed in Tiberg, H. (1984), 'Oil Pollution of the Sea and the Swedish Tsesis Decision', *Lloyd's Maritime and Commercial Law Quarterly* 218.
19 Supreme Court of New South Wales, 9 March 1982.
20 [1983] 1 AC 520.
21 [1986] 1 A.C.1.
22 For greater detail see, Summerskill, M. (1979), *Oil Rigs: Law and Insurance*, London: Stevens and Sons, especially Chapters 5 and 8.

International Convention on Civil Liability for Oil Pollution Damage
(Incorporating amendments made pursuant to the 1976 Protocol)

Brussels, November 29, 1969

PREAMBLE OMITTED

ARTICLE I

For the purposes of this Convention:

1 'Ship' means any sea-going vessel and any seaborne craft of any type whatsoever, actually carrying oil in bulk as cargo.
2 'Person' means any individual or partnership or any public or private body, whether corporate or not, including a State or any of its constituent subdivisions.

3 'Owner' means the person or persons registered as the owner of the ship or, in the absence of registration, the person or persons owning the ship. However in the case of a ship owned by a State and operated by a company which in that State is registered as the ship's operator, "owner" shall mean such company.

4 'State of the ship's registry' means in relation to registered ships the State of registration of the ship, and in relation to unregistered ships the State whose flag the ship is flying.

5 'Oil' means any persistent oil such as crude oil, fuel oil, heavy diesel oil, lubricating oil and whale oil, whether carried on board a ship as cargo or in the bunkers of such a ship.

6 'Pollution damage' means loss or damage caused outside the ship carrying oil by contamination resulting from the escape or discharge of oil from the ship, wherever such escape or discharge may occur, and includes the costs of preventive measures and further loss or damage caused by preventive measures.

7 'Preventive measures' means any reasonable measures taken by any person after an incident occurred to prevent or minimize pollution damage.

8 'Incident' means any occurrence, or series of occurrences having the same origin, which causes pollution damage.

9 'Organization' means the Inter-Governmental Maritime Consultative Organization.

Article II

This Convention shall apply exclusively to pollution damage caused on the territory including the territorial sea of a Contracting State and to preventive measures taken to prevent or minimize such damage.

Article III

1 Except as provided in paragraphs 2 and 3 of this Article, the owner of a ship at the time of an incident, or where the incident consists of a series of occurrences at the time of the first such occurrence, shall be liable for any pollution damage caused by oil which has escaped or been discharged from the ship as a result of the incident.

2 No liability for pollution damage shall attach to the owner if he proves that the damage:

(a) resulted from an act of war, hostilities, civil war, insurrection or a natural phenomenon of an exceptional, inevitable and irresistible character, or

(b) was wholly caused by an act or omission done with intent to cause damage by a third party, or
(c) was wholly caused by the negligence or other wrongful act of any Government or other authority responsible for the maintenance of lights or other navigational aids in the exercise of that function.

3 If the owner proves that the pollution damage resulted wholly or partially either from an act or omission done with intent to cause damage by the person who suffered the damage or from the negligence of that person, the owner may be exonerated wholly or partially from his liability to such person.

4 No claim for compensation for pollution damage shall be made against the owner otherwise than in accordance with this Convention. No claim for pollution damage under this Convention or otherwise may be made against the servants or agents of the owner.

5 Nothing in this Convention shall prejudice any right of recourse of the owner against third parties.

Article IV

When oil has escaped or has been discharged from two or more ships, and pollution damage results therefrom, the owners of all the ships concerned, unless exonerated under Article III, shall be jointly and severally liable for all such damage which is not reasonably separable.

Article V

1 The owner of a ship shall be entitled to limit his liability under this Convention in respect of any one incident to an aggregate amount of 133 units of account for each ton of the ship's tonnage. However, this aggregate amount shall not in any event exceed 14 million units of account.

2 If the incident occurred as a result of the actual fault or privity of the owner, he shall not be entitled to avail himself of the limitation provided in paragraph 1 of this Article.

3 For the purpose of availing himself of the benefit of limitation provided for in paragraph 1 of this Article the owner shall constitute a fund for the total sum representing the limit of his liability with the Court or other competent authority of any one of the Contracting States in which action is brought under Article IX. The fund can be constituted either by depositing the sum or by producing a bank guarantee or other guarantee, acceptable under the legislation of the Con-

tracting State where the fund is constituted, and considered to be adequate by the Court or another competent authority.

4 The fund shall be distributed among the claimants in proportion to the amounts of their established claims.

5 If before the fund is distributed the owner or any of his servants or agents or any person providing him insurance or other financial security has as a result of the incident in question, paid compensation for pollution damage, such person shall, up to the amount he has paid, acquire by subrogation the rights which the person so compensated would have enjoyed under this Convention.

6 The right of subrogation provided for in paragraph 5 of this Article may also be exercised by a person other than those mentioned therein in respect of any amount of compensation for pollution damage which he may have paid but only to the extent that such subrogation is permitted under the applicable national law.

7 Where the owner or any other person establishes that he may be compelled to pay at a later date in whole or in part any such amount of compensation, with regard to which such person would have enjoyed a right of subrogation under paragraphs 5 or 6 of this Article, had the compensation been paid before the fund was distributed, the Court or other competent authority of the State where the fund has been constituted may order that a sufficient sum shall be provisionally set aside to enable such person at such later date to enforce his claim against the fund.

8 Claims in respect of expenses reasonably incurred or sacrifices reasonably made by the owner voluntarily to prevent or minimize pollution damage shall rank equally with other claims against the fund.

9 (a) The "unit of account" referred to in paragraph 1 of this Article is the Special Drawing Right as defined by the International Monetary Fund. The amounts mentioned in paragraph 1 shall be converted into the national currency of the State in which the fund is being constituted on the basis of the value of that currency by reference to the Special Drawing Right on the day of the constitution of the fund. The value of the national currency, in terms of the Special Drawing Right, of a contracting State which is a member of the International Monetary Fund, shall be calculated in accordance with the method of valuation applied by the International Monetary Fund in effect at the date in question for its operations and transactions. The value of the national currency, in terms of the Special Drawing Right, of a Contracting State which is not a member of the International Monetary Fund, shall be calculated in a manner determined by that State.

(b) Nevertheless, a Contracting State which is not a member of the International Monetary Fund and whose law does not permit the application of the provisions of paragraph 9(a) of this Article may, at the time of ratification, acceptance, approval of or accession to the present Convention, or at any time thereafter, declare that the limits of liability provided for in paragraph 1 to be applied in its territory shall, in respect of any one incident, be an aggregate of 2,000 monetary units for each ton of the ship's tonnage provided that this aggregate amount shall not in any event exceed 210 million monetary units. The monetary unit referred to in this paragraph corresponds to sixty-five and a half milligrammes of gold of millesimal fineness nine hundred. The conversion of these amounts into the national currency shall be made according to the law of the State concerned.

(c) The calculation mentioned in the last sentence of paragraph 9(a) and the conversion mentioned in paragraph 9(b) shall be made in such a manner as to express in the national currency of the Contracting State as far as possible the same real value for the amounts in paragraph 1 as is expressed there in units of account. Contracting States shall communicate to the depositary the manner of calculation pursuant to paragraph 9(a), or the result of the conversion in paragraph 9(b) as the case may be, when depositing an instrument referred to in Article IV and whenever there is a change in either.

10 For the purpose of this Article the ship's tonnage shall be the net tonnage of the ship with the addition of the amount deducted from the gross tonnage on account of engine room space for the purpose of ascertaining the net tonnage. In the case of a ship which cannot be measured in accordance with the normal rules of tonnage measurement, the ship's tonnage shall be deemed to be 40 percent of the weight in tons (of 2240 lbs) of oil which the ship is capable of carrying.

11 The insurer or other person providing financial security shall be entitled to constitute a fund in accordance with this Article on the same conditions and having the same effect as if it were constituted by the owner. Such a fund may be constituted even in the event of the actual fault or privity of the owner but its constitution shall in that case not prejudice the rights of any claimant against the owner.

ARTICLE VI

1 Where the owner, after an incident, has constituted a fund in accordance with Article V, and is entitled to limit his liability.

(a) no person having a claim for pollution damage arising out of that incident shall be entitled to exercise any right against any other assets of the owner in respect of such claim;

(b) the Court or other competent authority of any Contracting State shall order the release of any ship or other property belonging to the owner which has been arrested in respect of a claim for pollution damage arising out of that incident, and shall similarly release any bail or other security furnished to avoid such arrest.

2 The foregoing shall, however, only apply if the claimant has access to the Court administering the fund and the fund is actually available in respect of his claim.

ARTICLE VII

1 The owner of a ship registered in a Contracting State and carrying more than 2,000 tons of oil in bulk as cargo shall be required to maintain insurance or other financial security, such as the guarantee of a bank or a certificate delivered by an international compensation fund, in the sums fixed by applying the limits of liability prescribed in Article V, paragraph 1 to cover his liability for pollution damage under this Convention.

2 A certificate attesting that insurance or other financial security is in force in accordance with the provisions of this Convention shall be issued to each ship. It shall be issued or certified by the appropriate authority of the State of the ship's registry after determining that the requirements of paragraph 1 of this Article have been complied with. This certificate shall be in the form of the annexed model and shall contain the following particulars;

(a) name of ship and port of registration;

(b) name and principal place of business of owner;

(c) type of security;

(d) name and principal place of business of insurer or other person giving security and, where appropriate, place of business where the insurance or security is established;

(e) period of validity of certificate which shall not be longer than the period of validity of the insurance or other security.

3 The certificate shall be in the official language or languages of the

issuing State. If the language used is neither English nor French, the text shall include a translation into one of these languages.

4 The certificate shall be carried on board the ship and a copy shall be deposited with the authorities who keep the record of the ship's registry.

5 An insurance or other financial security shall not satisfy the requirements of this Article if it can cease, for reasons other than the expiry of the period of validity of the insurance or security specified in the certificate under paragraph 2 of this Article, before three months have elapsed from the date on which notice of its termination is given to the authorities referred to in paragraph 4 of this Article, unless the certificate has been surrendered to these authorities or a new certificate has been issued within the said period. The foregoing provisions shall similarly apply to any modification which results in the insurance or security no longer satisfying the requirements of this Article.

6 The State of registry shall, subject to the provisions of this Article, determine the conditions of issue and validity of the certificate.

7 Certificates issued or certified under the authority of a Contracting State shall be accepted by other contracting States for the purposes of this Convention and shall be regarded by other Contracting States as having the same force as certificates issued or certified by them. A Contracting State may at any time request consultation with the State of a ship's registry should it believe that the insurer or guarantor named in the certificate is not financially capable of meeting the obligations imposed by this Convention.

8 Any claim for compensation for pollution damage may be brought directly against the insurer or other person providing financial security for the owner's liability for pollution damage. In such case the defendant may, irrespective of the actual fault or privity of the owner, avail himself of the limits of liability prescribed in Article V, paragraph 1. He may further avail himself of the defences (other than the bankruptcy or winding up of the owner) which the owner himself would have been entitled to invoke. Furthermore, the defendant may avail himself of the defence that the pollution damage resulted from the wilful misconduct of the owner himself, but the defendant shall not avail himself of any other defence which he might have been entitled to invoke in proceedings brought by the owner against him. The defendant shall in any event have the right to require the owner to be joined in the proceedings.

9 Any sums provided by insurance or by other financial security maintained in accordance with paragraph 1 of this Article shall be available exclusively for the satisfaction of claims under this Convention.

10 A contracting State shall not permit a ship under its flag to which this Article applies to trade unless a certificate has been issued under paragraph 2 or 12 of this Article.

11 Subject to the provisions of this Article, each Contracting State shall ensure, under its national legislation, that insurance or other security to the extent specified in paragraph 1 of this Article is in force in respect of any ship, wherever registered, entering or leaving a port in its territory, or arriving at or leaving an off-shore terminal in its territorial sea, if the ship actually carries more than 2,000 tons of oil in bulk as cargo.

12 If insurance or other financial security is not maintained in respect of a ship owned by a Contracting state, the provisions of this Article relating thereto shall not be applicable to such ship, but the ship shall carry a certificate issued by the appropriate authorities of the State of the ship's registry stating that the ship is owned by that State and that the ship's liability is covered within the limits prescribed by Article V, paragraph 1. Such a certificate shall follow as closely as practicable the model prescribed by paragraph 2 of this Article.

Article VIII

Right of compensation under this Convention shall be extinguished unless an action is brought thereunder within three years from the date when the damage occurred. However, in no case shall an action be brought after six years from the date of the incident which caused the damage. Where this incident consists of a series of occurrences, the six years' period shall run from the date of the first such occurrence.

Article IX

1 Where an incident has caused pollution damage in the territory including the territorial sea of one or more Contracting States, or preventive measures have been taken to prevent or minimize pollution damage in such territory including the territorial sea, actions for compensation may only be brought in the Courts of any such Contracting State or States. Reasonable notice of any such action shall be given to the defendants.

2 Each Contracting State shall ensure that its Courts possess the necessary jurisdiction to entertain such actions for compensation.

3 After the fund has been constituted in accordance with Article V the Courts of the State in which the fund is constituted shall be exclusively

competent to determine all matters relating to the apportionment and distribution of the fund.

Article X

1 Any judgement given by the Court with jurisdiction in accordance with Article IX which is enforceable in the State of origin where it is no longer subject to ordinary forms of review, shall be recognized in any Contracting State, except:
(a) where the judgement was obtained by fraud; or
(b) where the defendant was not given reasonable notice and a fair opportunity to present his case.

2 A judgment recognized under paragraph 1 of this Article shall be enforceable in each Contracting State as soon as the formalities required in that State have been complied with. The formalities shall not permit the merits of the case to be re-opened.

Article XI

1 The provisions of this Convention shall not apply to warships or other ships owned or operated by a State and used, for the time being, only on Government non-commercial service.

2 With respect to ships owned by a Contracting State and used for commercial purposes, each State shall be subject to suit in the jurisdictions set forth in Article IX and shall waive all defences based on its status as a sovereign State.

Article XII

This Convention shall supersede any International Conventions in force or open for signature, ratification or accession at the date on which the Convention is opened for signature, but only to the extent that such Conventions would be in conflict with it; however, nothing in this Article shall affect the obligations of Contracting States to non-Contracting States arising under such International Conventions.

[Articles XIII through XXI deleted]

8 Place of Commission of International Torts: The Substance Test and Its Extension to *Double Locality*

Peter Kaye

Introduction

Problems in locating place of commission of a tort are a familiar occurrence in complex multi-state cases, and both courts and commentators have been willing participants in the efforts to produce a satisfactory solution to the perennial difficulties caused by differently situated places of causative event and damage.

However, as if the situation were not already sufficiently complicated, English courts have recently uncovered a further layer of complexity to be contended with in international tort disputes; this is where not only are causative event and resultant damage located in different states (multi-state cases), but also either (or each) of those elements is itself split amongst a number of different states. It is therefore not immediately possible even to identify a particular place as that of the causative event (or alternatively, damage). This latter type of case adds significantly to the level of difficulty already present in respect of both choice of law and jurisdiction in international tort cases (notwithstanding improvements introduced under the European Judgements Convention and Rules of the Supreme Court (RSC) Order 11, in the jurisdiction sphere), and was expressly the subject of consideration by the English Court of Appeal in the case of *Metall und Rohstoff AG* v *Donaldson Lufkin & Jenrette Inc.*[1] Here Slade L J chose to designate the new situation as being one of 'double locality'.[2] Before that, Steyn J., as he then was, had also had occasion to deal with double locality – although not expressly referring to the issue as such – specifically in the context of tort jurisdiction under the European Judgements Convention, in the case of *Minster Investments Ltd* v *Hyundai Precision and Industry Co. Ltd.*[3]

How the courts responded to the newly recognised concept of double-locality torts in these cases is the subject of this chapter.

Determination of Place of Commission of Torts and of their Individual Components

In *Metall und Rohstoff AG*,[4] the plaintiffs of that name were a Swiss company trading on the London Metal Exchange through an English company, AML. The latter was a subsidiary in a group including the defendant Delaware corporations, Donaldson Lufkin & Jenrette Inc. (DLJ) and ACLI, each of which had its principal office in New York.

When the plaintiffs discovered that their chief aluminium trader had fraudulently dealt on his own account, and had passed on his losses to the plaintiffs, they successfully sued AML, which had connived at the fraud, for over £50 million. Ultimately they succeeded in recovering only £6.5 million, because of AML's insolvency.

The plaintiffs subsequently commenced proceedings against DLJ and ACLI, claiming damages for conspiracy, inducing breach of contract, abuse of process of the court, accounting as constructive trustees and procuring or inducing a breach of trust. Leave was given by Staughton J to serve process upon the defendants out of the jurisdiction under RSC Order 11, r 1(1)(f), on the ground that the claim was 'founded on a tort and the damage was sustained, or resulted from an act committed, within the jurisdiction'. The latter order was thereafter varied before Gatehouse J on the defendants' application to discharge it and to set aside service out of the jurisdiction, under RSC Order 12, r 8.[5] The defendants appealed against that part of the judge's decision to uphold service in respect of certain of the claims, and the plaintiffs cross-appealed against the outcome that other elements of their claim had been struck out.

The Court of Appeal (Slade, Stocker, and Bingham LJJ), delivering judgement through Slade L J, held that only the plaintiff's claim for damages for inducing or procuring breach of contract was able to be brought as one in tort. Consequently it was this particular head of the action which raised questions concerning place of commission of a tort and of its internal components, in the context of service of process out of the jurisdiction under RSC Order 11, r 1.[6]

Before dealing with the Court of Appeal's findings as to location of individual elements of causative event and damage under RSC Order 11 r 1(1)(f), it ought to be pointed out that notwithstanding amendments previously referred to as having been made to the wording of r 1(1)(f) so as to eliminate any reference to *place of commission of torts* thereunder, the Court of Appeal indicated that RSC Order 11, r 4(2) – requiring leave to serve process out of the jurisdiction to be refused unless it is sufficiently clear that the case is a 'proper one for service out of the jurisdiction' – nevertheless called for consideration to be given not merely to the issue of where the individual elements of causative event and damage were to be located (in order to found jurisdiction in tort under RSC Order 11, r1(1)(f)) but also *still* to that of where the alleged tort of inducement of breach of contract *as a whole* had been committed. There were two reasons for this.

First, for a case to be a *proper one for service out of the jurisdiction* under RSC Order 11, r1(1), one of the matters that had to be proved was that the case fell within a definite ground included within r 1(1) – here r 1(1)(f).[7] Since this, as seen, required the damage to have been sustained, or to have resulted from an act committed, within the jurisdiction, in actions founded on a tort,[8] the *main* question for the court in the present case for such purposes was *whether the relevant act or damage had been committed or sustained* in the forum, rather than whether the tort as such had been committed there.[9] Nevertheless, the latter factor would remain important, as a matter to be taken into account by the court in deciding whether or not to exercise its *discretion* to grant leave for service out – as *forum conveniens* – under Order 11, r 1(1)(f), even where that ground was satisfied in relation to the forum. Accordingly, place of commission of the tort was still required to be determined, as well as that of its individual elements of causative event and damage.[10]

Secondly, for the case to be a proper one for leave to be granted for service out under RSC Order 11, r1(1), in accordance with RSC Order 11, r 4(2), the plaintiffs also had to show that they had a good arguable claim on the merits – a good chance of succeeding at trial.[11] Once more, therefore, the court would need to determine place of commission of the alleged tort; yet, this time (albeit in a general jurisdictional context) for choice of law purposes. For, if place of commission were England, English law alone, according to which the plaintiffs *could* show a good arguable case on the facts, would govern the claim. But if New York were held to be *locus delicti*, the 'double actionability' rule, requiring liability to exist under both English *lex fori* (had the wrong been committed in England) and New York *lex loci delicti*, in accordance with *Phillips* v *Eyre*[12] and *Boys* v *Chaplin*,[13] would then apply. In this event the plaintiffs would be unable to make out a good arguable case, since the action would be time-barred under New York law's statute of limitations. This statute English courts were required to treat as substantive, not procedural, in accordance with s 1 of the Foreign Limitation Periods Act 1984, and consequently as applicable to the case.[14]

Ascertainment of place of commission of the tort, or of its individual components, as England or New York, therefore, would have a profound effect upon the outcome of the proceedings. In giving its decision as to the correct method of determining place of commission of torts and of their internal elements for the preceding purposes, the Court of Appeal proceeded on the basis of the following principles.

English Law is to apply Exclusively to Ascertainment of Place of Commission

The Court adopted Dicey and Morris's approach, to the effect that ascertainment of place of commission of a tort concerned interpretation of a connecting factor, and was always therefore to be answered in accordance with English law, on normal principles.[15] This seems broadly acceptable. If English courts are called upon to decide on location of torts or of their individual elements, it is difficult to see how they could be justified in applying any test other than that which is considered to be appropriate under the English conflict of laws.

However, if the proposition also entails that in reaching a conclusion on place of commission, the court should only take into account those places in which acts and elements of liability, *as this latter would be established under English law,* are located, in total disregard of their material relevance or otherwise under the laws of any other states in which connected acts and damage have taken place, then its wholesale acceptability, to this extent, might be rather more questionable.

English Law on Ascertainment of Place of Commission is to Locate the Substance of the Tort

Where causative event and damage are situated in different states ('multi-state' cases) In these circumstances, the Court of Appeal noted that the traditional test in *George Monro Ltd* v *American Cyanamid and Chemical Corpn*,[16] requiring place of act, rather than damage, to be taken to be that of commission of the tort of negligence, was no longer to be followed; and that the courts would instead seek to ascertain *where in substance the cause of action arose* on a consideration of the whole series of events.[17] Established authorities were cited by the court in support of this proposition.[18]

Where several acts, alleged to form part of the causative event as a whole, have occurred in more than one country. This is what the Court of Appeal intended to be meant by 'double locality' cases. The court found that there existed no authoritative guidance on how the double actionability rule in *Phillips* v *Eyre* and *Boys* v *Chaplin* was to operate in such double locality situations, because in those two cases themselves relevant elements of the tort had all taken place in the foreign state concerned.[19]

Unrestricted by direct authority therefore, the court held that the 'now well familiar' substance test, previously applied in cases such as *Distillers Co (Biochemicals) Ltd* v *Thompson, Castree* v *Squibb* and *The Albaforth*,[20] should govern in double locality situations;[21] if the substance of the tort was then found to have been committed in England, the double actionability rule in *Boys* v *Chaplin* would have no application, and the fact that some of the relevant events occurred abroad would thenceforth have no bearing on the defendant's liability in tort. *Boys* v *Chaplin*'s double actionability rule, as a matter of justice, comity and public policy, was intended to prevent a person from being held liable under the English law of tort for an act which was lawful by the law of the foreign state in which it was performed. Conversely, however, it was unreasonable for such a person to be exempted from liability when his acts *harmed people in England*, in which the *substance* of the tort took place; in such circumstances the actor should rightly be expected to have some regard to the laws of England, not just to those of the place of the act. Thus, whilst comity was important, courts should not:

> be obliged to turn a blind eye to damage intentionally or negligently caused to persons within this jurisdiction merely because the acts which did the damage were performed abroad in a country which rendered them non-actionable.[22]

It was appreciated that application of the substance test could give rise to difficulty on the facts of some cases; but it had to be realised that double locality cases were bound to cause problems and there was no reason to suppose that it would create more injustice or greater difficulties than any other test.[23]

Thus it was that the Court of Appeal sanctioned the operation of the 'substance of the cause of action in tort' test in multi-state and double locality cases, the implications thereof being that:

(1) where the substance of the tort is held to be located in England, the double actionability rule will cease to apply to choice of law, and laws of foreign states in which any acts or elements in the chain of events leading to harm occurred are irrelevant as to liability;

(2) although Slade LJ referred expressly to double locality cases in which the *causative event* was divided amongst different states, it can surely be reliably inferred therefrom that instances in which *damage* elements are so divided – for example, in a conspiracy or defamation case – are likewise included within the principles applicable to double locality; and

(3) in the matter of jurisdiction, in so far as it is relevant to exercise of discretion, place of commission of the tort is solely in the country of substance; and furthermore, place of causative act and place of damage are also to be determined on this basis, so that plaintiffs therefore do not have the option to choose to sue in *any* of the states in which acts or elements of damage took place, if these differ from that of the substance of either.

On the facts of *Metall und Rohstoff AG*, the Court of Appeal concluded that the substance of the cause of action in tort for inducement of breach of contract was committed in England; there were *some* acts of inducement (in respect of one of the contracts involved) and breaches of contract in New York; but other acts of inducement, and the main breaches of each contract in question, together with the resultant damage, occurred in London. So looked at as a whole, the tort of inducement was in substance committed in London.[24]

Critique of the Substance Test in Double Locality Torts

Precise Meaning of 'Double Locality'

It is not entirely clear from Slade L J's judgement *exactly* which types of case are meant to be included within the 'double locality' concept. On the one hand, Slade L J referred to such cases as those where several *acts* alleged to form part of one tort have occurred in more than one country.[25] Yet, on the other hand, he then proceeded to include as an alternative, those where the *damage or injury* has occurred in a country different from the place of one or more of the relevant *acts*.[26] It is felt that Slade L J would have done better to use terms which clearly limited the concept of double locality torts to the former situation, for two reasons.

First, in the latter type of case mentioned by him, where causative act and damage take place in separate states, there is – as has been seen – abundant authority for applying the substance test. The decisions in, for example, *Cordova*, *Diamond* and *Castree* have previously been referred to, and in the view of this writer it would be preferable for this sort of fact situation to be designated as 'multi-state' rather than double (*or more*) locality. However there has been no express line of authority sanctioning the substance test in those cases in which the chain of causative events, taken as a whole, amounts to substance – or, it may be inferred, where damage as a whole does so – but event (or damage) as substance consists of individual elements located in different states. This was acknowledged by Slade L J.[27] Furthermore, the description of this latter type of case – in which causative event (or damage) *as a whole* is considered to amount to substance of the tort and yet is itself split, requiring a further exercise of selection of the *main* act (or damage) as substance, according to the Court of Appeal's preferred course – as being one of 'double locality' tort, can be seen to be particularly accurate and appropriate.

Secondly, applicability of the substance approach may be more problematical in double locality cases than in multi-state, since in the former it may well be difficult to select a particular element from amongst those in the chain which is capable of being considered more weighty than others, where collectively they can be said to amount to the substance.

Double Locality and Choice of Law

In *Metall und Rohstoff AG*, it will be recalled that ascertainment of place of commission of torts remained relevant *inter alia* in satisfying the requirement of a good arguable case on the merits for service out to be permitted under RSC Order 11. Plainly, there is much sense in applying the substance test to double locality cases in the matter of choice of law, where the object is to assess liability under a singular *lex loci delicti*, rather than in accordance with any of a number of optionally available applicable laws of states in which any of the acts in the overall chain of events have taken place. It is submitted, furthermore, that this approach is, in any event, virtually inevitable in choice of law. For, there, the question to be asked is not – as in jurisdiction – 'which of differently situated places of causative event and damage, as separately ascertained, constitutes the substance of the tort', but 'where in substance did the cause of action in tort take place', whatever may be the separate location of act and damage, or of their individual internal components.

Double Locality and Jurisdiction

Brussels Convention cases In *Bier BV* v *Mines de Potasse D'Alsace SA*,[28] the European Court held that *both* the place of causative event and that of damage should be capable of conferring jurisdiction as that in which 'the harmful event occurred' in tort cases under Article 5(3) of the Convention.

Each one, it felt, was as appropriate as the other. Consequently, the plaintiffs could sue in France, where the pollution waste was allegedly discharged into the Rhine by the defendants, or in the Netherlands, where the resultant damage to the plaintiffs' horticultural business was sustained. Thus, in double locality cases, the application of a substance test to individual elements comprising causative event and damage would seem to run counter to the European Court's favoured overall multi-state approach, of affording plaintiffs an opportunity to choose a particular forum from amongst those qualified to adjudicate.

However, despite these misgivings as to application of a substance test to double locality torts in Brussels Convention cases, it is to be noted that one year prior to the decision in the *Metall und Rohstoff AG* case, Steyn J, in effect, endorsed just this approach – without however expressly designating such cases as 'double locality', in a judgement specifically concerning the meaning of *place where the harmful event occurred* in tort under Article 5(3) of the Convention. The decision in question was that of *Minster Investments Ltd* v *Hyundai Precision and Industry Co.Ltd*,[29] in which the plaintiff English companies sued the first defendant, a South Korean company with a branch in London. The dispute concerned the purchase of containers, which had failed to comply with contract specifications. The plaintiffs joined the second defendants, a French company with a South Korean office, which had contracted with the first defendants to test the containers for contractual compliance. The plaintiffs claimed that the second defendants had been negligent, in failing to carry out their checks with due care and in providing the first defendants with a certificate of compliance in Korea. This, it was argued, they must have known would be sent by the first defendants to the plaintiffs in England, who would then authorise payment to be made to the first defendants under the container contract, as had in fact happened.

The second defendants challenged the jurisdiction of the English courts in the negligence action against them. Since their seat was situated in France and Article 53, para 1 of the Brussels Convention provided that seat was to be treated as domicile for purposes of the Convention, Article 2 thereof conferred jurisdiction upon French, not English, courts, on the basis of their domicile. The only possible ground for exercise of jurisdiction by English courts under the Convention was that founded upon Article 5(3). This would confer jurisdiction upon the courts for the place where the harmful event in tort occurred; and this, according to the second defendants, was not England, but Korea, where the allegedly negligent certification was prepared.

The judge held that the Convention was applicable in accordance with Article 34(1) of the 1978 Accession Convention, on the ground that the proceedings were commenced *following* entry into force of the Convention in the United Kingdom on 1 January 1987 (notwithstanding that an original application for leave to serve out had been made and withdrawn prior to that date). Steyn J went on to consider where it was that the *harmful event* should be held to have occurred on the facts, for purposes of jurisdiction under Article 5(3).[30] He recorded that the second defendants' work had been carried out in France and Korea, but that it had to be assumed that they would have contemplated that the certificates prepared would be sent to the plaintiffs who were in England, and who would then authorise payment to be made to the first defendants in Korea, in reliance upon the certificates.[31] As in the case of many international torts, therefore, the facts displayed connections with several states – here, France, Korea and England – and the expression 'place where the harmful event occurred' in Article 5(3) would consequently give rise to many problems.

In reaching his decision on the question, Steyn J said that he would confine himself strictly to the particular circumstances of the case, since neither English nor European jurisprudence was considered to have any direct bearing on the matter at issue. National English case law – for example, *Cordova*, *Diamond* and *The Albaforth*[32] – was of minimal relevance, because the Convention was 'intended to be a self-contained code' which was designed to prevent conflicts of jurisdiction.[33] As for European jurisprudence, in *Bier BV* v *Mines de Potasse d'Alsace S.A.*, the European Court had held *place where the harmful event occurred* in Article 5(3) to cover 'both the place where the damage occurred and the place of the event giving rise to it'. Thereby it afforded the plaintiffs the option of suing

> either in the courts for the place where the damage occurred or in the courts for the place of the event which gives rise to and is at the origin of that damage.[34]

However, although this had *some* bearing on the matter and did provide guidance which would be most helpful in many other cases, it had nevertheless to be read, like any other judgement, in the context of the issue which had been before the European Court. Consequently, it would not solve *all* problems. Indeed, the very words 'event giving rise' in the European Court's judgement in *Bier* were capable of more than one interpretation in the context of the present case. Was the 'event' giving rise to damage the negligent work performed by the second defendants in France and Korea, or was it the receipt of the certificates by the plaintiffs in England and their reliance thereon and consequent instruction given from England to pay the first defendants in Korea? Accordingly, the language of the European Court in *Bier* was not to be treated as if it had *statutory force* and as if it afforded comprehensive guidance which was useful in *every* single case. Instead, Steyn J preferred to take account of the 'broad approach' of the European Court in *Bier* and to base his decision on the very words of Article 5(3), as enacted in the 1982 legislation.[35]

Proceeding on this basis, Steyn J went on to reject the idea that the *first* of the causative events should always be selected as the *sine qua non* of the commission of the tort, because such a rigid rule could lead to artificial results if the first act was relatively insignificant.[36] Instead, 'common sense and policy' required the court to ask 'where in substance the cause of action in tort arises, or what place the tort is more closely connected with'.[37] Further, in applying this substance test, the court was to look at the true nature of the case against the second defendants, and was not to place undue weight on the niceties of the way in which the case was pleaded. Thus, essentially what was alleged by the plaintiffs against the second defendants was liability arising from negligent misstatement or advice and reliance thereon – within the scope of the doctrine in *Hedley Byrne & Co. Ltd* v *Heller & Partners Ltd.*[38] – and not the 'historical carelessness' in Korea which led to the misstatement or wrong advice. Consequently, the event which *in substance* caused harm to the plaintiffs in *Minster* was the receipt in England of the negligently prepared certificates of the second defendants, relied on by the plaintiffs, as intended; so that, on a realistic appraisal of the plaintiffs' cause of action against the second defendants, the 'place where the harmful event occurred' within the meaning of Article 5(3) was England. Under Article 5(3) the court possessed jurisdiction against the second defendants.[39]

So it was that Steyn, J. effectively sanctioned application of the substance test in double locality causative event – and, by inference, damage – cases, for the purposes of Article 5(3) of the Convention. He regarded himself as being fully entitled to do this, since *Bier* was merely a *multi-state* case, involving occurrence of singular causative event and damage in different states. The European Court had not there been concerned with a case of double locality causative event (or damage), in contrast to the proceedings in *Minster*, where the causative event was split between Korea (and France) and England. This was why the English court would be justified in construing the wording itself of Article 5(3) and in simply following the broad approach of *Bier*; the latter was not, in particular, concerned with double locality.

As to this method of approach it is considered that there *may* perhaps be a greater policy justification for its adoption in Convention cases than there is in respect of national jurisdiction under RSC Order 11, r1(1)(f), since the former, unlike the latter, is mandatory rather than discretionary, so that jurisdiction based upon a relatively minor element of causation or damage would be unavoidable in the former case. Nevertheless, there is cause for some concern to be felt over the judgement's scope and legitimacy. In the first place, it will be recalled that the 'broad approach' of the European Court in *Bier*, which Steyn J purported to follow (albeit in a double locality case, rather than in the multi-state situation which had prevailed in *Bier*), would seem to have been to permit plaintiffs to opt for competing contact points – rather than to limit them to fora of the state of act or damage in which the substance of the tort could be held to be located. Consequently, as commented earlier, restriction of double-locality elements of act (or damage) to the substance thereof appears to be quite *contrary* to the spirit of *Bier*.[40]

In the second place, it is uncertain from Steyn J's judgement, as to whether, on the one hand, it was merely the double-locality event (or damage) which was to be confined to the place of *its* substance, leaving courts of the place of damage (or event) optionally available to be chosen in the alternative; or, on the other hand, whether in the event of double locality, the approach laid down was one of ascertainment of the substance of the tort *as a whole*. The language used by Steyn J seemed to indicate that the latter was intended. However, this would be even less acceptable than the former construction – itself criticised here as being contrary to the spirit of *Bier*! This is, firstly, because if the intention was simply to limit whichever of act or damage was subject to double locality, to the substance of the tort as a whole, leaving courts of the other open to be optionally chosen to adjudicate, in accordance with *Bier*, then if *none* of the various acts comprised in the double-locality event (or damage) amounted to the substance of the tort, which latter was instead constituted by the damage (or *vice versa*), this would in effect mean that one of the plaintiff's jurisdiction opportunities would be closed off, contrary to *Bier*. Secondly, Steyn J may have actually been saying that in such circumstances, in which either act or damage was subject to double locality, the optional approach in *Bier* – in which the state of either act or damage was available to the plaintiff – could simply be abandoned in favour of a single test of substance. If this interpretation is followed, then just because the European Court was not dealing with a double locality situation in that case, this would nevertheless be a rather disturbing application of strict national English principles of *stare decisis* to uniform Community jurisprudence. Steyn J stated that in the case before him the language of the European Court would not have statutory force;[41] but it would be well for it to be remembered that by virtue of s 3(1) of the Civil Jurisdiction and Judgements Act 1982 – requiring any question as to the meaning or effect of any provision of the Convention, if not referred to the European Court, to be determined 'in accordance with the principles laid down by and any relevant decision of the European Court' – the words of the European Court come very close to having statutory force.

Accordingly, if in so-called double locality cases English courts desire to depart from the spirit or from the effects of the European Court's judgement in *Bier*, it is submitted that the proper course of action is for interpretation of Article 5(3) to be referred to the European Court of Justice for a preliminary ruling thereon under Article 3 of the 1971 Interpretation Protocol, should the matter come before an appellate tribunal for decision.

RSC Order 11, r 1(1)(f) In *Metall und Rohstoff AG* [42] Slade L J correctly stated that the wording of r 1(1)(f), applicable when the Convention is not, – and permitting leave to be given for service out of the jurisdiction, in actions founded on a tort, where the damage was sustained or resulted from an act committed within the jurisdiction – was introduced in order to align national tort jurisdiction with that conferred by Article 5(3) of the Brussels Convention, as interpreted by the European Court in *Bier*.[43] Again, however, it is considered that application of the substance test to double locality, and exclusion of optional choice of contacts, is *not* necessarily in accordance with the true spirit of *Bier* – quite the opposite in fact.

Furthermore, in the case of RSC Order 11, r 1(1)(f), jurisdiction is merely discretionary. Even if the ground is held to be satisfied in relation to the English forum's territory, on the basis of location there of some relatively minor element of causative act or damage, the court can always decline to assume jurisdiction thereunder. This it can do on the basis that the connection with England is nonetheless too insignificant, as it did in the defamation case of *Kroch* v *Rossell et Cie*[44] – and that England accordingly is not *forum conveniens* as required under Order 11. In fact the substance test could then quite legitimately be applied both to place of commission of the tort as a whole and to individual double-locality elements thereof, in determining whether England was *forum conveniens* for such purposes.

Thus, in *Metall und Rohstoff AG* itself, the Court of Appeal applied Lord Goff's principles of *forum conveniens* set out in *Spiliada*,[45] requiring the plaintiff in Order 11 applications to demonstrate that England was clearly more appropriate than New York.[46] Taking into account plaintiffs' and defendants' respective residences, availability of witnesses and methods of gathering their evidence, extent of legal expertise in England, and the time bar on actions in New York, its conclusion was that England, *as locus of the substance of the cause of action in tort*, was the most appropriate forum for trying the claim for inducement of breach of contract.[47]

As a postscript to the *Metall* and *Minster* cases, in *Shevill and Others* v *Presse Alliance SA*[48] the French domiciled defendants argued against English courts' Article 5(3) jurisdiction, on the basis *inter alia* of France as country of substance of the harmful event as cause of action in tort of defamation, following *Minster*. The plaintiffs had alleged libel by the defendant French publishers of *France Soir* – a French evening newspaper with a circulation of 200,000 copies in France and 15,000 elsewhere, but only 250 in England (probably a mere 10 in Yorkshire, where the first plaintiff, Miss Fiona Shevill, an employee of the fourth plaintiff, had her home) – in respect of publications in France, England and Wales, and elsewhere. Subsequently, the statement of claim was amended so as to limit the cause of action to publication in England and Wales – plainly believed by the plaintiffs to be an advantage in the event of any dispute over the jurisdiction of English courts. The defendants asserted a) that *substance* of the cause of action was the *French* publication, and confinement of the substance examination to the English publication, as pleaded, was artificial and incorrect, and b) in accordance with the opinion of Advocate General Warner before the European Court in *Netherlands State* v *Rüffer*[49], and with the comments of the Court itself in that case, harmful event should be given an independent, Community meaning, distinct from any particular national definitions, and accordingly, that the English rule of treating each separate publication as a cause of action in tort was inappropriate for Article 5(3), and c) similarly, that the English law on substance, not requiring damage to be proved at all once the libel was established, or at least presuming damage to have occurred, should not obscure the fact that actual damage may have occurred substantially in another country, nor the requirement of some actual damage in England, for Article 5(3) jurisdiction purposes. The Court of Appeal, delivering judgment through Purchas LJ, rejected the defendant's arguments against English jurisdiction and held the latter to exist under Article 5(3) (although, the claim by the second plaintiffs, in whose favour there could be no good arguable case for any damage at all on the merits, was stayed).

In the first place, it was stated, the court should look at the cause of action as pleaded at the time of the application and not as things stood according to the unamended statement of claim. Thus, at the former date, it was the English publication which was complained of, not also the French and others. It might be thought that such finding should be held to conflict with the approach of Steyn J in *Minster* previously referred to, which was to look at the true nature of the case, without placing undue weight upon the niceties of pleading. However, such a conclusion would be incorrect; for, there is a difference between, on the one hand, assessing the substance rather than merely the form of what has been pleaded, as in *Minster* (negligent advice rather than act of certification), and, on the other hand, going beyond both form *and substance* of the plaintiff's cause of action as pleaded, quite properly held to be incorrect in *Shevill* v *Presse Alliance SA*. Thus, if a plaintiff decides not to claim in respect of particular aspects of a wrong alleged to have been carried out against him, he may, as a consequence, benefit jurisdictionally, but he will in the process have relinquished any hope of recovery for the abandoned part of his possible cause of action on the merits.

Secondly, the English rule which would look upon each separate publication as a tort was held not to be peculiar to English law and consequently not necessarily in conflict with adoption of an autonomous Community concept of tort for purposes of Article 5(3) (and Convention provisions on *lis alibi pendens* would operate in respect of any contemporaneous French libel proceedings). It is submitted, however, that even if the rule of individual libel publication as a separate tort *were* to be found to be peculiar solely to national English law, the need for an independent Convention tort concept would nonetheless still neither require nor justify disregard of the English rule, if otherwise applicable, since the nature of the cause of action and claim brought must always be established according to applicable national legal systems' norms, even though classification of these latter, as tortious or otherwise, for purposes of Convention Article 5(3), may then be carried out according to the independent Convention definition of tort (Kaye, Civil Jurisdiction and Judgments (1987) Professional Books, pp 563–6).

Thirdly, it was pointed out, whereas the existence of damage to the plaintiffs' reputation in England might be relevant to assessment of damages on the merits of the claim, it was untrue to state that such damage was *required* to be shown for Article 5(3) jurisdiction purposes: to which it should be added, however, as the defendants themselves appeared to contend, that if actual damage were able to be proven, place of harmful event under Article 5(3), to the extent that it was founded upon damage as opposed to causative event,[50] should be based upon where damage has *in fact* taken place rather than wherever it may be assumed to have occurred for purposes of merits adjudication.

Conclusion

RSC Order 11, r1(1)(f) has expressly eliminated previous reliance upon the concept of *place of commission* of torts in satisfying that particular head of jurisdiction. Despite this, *Metall und Rohstoff AG* has confirmed that location of place of commission remains relevant under the English conflict of laws, for the following reasons:

(i) as a factor to be taken into account by the court in its overall assessment of whether or not to exercise its discretion to permit service out of the jurisdiction under r1(1)(f) (and probably also, therefore, as a material element in the court's decision upon whether or not to grant a stay of proceedings on the ground of *forum non conveniens*, where the defendant is served within the jurisdiction), and

(ii) as necessary to be ascertained for purposes of determining applicable law, under the double actionability principle, whether in a purely choice of law context, or in order to demonstrate existence of a good arguable case on the merits under RSC Order 11, r1(1).

Further, in accordance with the decision of the Court of Appeal in *Metall und Rohstoff AG* and with the earlier judgement of Steyn J in *Minster Investments*, the 'substance' test of locating torts is apparently to be regarded as governing not only place of commission of the tort as a whole (where this is sought to be determined) but also that of the tort's individual components – namely, causative act and damage – where either or both of these are divided ('double locality') and require to be located for choice of law or jurisdiction. Also this will be so whether as part of the overall tort-location enquiry, or independently, as under RSC Order 11, r1(1)(f) or Article 5(3) of the Brussels Convention in conformity with the European Court's decision in *Bier*.

Where application of the substance test to double-locality elements of torts is concerned, in the case of choice of law, substance of the cause of action in tort appears to have gained acceptance as the test to be applied to determination of *locus delicti*. In this respect there is much to be said in favour of the adoption of a consistent policy in relation to location of place of causative event or damage, where either (or both) of these elements from which the substance is derived is itself split amongst different states in a double locality case. Indeed, the very generality of the approach of determining substance of the tort as a whole for choice of law, makes its further application to individual elements of the tort virtually an inevitability.

However, a number of difficulties have arisen in relation to operation of the substance test *vis-à-vis* the internal double locality elements of causative event or damage, where jurisdiction under either Article 5(3) of the Brussels Convention or RSC Order 11, r1(1)(f) is involved, other than for purposes of assessing *forum conveniens* for exercise of discretion under Order 11. These difficulties arise from the point of view of policy and as a matter of statutory construction of those provisions, both of which – as interpreted by the European Court in *Bier* in the former case – specifically accord jurisdiction to courts of the places of act *and* damage in multi-state cases. Naturally, there is always a strong desire to secure that jurisdiction is concentrated within the most appropriate fora, to the exclusion of those having a significantly lesser connection with the parties and case. Yet, on the other hand, restriction of individual elements of causative act and ɔ the most substantial forum for jurisdiction-conferring purposes to arbitrary and difficult decisions at that micro-level, and to a *reduction* of jurisdictional opportunities within the European Community, where substance of the event or damage is held to be located without.

British courts should, therefore, show some hesitation in future proceedings, before giving wholehearted approval to the substance method in double locality cases in a jurisdictional context – and they should at least be prepared to submit its acceptability to the European Court itself in Convention cases, lest too great a degree of divergence from uniform Community practice be permitted to develop.

Notes

1 [1989] 3 WLR 563 (CA).

2 *Ibid.*, at p 589.

3 [1988] 2 Lloyd's Rep 621.

4 *Supra cit.*

5 [1988] 3 WLR 548. Service out was allowed to stand in respect of claims for the torts of conspiracy and inducing breach of contract, which were held to be established for purposes of RSC Order 11, and for an account as constructive trustees, which was merely a remedy and need not therefore be classified as tort; not so however in the case of the claim for abuse of the court's process by the defendants, which was held not to have been substantiated, and of that for procurement of breach of trust, which was not a tort.

6 [1989] 3 WLR 563, p 591. There was held to be no such tort as procurement of breach of trust, and accounting as constructive trustees was also not a matter for the law of torts (*ibid.*, pp 616 and 623); nor was there a good arguable case on the merits (as required for service out of the jurisdiction, in accordance with RSC Order 11, r4(2)) to support a claim of abuse of process of the court, so as to expose the *defendants* to liability in damages under the principles governing malicious *prosecution* in *Grainger* v *Hill* (1838) 4 Bing NC 212 (*ibid.*, p 613 *et seq*); while, although conspiracy was a tort, nevertheless, as it had been pleaded, the plaintiffs had no good arguable case for service out under RSC Order 11, r1, because they had failed to contend that the defendants' sole or predominant purpose was to injure them, as was required for the tort of conspiracy to be made out in accordance with the decision of the House of Lords in *Lonrho Limited* v *Shell Petroleum Company Limited (No 2)* [1982] AC 173 (*ibid.*, p 609).

7 *Ibid.*, pp 579–80.

8 A formulation which was designed to take account of European Court case-law on the Brussels Convention, sanctioning place of causative event *or* damage as that of the harmful event in tort (see *Bier BV* v *Mines de Potasse D'Alsace SA*, Case 21/76 [1978] QB 708; [1976] E.C.R. 1735) – *ibid.*, p 581–2, Slade LJ.

9 *Id.*

10 *Ibid.*, pp 580, 626 and 630. Gatehouse, J. also, at first instance, [1988] 3 All ER 116, at pp 119–20, [1988] 3 WLR. 548, at p 555, made the point that in spite of the fact that under the re-worded Order 11, r.1(1)(f), place where the tort was committed (as

that of the tort's substance) was no longer the sole consideration, it remained nonetheless a powerful factor, in guiding the courts upon whether or not to exercise their *discretion*, being '*prima facie* the natural forum for the determination of the dispute.' Presumably, therefore, since the principles for service out of the jurisdiction under Order 11 and for stays of action on the ground of *forum non conveniens* bear a 'marked resemblance' (*Spiliada Maritime Corp.* v *Cansulex Ltd* [1987] 1 AC 460, at p 480, (HL[E]), *per* Lord Goff), place of commission of a tort, as that of substance thereof, is also relevant, where a plea of *forum non conveniens* is raised by a defendant tortfeasor served within the jurisdiction.

11 [1989] 3 WLR 563, p 579.

12 (1870) LR 6 QB 1.

13 [1971] AC 356.

14 [1989] 3 WLR 563, p 582.

15 See Dicey and Morris, (1987) The Conflict of Laws, (11th Edn) Stevens, p 1382 – [1989] 3 WLR 563, pp 585, 588 and 590.

16 [1944] 1 KB 432.

17 [1989] 3 WLR 563, p 586 *et seq.*

18 *Cordova Land Co Ltd* v *Victor Brothers Inc.* [1966] 1 WLR 793; *Distillers Co (Biochemicals) Ltd* v *Thompson* [1971] AC 458; *Diamond* v *Bank of London and Montreal Ltd* [1979] 1 QB 333; *Castree* v *E R Squibb & Sons Ltd* [1980] 2 All ER 859; *The Albaforth* [1984] 2 Lloyd's Rep 91.

19 [1989] 3 WLR 563, pp 585 and 589.

20 *Supra cit.*

21 [1989] 3 WLR 563, p 590.

22 *Ibid.*, p 591.

23 *Ibid.*, p 590.

24 *Ibid.*, p 626–30.

25 *Ibid.*, p 589.

26 *Ibid.*

27 *Ibid.*, pp 589 and 590.

28 Case 21/76 [1978] QB 708; [1976] ECR. 1735.

29 [1988] 2 Lloyd's Rep. 621.

30 *Ibid.*, p 623, col. 1.

31 *Ibid.*, p 623, col. 2.

32 *Supra cit.*

33 [1988] 2 Lloyd's Rep. 621, p 623, col. 2.

34 *Ibid.*, p 624, col. 1.

35 *Ibid.*, pp 623–4.

36 *Ibid.*, p 624, col. 1.

37 *Ibid.*, p 624, col. 2.

38 [1964] AC 465.

39 [1988] 2 Lloyd's Rep. 621, p 624, col. 2.

40 Although, it should here be added that in the case of double locality *damage*, whilst it is felt that this ought not to be reduced to the single element forming the substance thereof if the spirit of *Bier* is properly to be adhered to, nevertheless, for sound reasons of common sense, only the place or places in which it can be shown that damage was *first sustained* should be taken into account. This should be to the exclusion of that or those in which it subsequently becomes apparent, since this would be an unreliable criterion, and possibly open to manipulation by plaintiffs: see Kaye, Civil Jurisdiction and Enforcement of Foreign Judgments (Professional Books) (1987), p 582–4. Fur-

thermore, in *Dumez France and Tracoba* v *Hessische Landesbank (Helaba)*, Case 220/88 [1990] E.C.R. 49, the European Court held – though not strictly relevant to double – locality damage, *in denying the very existence of 'damage' at all for Article 5(3) jurisdiction – conferring purposes* – that indirect and consequential financial damage suffered by the plaintiffs, as parties other than the direct victims of the harmful act complained of, was insufficient to amount to damage as the *harmful event* in tort, delict or quasi-delict under Article 5(3).

41 [1988] 2 Lloyd's Rep 621, p 624, col. 1.
42 *Supra cit.*
43 *Supra cit*, at pp 581–2.
44 [1937] 1 All ER 725.
45 *Supra cit.*
46 [1989] 3 WLR 563, p 624.
47 *Ibid.*, p 630. See also note 10, *supra*.
48 The Times (1991) 13th March.
49 Case 814/79 [1980] ECR 3807. See too *Kalfelis* v *Bankhaus Schröder, Münchmeyer, Hengst & Co*, Case 189/87 [1988] ECR 5565, 5585.
50 *Bier* v *Mines de Potasse*, Case 21/76 [1976] ECR 1735.

Index